METHODS FOR TEACHING

A Skills Approach

Third Edition

David Jacobsen
University of North Florida

Paul Eggen
University of North Florida

Donald Kauchak
University of Utah

Merrill, an imprint of
Macmillan Publishing Company
New York

Collier Macmillan Canada, Inc.
Toronto

Maxwell Macmillan International Publishing Group
New York   Oxford   Singapore   Sydney

Cover Photo: Richard Hutchings

This book was set in Aster and Univers.

Administrative Editor: Jeff Johnston
Production Coordinator: Sharon Rudd
Art Coordinator: Ruth Kimpel
Cover Designer: Brian Deep

Photo Credits: Wellington Merton, pp. 54, 338; Danile T. Pitler, all other photos.

Library of Congress Catalog Card Number: 88-62270
International Standard Book Number: 0-675-20969-2
Printed in the United States of America
    4 5 6 7 8 9 — 92 91

Preface

Planning.

Implementing.

Evaluating.

Effective classroom teaching requires professional commitment. Although exciting experiences may occur spontaneously, such happenings serve as the exception, not the rule. If teachers are to sustain a success-oriented environment throughout the academic year, they must continually and thoroughly address the teaching act which is founded upon the planning and implementing of instructional activities and the evaluating of student performance.

These planning, implementing, and evaluating components represent a continual process in which professional teachers strive to increase the quality of their instruction, that is, facilitate learning in increased numbers of students. The purpose of this textbook is to provide tools that will enable the inservice as well as the preservice teacher to effectively plan, implement, and evaluate. In doing so, the teacher will constantly be considering the goals to be achieved, the resources needed, and whether or not the goals were met.

Needless to say, it is impossible for one textbook to cover the entire waterfront; however, we believe we have offered a foundation that will foster successful classroom teaching and provide a solid framework for in-depth study in the areas presented.

In addition to updated research on teacher effectiveness throughout the text, there are a number of additions to the third edition including

The Teacher's Role

Gronlund's Instructional Objectives

The Affective Domain

The Psychomotor Domain

The Madeline Hunter Planning Model

Motivating Students

Guided Discovery: Developing Thinking Skills

Classroom Management: Teacher Strategies

Establishing Classroom Procedures

Assertive Discipline

Teaching Alignment: Matching Curriculum Instruction and Tests

Multicultural Education

Cooperative Learning

Learning Styles and Hemispheric Brain Research

Finally we have attempted to produce a methods book that is even more practical and applicable to classroom teaching. Additional examples and scenarios have been produced and alternatives have been offered throughout the text.

We would like to express our gratitude to our reviewers, Ann Lally, Morsley Giddings, Franklin Carlson, and Duane Giannangelo and to the hundreds of students and teachers who provided critical feedback and served as invaluable sources in the preparation of the third edition.

D. A. J.
P. D. E.
D. P. K.

Contents

UNIT THREE: EVALUATING

1 ‖ Introduction: A Model for Teaching

You've probably begun to read this material because you're either enrolled in an undergraduate general methods course or you're a teacher interested in updating your skills. Whichever position you're in, we want to put your mind at ease by describing an assumption we're making. As we write this material, we're assuming that while you've had experience with teaching—as we all have had as students, parents, aides, or tutors—you may not have done any formal teaching yourself. Based on this assumption, we're going to provide you with the background needed to launch you into further study of the teaching profession and to provide the basic tools needed to make intelligent decisions about planning teaching activities, performing or implementing those activities with children, and evaluating their success.

With this thought in mind, a basic theme of this text will focus on the process you go through and the kind of thinking you do as you study the material. We hope that when you have finished your study you will have conceptual or intellectual tools that will allow you to continue to grow as a professional throughout your career.

For those of you who have had formal experience with teaching, we hope this material will help make your work more systematic and will further assist you in making even better decisions about teaching.

THE TEACHER'S ROLE

An often held and stereotypical view of a teacher is that of a learned person disseminating information to a group of people hungry for knowledge. The group is often viewed as passive, and the main activity in such a learning environment involves the teacher *telling* the students what they need to know. However, many educators agree that this view is extremely narrow and that *telling* is only one of many tools a teacher may employ.

The central role of a teacher is to promote growth and achievement—i.e., learning, which is an internal process. This being the case, teachers don't teach students to learn; they disseminate information, demonstrate desired behaviors, model appropriate behaviors, and facilitate student achievement.

How do we learn? Epistemology, a branch of philosophy, is concerned with sources of knowledge. We learn through such things as revelation, intuition, rationalization, empiricism, and acceptance of authoritative information. Intellectually speaking, all of these sources involve degrees of internalization. Interestingly, such processing can include operant as well as perceptual learning theories.

For example, most parents *condition* their children to say such things as please and thank you. This can be effectively accomplished through parental modeling in which the parents themselves use these terms and establish for children the desirability of these socially acceptable behaviors. The initial motivation for the children may well involve the concept of extrinsic worth. When using *please* and *thank you* the children get what they want and also may find that they please their parents when doing so. However, the parents have not actually *taught* the children; they have facilitated the children's ability to internalize the extrinsic worth of incorporating these terms into their verbal repertoire.

Although there are educators who are critical of motivational factors based upon extrinsic worth, much of what we do may be founded upon or initiated by an extrinsic internalization. Is it uncommon for people, adults as well as children, to want to please their teachers? And isn't it also possible that human nature is such that we derive a great amount of pleasure by being perceived by others in a positive light? In and of itself, that may be fine, but many educators further believe it is equally important to make the transition from the extrinsic to the intrinsic.

For example, providing a reward for children who successfully tie their shoes can be effective in initiating the desired behavior, but the terminal behavior should be based upon intrinsic, and not extrinsic, motivation. In other words, the bottom line involves the children "feeling good" about their ability to put on their shoes. They thereby enhance their self-worth, their positive image of themselves.

It is in this area that teachers provide a critical function. Teachers facilitate the internalization process and most effectively do so by promoting a positive self-concept. In doing so, the teacher may stimulate a child's interest and, more importantly, promote achivement and success.

As a further example, some educators would say, You can't teach a child to ride a bicycle. Once again, this would depend upon one's definition of the teacher's role. As stated earlier, teachers cannot internalize concepts or behaviors for students because internalization is a unique process that all of us must undertake for ourselves. However, there are many things we, as teachers, can do.

We can demonstrate bicycle functions such as use of brakes and pedaling. We can have the child sit on the bike with us, roll it slowly, and lean from side to side, thereby demonstrating balance. We can put the child on a stationary bicycle and allow him or her to actually experience pedaling and using the brakes. We can run alongside the child, aid in corrections, and constantly encourage and reinforce appropriate behaviors. In short, what we do is demonstrate or model riding a bicycle; provide a knowledge base regarding operation; and provide appropriate, sufficient, and supportive practical experiences. Only then does the child *learn* to ride a bicycle.

Rudolph Dreikurs provided us with a classical example of moving in line with one's expectations, and it too involved learning to ride a bicycle (Dreikurs, 1968). He stated that when many children learn to ride a bicycle, they go down a street, and there is a rock in the middle of the road. It is much easier to miss the rock, but more often than not, they will hit it because they may be moving in line with their expectation—which is to hit the rock when learning to ride.

Likewise, many of our students are prone, concretely or abstractly, to hit the rock. We cannot *teach* them to do otherwise, but what we can do is provide educational experiences that promote positive learning environments laden with a variety of extrinsic motivational factors that the student will hopefully transfer to the intrinsic plane. In this way, teachers enhance and, to some degree, direct the internalization process, the final product of which is original to the child.

Throughout history, the great "teachers" have facilitated that which students think or do (intellectually, attitudinally, and physically), and the educator's utility has been found in paving the way for a student's transfer from what he or she does to what he or she becomes.

Now let's proceed to an introductory illustration of teachers in action.

THE TEACHING ACT

Because your background may be limited or may be quite informal, our first step in a systematic description of teaching begins with a brief look at the teaching act itself. To do this, let's look at three scenarios of teachers working in classrooms.

Examples

Scenario 1. Mrs. Shafer is a pleasant woman in her middle thirties who teaches at Plainview Elementary School. Plainview is an older school in a lower-middle-class neighborhood of Laqua, Florida. While the school is not new, the administration has kept the grounds and building very attractive. Everyone cooperates in keeping the small areas of grass from being trampled on and killed, and the paved and cemented areas are kept free from debris. There are no broken windows, and the water fountains and lavatories work well and smell fresh.

Mrs. Shafer's room has a high ceiling which makes it seem big, but she has grouped large boxes to make cubbyholes and privacy corners for her children. She asked for and received permission to paint designs and graphics (sayings or pictures such as rainbows) on her walls in addition to her use of several large bulletin boards for decoration.

Mrs. Shafer is presenting a unit in geography, and students have studied various geographic regions and their physical features. The children are now familiar with regions such as the American central plains, the Russian steppes, and the Argentine pampas; and the American Rocky Mountains, the Swiss Alps, and the South American Andes. They know how the regions are similar and how they differ. She now wants the children to understand the influence of geography on the people's life-styles and habits. She decides she will use pictures of people in different regions and will try to get students to compare the region with the appearance and activities of the people. She gathers her pictures and begins the lesson. She starts by showing a picture of some children playing in front of some grass huts.

"Look at the picture, everyone," Mrs. Shafer says, smiling. "Tell me anything at all you see about the pictures."

"They're in Africa," Carol says immediately.

"Excellent, Carol, but how do you know that?"

"My dad is in the navy, and we lived in Greece, and we took a trip to Africa, and we saw houses like those."

Jimmy's eyes open wide. "You went to Africa? I've never been out of Laqua in my life."

Mike adds, "I've never been there, but I've read about it, and those children could live in India maybe 'cuz they don't wear many clothes in India either."

David is whispering and grinning at Billy as Mike is talking, and Mrs. Shafer gives him a stern look.

"What did we agree was one of our important rules, David?" Mrs. Shafer asks.

"We always respect others," David says quietly.

"And what is one way we do that?"

"We listen to what they have to say whether we agree or not, and then express our opinion when it's our turn."

"Very good, David," Mrs. Shafer says with a smile. "That's a good reminder for all of us. Now let's go on. What else do you see in the picture?"

The children continue dpescribing what they see, and then Mrs. Shafer shows two Russian children playing with a sled in front of a mosque. Again she asks for a description of what the children see. She continues this process, showing pictures of Indian shepherds in Ecuador and Bedouin tribesmen in Arabia. She asks the students to compare all of the pictures by showing similarities and differences. Finally she asks the children to summarize what they saw.

"Well, people live in different places and their houses are different," Joan suggests.

"Fine, Joan. Now, anything else?"

"They dress different," Kim adds.

"O.K."

"They're playing different games and stuff," Susan says.

"Very good. What more can you say about what we've seen—people's houses, clothes, games they play, and so on?"

"Well," Jimmy says somewhat hesitantly, "they're things about people."

"Fine, and what things about people?"

"Oh, how they live and everything."

"Very good. So we're saying geography and climate affect people's lifestyles."

Mrs. Shafer goes into a discussion of Florida's climate, geography, and lifestyle and asks the children to compare that to how they would expect to live in northern Michigan or Minnesota.

After a number of comparisons are made, Mrs. Shafer announces, "Now, everyone, I have two short paragraphs that I want you to read. Then I want you to write four examples from the paragraph that show how geography and climate affect life-style."

The paragraphs she gives the children are as follows:

> José and Kirsten are two children about your age who live in faraway lands. Kirsten lives in the mountains of Norway, which is quite far north. José lives on the flat plains of western Mexico where it is very hot and dry. Kirsten loves to ski and does so nearly every day in the winter. In the summer she and her brother put on light wool sweaters and go hiking in the mountains. They love to sit atop the peaks and look down over the valleys. In the evenings Kirsten's mother builds a fire, and everyone in the family reads quietly.
>
> José loves to play, just as Kirsten does. He swims every afternoon in a pond formed by a spring near his village. He becomes impatient because he has to wait until after the nap his mother takes every day at noon. The children go outside and play in the evening, enjoying the breeze that cools the village. They usually play until it is so dark they can't see.

Mrs. Shafer collects the students' papers and ends the class by saying she will introduce the idea of *culture* the following day and relate culture to geography and climate. She reviews the papers during her planning period and finds the following acceptable responses:

1. Kirsten skiing in the winter
2. Kirsten's family sitting and reading by the fire in the evening
3. Kirsten and her brother hiking in the mountains
4. José's mother napping every noon
5. José playing in the evening
6. José swimming in the afternoon

Scenario 2. Mr. Adams works in a kindergarten classroom. He has his room arranged in sections. Today is Monday, so Mr. Adams arrives at school early to set up his room for the week. He changes his activities on a weekly basis and spends his Friday afternoons and Monday mornings getting them ready. This week he wants to put particular emphasis on manipulative skills and wants to be sure all of the children can perform tasks such as buttoning coats and tying shoes. In one corner he puts some flashlight bulbs in little holders, some dry cell batteries, and some wire. In another corner he places a large flannel board with different numbers of beans glued on it so children can match numerals such as 2 or 3 with the appropriate number of beans. He arranges similar activities in the other corners of the room.

As the children come in, Mr. Adams asks them what activities they would like to choose and sends them each to a corner to begin. He then sits down on the floor with three boys to help them learn to tie the shoelaces on a large doll they've named Fred. Each day the children button Fred's shirt, tie his shoes, brush his teeth, and wash his hands after Mr. Adams has taken him to the bathroom.

Jimmy is struggling to get Fred's shoe tied and appears slightly uninterested to Mr. Adams. He feels his forehead, which appears to be warm, and immediately takes him by the hand down to the nurse's office. Jimmy is often ill, so Mr. Adams is sensitive to his behavior when he appears listless.

As he returns, he sees Scott throw a beanbag at Lisa. Mr. Adams admonishes him gently saying, "Scott, you're not supposed to throw the beanbag at Lisa; you're supposed to throw it so she can catch it."

"She threw it at me first."

"Did you, Lisa?"

Smiling shyly, Lisa nods.

"Throw it *to* each other and count to see if you can do it ten times each without missing."

Mr. Adams continues working with groups of children until 11:30 when it is time for dismissal. He helps the children get safely on the bus and then goes back to his room.

Taking stock of his morning, he grins to himself as he recalls that David had improved significantly in tying Fred's shoes. He takes out a sheet that has the children's names on it and puts a check by David's name. He notices as he glances at the sheet that Bobby had trouble walking the balance beam and prepares a note for his mother suggesting some exercises he could do at home. With this done, he prepares for his afternoon class.

Scenario 3. Mrs. Tyler is a history teacher in a large high school. She is working on a unit in group processing, and while her ultimate goal is for the students to understand the effects of group processing on democratic decision making, her particular interest in this lesson is to have her students learn to understand their own views more clearly and to learn to cooperate by making decisions in groups. To accomplish this, she splits the class into two groups and presents each group with a perplexing situation. The situation describes a shipwreck with some sick and injured people. The party is marooned on a deserted island, short of food and water fit for drinking. Fortunately, they're rescued, but the ship can only handle part of the people in one trip. In all likelihood, many of the sick and injured won't survive the trip back to civilization, but they'll surely die if left on the island. If the healthy are left until the second trip, many will die of starvation or thirst before the ship returns. She asks the students to discuss the issue during the class period, recording notes and decisions. Each group is to report the following day.

As the groups discuss the problem, Mrs. Tyler listens and periodically raises questions if the students appear to drift away from the task at hand or raises questions that aren't considered by the group.

The next day Mrs. Tyler has the students discuss the process they went through, their feelings as they were involved in the discussion, and the bases for the decisions they made. As the year progresses, Mrs. Tyler makes short notes about each student describing the student's progress in working in group situations.

Analysis

We have described three teachers involved in activities with students at three different levels and in three different content areas. Let's analyze the three scenarios and see how they illustrate the framework we want to provide for later chapters in this book.

Teacher Emphasis.   First, let's look again at what the three teachers did. Mrs. Shafer wanted her students to understand the influence of geography and climate on life-style. Mr. Adams had his children doing a variety of things; some worked with trying to light the bulb, some counted beans, and others worked on skills like tying shoes and buttoning coats. Mrs. Tyler wanted her students to learn to cooperate in groups and involved them in a decision-making activity. We can see from the earlier examples that the differences among these three areas in many classrooms are those of emphasis rather than exclusion. For example, while Mrs. Shafer wanted her students to learn about the relationship between geography, climate, and life-style, she also viewed respect for others as important. She demonstrated this view when she reminded David and Billy to listen when Mike was talking. Also, in order to perform skills such as carpentry and hitting a tennis ball properly, knowledge of technique is required. All of this serves to show that the three areas — knowledge, skills, and attitudes — are closely interrelated and cannot be completely separated in any reasonable way.

All three of the areas are extremely important and should be emphasized as much as possible in schools. However, a discussion of the learning of knowledge, skills, and attitudes is beyond the scope of a single text, so we have chosen to emphasize the area of knowledge and information more than the others. The reason is simple. While skills and attitudes are important and are considered important by public school officials, relatively greater emphasis is placed on the acquisition of knowledge and the ability to think. For this reason we have chosen to concentrate on this area.

Based on the three scenarios, we see that students' learning can be more varied than we might expect at first glance. Mrs. Shafer's students were learning *information* or *knowledge* and how it can be used to explain objects and events that occur in the world. By comparison, many of Mr. Adams's activities were related to *manipulative skills* such as buttoning Fred's coat and tying his shoes. Many other such skills are taught in schools — typing, carpentry, leatherwork, mechanics, and physical education skills in all the sports areas. Mrs. Tyler's activity was different from both Mrs. Shafer's and Mr. Adams's. She wanted her students to acquire certain *attitudes* and *values*, such as cooperation, willingness to listen to a contrasting view, and respect for others.

So, we see now that students can learn much more than information in schools. Student learning can roughly be described as existing in three forms: (1) information and knowledge, (2) manipulative skills, and (3) attitudes and values.

Learning Environments. Let's look again at the three scenarios and see how the learning environments differed. Mrs. Shafer worked with her whole class, while Mr. Adams worked with small groups and had learning centers set up. Mrs. Tyler worked with two large groups. Adding one-to-one encounters to our list, the possible grouping arrangements appear as follows:

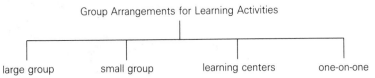

Group Arrangements for Learning Activities

| large group | small group | learning centers | one-on-one |

The material in this text is designed to be used with all group arrangements. We will discuss these arrangements in more detail in later chapters.

Other Influences on Learning. While the group arrangement affects the way children learn, many other factors influence what children take away from school. For instance, in Mr. Adams's activity, Jimmy appeared listless, and it turned out that he didn't feel well. Health is certainly a factor that affects learning. Nutrition is another factor, and its importance, in addition to promoting general health, is evidenced by schools implementing breakfast and free lunch programs for needy children.

Think for a moment now about the way Mrs. Shafer and Mr. Adams arranged their rooms to present them in the most attractive way possible. The physical environment has been shown to be an important factor affecting both student learning of information and attitudes toward school.

Again, think about Mrs. Shafer's lesson. In discussing the picture of children playing in front of the grass huts, Carol reacted quite differently from Jimmy because she had been to Africa and had seen live examples of huts and children similar to those in Mrs. Shafer's picture, while Jimmy had no frame of reference whatsoever. Mike's reaction was somewhere in between. He had no firsthand experience but was familiar with the ideas from pictures and stories. This all illustrates how background experience can affect what children learn. In the situation just described, Carol was certainly in the best position to derive the most benefit from the lesson because of her prior experience, while Jimmy was in the least advantageous position. Obviously, we as teachers cannot control students' backgrounds, but we can provide the most realistic examples possible, as Mrs. Shafer did, and promote as much student involvement as possible, again as Mrs. Shafer did. This illustrates the role of the teacher in influencing student learning, which brings us to the central theme of this text.

As you reflect on your role as a teacher in the schools, you see that as an individual teacher you can do little about children's health, nutrition, outside experiences, or emotional makeup. You can, however, significantly influence their learning by providing school experiences

Teachers should provide positive learning experiences.

that promote thinking and by making learning as positive an experience as possible. This is what this book is all about. In succeeding chapters we will help you learn to plan, implement, and evaluate activities to promote as much student learning as possible. We will describe this process according to a three-step model or approach. This approach outlines the steps a teacher takes in developing any learning experience, and the majority of the remaining material in this text will be devoted to discussion and illustration of the three steps.

THE THREE-PHASE APPROACH TO TEACHING

The model of teaching we are presenting is simple, and we realize curriculum development experts would include additional steps. However, the approach is understandable, practical, and workable in the planning of single lessons or units, and we have chosen it for these reasons.

The three basic steps in the three-phase approach to teaching are these:

1. The planning phase
2. The implementing phase
3. The evaluating phase

These three phases are sequential and interrelated. In other words, a teacher, in developing any learning experience, first plans, then implements those plans, and finally evaluates the success of the activity.

In each of these phases effective teachers ask themselves a series of questions that are constantly kept in mind as the process develops. We are going to use these questions in our development of the remainder of the text. Keep this idea in mind and look now at each of the steps more closely.

Planning

All teaching begins with some kind of planning. At this point, a teacher asks himself:

What do I want the students to know, understand, appreciate, and be able to do?

The answer to this question will be the teacher's goal. The first step of the planning phase is the establishment of some kind of goal. This goal may be as mundane as keeping the students quiet for an hour or as lofty as developing students' moral or spiritual values. Whatever the intent, the establishment of some type of goal or purpose is the first priority in teaching.

You may wonder or ask yourself, What determines the goal? or, From where does it come? The answers to these questions can become very philosophical, and we consider this issue in Chapter 2. In addition, methods for precisely stating teaching goals are described in Chapter 3.

Each of the teachers in our introductory scenarios established goals. Mrs. Shafer wanted her students to understand the influence of geography on life-style and habits, Mr. Adams wanted his children to develop their manipulative skills, and Mrs. Tyler wanted her students to work cooperatively in groups.

A second step in the planning phase is selecting a strategy and gathering the supporting materials. Mrs. Shafer wanted her students to discover the relationship between climate and life-style and attempted to accomplish this by showing pictures and asking questions. Her pictures were her supporting materials. Mr. Adams chose as his strategy the simple procedure of practice, with the doll being the supporting materials, and Mrs. Tyler's strategy was to actually have the students involved in a group decision-making process. To accomplish her aim, Mrs. Tyler needed no materials other than pencil and paper and the problem-solving situation. Chapters 2 through 5 are all devoted to the planning process.

Research evidence supports the value of the planning process. Peterson, Marx, and Clark (1978) found that teacher behaviors in the classroom depend on the plans teachers make. Clark and Yinger (1979) and McCutcheon (1980) both found that planning tends to give teachers confidence and security. For those of you who have not yet taught and are approaching the experience with understandable apprehension, the research results are encouraging. The implication for you is to plan carefully so that your feelings of uncertainty can be significantly reduced.

Implementing

Having determined the goal and selected an appropriate means to reach that goal, the teacher then must consider implementing that strategy. The teacher attempts in the implementation phase to accomplish the teaching goal through the selected strategy. The teaching activity in the implementation stage is the actual performance of the strategy the teacher has selected. Mrs. Shafer implemented her activity when she actually showed the pictures and asked the students questions. Mr. Adams implemented his activity when he had the students practice on Fred, and Mrs. Tyler was in the implementation phase when the students actually worked on making the group decisions. The implementation phase is simple to describe but may be much more difficult to perform. Essentially, this phase occurs when you actually do a teaching activity with the idea of reaching a preestablished goal. Interestingly, a surprising number of teachers do activities with little thought of what goal they're trying to reach. Mintz (1979), Peterson et al. (1978), and McCutcheon (1980) all found that teachers do not typically start the planning process with a consideration of goals but rather with a concern for activities, content, or materials. A goal for us in writing this text is for you, as preservice and inservice teachers, to make your planning, implementing, and evaluating of learning experiences for your students a systematic and considered process rather than a contingency or "seat-of-the-pants" approach. The research suggests that while planning and carrying out meaningful goal-oriented programs isn't often systematically done, such action is possible and will be rewarded with positive results.

The question the teacher asks in anticipating the implementation of activities is, How will I get the students to reach the goal? The answer to the question will be the teaching procedure, strategy, or technique that is used. Deciding the most appropriate method to use depends on the goal, the students' characteristics, the teacher's style, and other factors. We will formally discuss teaching procedures in Chapters 6, 7, and 8.

In addition to considering and implementing a teaching strategy to reach a predetermined goal, teachers must organize and manage their classrooms so the learning process can proceed smoothly. Management procedures range from something as simple as a word spoken to a student to complex procedures that require the creation of unique environments.

Mrs. Shafer was involved in classroom management when she gave David a stern look for whispering while another student was talking, and Mr. Adams employed management procedures when he gently corrected Scott for throwing the beanbag at Lisa rather than to her. Additional management features were illustrated in the way Mr. Adams arranged his room. Rather than having children organized in rows of semicircles, he had them in small groups working at stations.

As the anecdotes involving Mrs. Shafer and Mr. Adams illustrate, classroom management and instruction are essentially inseparable. Without attending to the learning task, students cannot learn, and organizing a learning activity invariably incorporates some management considerations on the part of the teacher. It is for these reasons that management of classrooms is included in our discussion of the implementing phase of teaching. Management procedures are discussed in Chapters 9 and 10.

Evaluating

The third stage in the teaching act is evaluation. Here the teacher attempts to gather information that can be used to determine if his teaching has been successful. This can be done in a number of ways including administering tests or quizzes or noting students' reactions to questions or comments. Each of these methods can be used by the teacher in making decisions concerning whether or not the goal established in the planning stage was reached.

At this point the teacher is asking, How will I determine if the students know, understand, or appreciate the goal I have identified? The answer to this question specifies the way in which the students' understanding will be measured and evaluated.

For instance, Mrs. Shafer gave the children an unfamiliar paragraph and asked them to identify illustrations of the relationship between geography and life-style in it, Mr. Adams observed the children performing the manipulative tasks and checked the names of those who were successful, and Mrs. Tyler observed the students and made notes regarding their progress in group situations.

In all these instances the evaluation procedures used by the teachers were chosen so as to be congruent with the established goals and the selected implementation strategies. We discuss evaluation procedures in more depth in Chapter 11.

SUMMARY

The scenarios in which the three teachers performed each of these phases can be summarized as follows:

	Planning	Implementing	Evaluating
Mrs. Shafer	Wanted students to know how life-style and geography relate. Selected pictures and planned discovery.	Had children observe pictures and discover relationship.	Gave children a paragraph and had them identify illustrations in it.
Mr. Adams	Wanted students to develop manipulative skills. Decided on practice. Decided to use the doll.	Had students practice on the doll.	Observed students and checked their names on a checklist.
Mrs. Tyler	Wanted students to learn to work in groups. Chose a dilemma for groups to discuss.	Had students discuss the dilemma and arrive at group decision.	Observed students work in groups during the year.

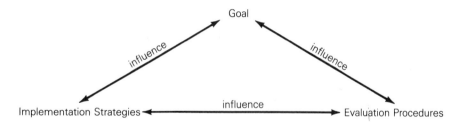

Figure 1.1   The Three-Phase Approach to Teaching

Although described as three separate phases, the continuity and interrelationship of the phases should be emphasized. The goal that a teacher has for a particular group of students should determine both what is taught and how it is taught and should influence the manner in which the learning is evaluated. This relationship is shown in Figure 1.1.

Some of the relationships shown in Figure 1.1 are readily apparent, while others may require some discussion. The effect of goals on implementation strategies and evaluation procedures is apparent in that the goal being taught influences how the lesson is taught and how the effectiveness of the lesson is measured. However, other relationships in the diagram may not be so apparent. Evaluation procedures also influence the goals chosen and the implementation procedures used. For example, if evaluation procedures show that the desired learning has not taken place, the teacher may wish to reconsider both the goals and the implementation procedures. Perhaps the goals were overly ambitious or inappropriate for the students. On the other hand, the teaching strategy may have been unsuitable for attaining the chosen goal. With feedback from one phase of the teaching act, the teacher can critically examine the effectiveness of the other components.

The three-phase approach to teaching as described here is a sequentially related series of steps which proceed from the establishing of goals to a verification of the attainment of these goals. Stated another way, teaching is a logical operation in which goals are determined, attempts are made to reach those goals, and the effectiveness of those attempts is evaluated. Each of the steps can be identified with questions such as

What do I want the students to know or understand?

How will I get the students to the goal?

How will I determine whether or not they know or understand what I have identified in the goal?

Two major themes or goals will serve as structure for the text. The first is to develop in readers the mental tools needed to serve as a foundation for continued professional growth. The second is to describe and apply the results suggested by research in teaching effectiveness.

Research on Teaching Effectiveness

The education profession is at the most exciting and unique time in its history. Admittedly, it is under fire as a result of studies done by groups such as the National Commission on Excellence in Education (1983). However, the studies uniformly point out that teachers deserve higher salaries, better working conditions, and more prestige. Because of these studies and other factors, the public is finally becoming aware of the needs of the profession. Our view is that the future of education is brighter than ever before.

In addition to studies and public awareness, a substantial body of research literature is also exerting a prominent influence on educational decisions. This literature falls under a somewhat general category called *teacher effectiveness*. Simply stated, the research identifies what "good" or effective teachers do compared to what is done by those who are less effective. Historically, education has been very vulnerable to opinion, influenced by prominent thinkers, or at the worst, even whim. This is no longer the case. Because of this second theme we cite throughout the text appropriate studies that document teaching effectiveness.

ORGANIZATION OF THE TEXT

The material that follows has been organized into four units, which are as follows:

Unit 1: Planning (Chapters 2–5)

Unit 2: Implementing (Chapters 6–10)

Unit 3: Measurement and Evaluation (Chapter 11)

Unit 4: Directions (Chapter 12)

In an attempt to streamline the readability of the text, we have implemented a standard format that is used for each chapter. The format includes the following:

1. *Introduction.* An orientation to the material and a rationale for its inclusion in the book.
2. *Objectives.* A listing of the skills you will have upon the conclusion of the chapter.

3. *Content.* Materials which facilitate the objectives by providing explanations, descriptions, and examples.
4. *Exercises and Feedback.* Opportunities to practice the skills with explanations and answers provided. Feedback for all exercises is given at the end of each chapter.
5. *Summary.* Brief statements relating the work to the overall conceptualization of the book.

As just stated, the first step to effective teaching is planning, and the planning phase begins with the identification of content areas. Turn now to Unit 1, Chapter 2, where content analysis will be discussed in detail.

REFERENCES

A nation at risk: The imperative for educational reform. (1983). Washington D.C.: National Commission on Excellence in Education.

Broudy, H. (1972). *The real world of the public schools.* New York: Harcourt Brace Jovanovich.

Clark, C., & Yinger, R. (1979). *Three studies of teacher planning.* East Lansing, MI: Michigan State University, Institute for Research on Teaching.

Davies, I. (1973). *Competency based learning: Technology, management and design.* New York: McGraw-Hill.

Dreikurs, Rudolph. (1968). *The courage to be imperfect [Speech].* Tempe, AZ: Arizona State University.

Goodlad, J., & Klein, M. (1970). *Behind the classroom door.* Worthington, OH: Charles A. Jones.

Holt, J. (1964). *How children fail.* New York: Dell.

Hyman, R. (Ed.). (1971). *Contemporary thought on teaching.* Englewood Cliffs, NJ: Prentice-Hall.

Jackson, P. (1968). *Life in classrooms.* New York: Holt, Rinehart & Winston.

Kounin, J. (1970). *Discipline and group management in classrooms.* New York: Holt, Rinehart & Winston.

Mager, R. (1962). *Preparing instructional objectives.* Belmont, CA: Fearon.

McCutcheon, G. (1980). How elementary teachers plan their courses. *Elementary School Journal, 81,* 4–23.

Mintz, A. (1979). *Teacher planning: A simulation study.* Unpublished doctoral dissertation, Syracuse University.

Nyquist, E., & Hawes, G. (Eds.). (1972). *Open education.* New York: Bantam.

Peterson, P., Marx R., & Clark, C. (1978). Teacher planning, teacher behavior, and student achievement. *American Educational Research Journal, 15,* 417–432.

Popham, J., & Baker, E. (1970). *Systematic instruction.* Englewood Cliffs, NJ: Prentice-Hall.

Ragen, W., & Shepherd, G. (1977). *Modern elementary curriculum* (5th ed.). New York: Holt, Rinehart & Winston.

Ryan, K., & Cooper, J. (1975). *Those who can, teach* (2nd ed.). Boston: Houghton Mifflin.

Silberman, C. (1970). *Crisis in the classroom.* New York: Random House.

Smith, B., Cohen, S., & Pearl, A. (1972). *Teachers for the real world.* Washington, DC: American Association of Colleges of Teacher Education.

Thomas, J. (1975). *Learning centers.* Boston: Holbrook Research Institute.

UNIT
ONE

PLANNING

2 ‖ The Goals of Instruction

INTRODUCTION

The purpose of this chapter is to help you think about your own teaching goals. We will discuss the different types of goals found in our schools today, which will provide you with the tools necessary to select and analyze goals for your own teaching. These goals then will serve as the starting point for the construction of objectives, which is the focus of Chapter 3. In subsequent chapters we will then discuss the process of translating objectives into teaching strategies that can be implemented in elementary and secondary classrooms.

Before we launch into our discussion of goals, brief mention should be made of the distinction between goals and objectives. Goals are broad statements of educational intent. Typically, they are described in general, abstract terms, for example:

> To understand the importance of the Civil War in U.S. history.

> To appreciate the importance of good study habits.

> To know basic principles of proper nutrition.

Objectives, by contrast, are typically stated using behavioral terms, in an attempt to define educational outcomes precisely, for example:

> Students will identify examples of participles, gerunds, and infinitives.

> Students will match major historical events with appropriate U.S. presidents.

> Students will apply the Pythagorean theorem to various word problems.

In these instances verbs like *identifying, match,* and *apply* specify what is expected of students as they attain the objective. We talk more in the next chapter about the relationship of goals to objectives.

OBJECTIVES

After completing Chapter 2, you should be able to accomplish the following objectives:

1. For you as a pre/inservice teacher to become aware of the three major sources of goals for the school curriculum so that, when provided with a list of goals, you will be able to classify each as

to whether the primary source has been the child, the society, or the academic disciplines.

2. For you as a pre/inservice teacher to become aware of the three domains so that, without aid, you will be able to provide a characteristic for each of the affective, psychomotor, or cognitive domains.

3. For you as a pre/inservice teacher to understand abstractions and facts so that, when given a list of statements, you will be able to correctly identify each type of content.

SOURCES OF GOALS

Every teacher has some kind of goal when she teaches, but the goals selected by various teachers differ in their value to the student. For example, some teachers have as their goal keeping the kids busy and quiet until the bell rings; other teachers have as their goal getting through a textbook or covering a chapter in the following week. The value of each of these goals is questionable at best and is hard to defend from a professional standpoint. Our purpose here is to describe some possible sources for the establishment of educationally defensible goals and discuss the significance of these sources for today's schools.

The Child as a Source of Goals

Two basic questions every teacher should ask in considering the goals of instruction are What are schools for? and How does my class fit into the larger picture? One pair of answers to these questions is that schools are for people, and the function of the school and its classrooms is to help young people develop to the fullest extent of their potential. In other words, one source of goals for instruction can be found in the students themselves. In tapping this source of curriculum goals, the teacher is basically asking the question: How can the knowledge and skills that I possess as a teacher help the students I'm teaching develop into healthy and functioning adults?

If you thought about this question for a while, we think you'd realize that the answer to this depends upon a number of factors such as the level of the students and the subject being taught. A detailed discussion of how the needs of students at different levels and in different types of classes determine the goals of instruction is beyond the scope of this chapter, but a few illustrations may be helpful.

Probably the area of the curriculum where the learner has had the greatest effect on goals is in the area of early childhood. Here, a large part of the school day is devoted to helping the child grow emotionally, intellectually, and physically. Special attention is paid to the developmental levels of the students, and learning tasks are designed to match these levels and help children progress to the next. In addition, special attention is paid to the emotional growth of individuals, and attempts are made to help students develop healthy attitudes about themselves and others. Some representative goals in the early childhood curriculum that have the student as a primary source include the following:

Kindergarten students will develop good eye-hand coordination.

Kindergarten students will understand families and how children are a part of families.

Kindergarten students will develop speaking and listening skills.

Another area of the curriculum that stresses the child as a source of goals is the area of health science. A primary focus of the health curriculum is to help the child understand his body and the changes which are occurring in that body. Some examples of student-related goals in this area of the curriculum include the following:

Health science students will understand the importance of proper nutrition in the diet.

Health science students will appreciate the importance of hygiene in maintaining the body's functionings.

Health science students will understand the role of exercise in maintaining physical fitness.

Each of these goals focuses on the area of health and uses the child as a starting point for that focus. Lists like these could be constructed for each subject matter area and grade level. The extent to which a particular teacher's goals approximate this list would indicate, to a large extent, the degree to which that teacher believes that schools are designed to help students develop into physically and psychologically healthy adults.

Society as a Source of Goals

Another way to approach the task of establishing teaching goals is to examine the society that students live in and will ultimately function in, and decide how schools can help students to effectively meet the challenges of that society. Proponents of this view of the curriculum claim that the role of the school is to prepare students for life, and the content of the schools should be matched to the demands of everyday living. The value of goals established by this approach is measured in terms of their usefulness to the individual in functioning in today's

Democratic societies are founded upon an educated and knowledgeable populace.

world. Knowledge for its own sake is rejected; instead, knowledge becomes valuable to the extent that it is practical. A present-day interpretation of this approach of selecting goals is called life management and focuses on those goals that will help an individual manage his life in a complex technological world. A major focus of this curriculum is helping students to understand how basically abstract processes like math and reading have potential utility for functioning in the worlds of work and play.

One of the areas of the curriculum where societal influences have had a major impact on the curriculum is in the area of home economics. Here, students are trained to attack the problem of functioning in today's modern society in a systematic and scientific way. Some examples of goals in the home economics curriculum that reflect a societal influence are

Home economics students will compare different loan conditions and select the one that is best for a particular situation.

Home economics students will plan menus that are nutritionally and economically practical.

Each of these goals has as its focus the development of skills that will be useful to each individual in living in modern-day society.

Another more traditional area of the curriculum where societal demands have had an influence is the field of mathematics. With this orientation, mathematics' place in the curriculum is determined by the extent to which it can help students function in 20th-century America. Emphasis is placed on the application of math skills rather than their theoretical implications. The following are some goals from the area of math that reflect a societal influence:

Math students will be able to balance their checkbooks.

Math students will use ratios to adjust recipes and adapt plans.

Math students will understand distance, rate, and time problems.

Math students will be able to use various area formulas to solve everyday problems.

In each of these examples mathematics is seen not as an end, but rather as a means toward some other goal. A third type of orientation to goal setting, the academic focus, views the various disciplines as ends in, and of, themselves. This approach to goal setting is described in the next section.

The Academic Disciplines as Sources of Goals

A third way to generate goals for instruction is to examine the various academic disciplines and determine which knowledge in these disciplines is most important or central to understanding these different content areas. Proponents of this approach to goal setting contend that the function of the schools is not so much to help students adjust to society or to give them short-range skills that will quickly become outmoded in today's rapidly changing world but rather to transmit to students the knowledge that has stood the test of time. These same people call attention to the immense number of changes that have occurred in the last 20 or 30 years and point out that anything other than an academically oriented curriculum, which transcends these changes, would soon be outmoded. In addition, they state that a number of other institutions, like the family and the church, are much better suited to teach life adjustment skills and that the schools should teach only basic knowledge and skills.

If a teacher were to use an academic approach to select teaching goals, she would probably turn to the texts and notes she used as a college student and try to determine which ideas were central to her discipline. These would then become the goals of the curriculum and the major focus of her teaching. Some examples of academically oriented goals include the following:

Social studies students will know the differences between Marxism and socialism.

Economics students will understand the law of supply and demand.

Science students will know the characteristics of the major animal phyla.

Music students will be able to classify major musical works as baroque, classical, or romantic.

Math students will know how to solve for unknowns in quadratic equations.

Sometimes goals are selected for inclusion into an academically oriented curriculum because they form the foundation or basis for other goals. For example, teaching young children the concepts of *right* and *left*, *up* and *down*, *big* and *little*, and *square* and *circle* can be justified in terms of their future value in the teaching of reading in addition to their more immediate utilitarian value. (Think for a second how you would explain the difference between a *d*, a *p*, and a *q* if kindergarten or first-grade students didn't know the difference between left and right or up and down.)

Another example from the early childhood curriculum which further illustrates the use of prerequisite goals is the common activity in preschool and kindergarten classes of having children color in figures. The major purpose of this activity is not to provide some type of artistic experience for students but rather to develop their eye-hand and small muscle coordination. Both of these are important in the later learning of reading and writing skills.

Both of these latter examples were provided to broaden the concept of an academically oriented curriculum to include a broad spectrum of goals in the schools which is designed to provide students with background experiences for later, more traditional, academic goals.

EXERCISE 2.1 _____

Examine the goals and try to determine whether their primary focus is the child (c), society (s), or the academic disciplines (a). When you're done, you can check your answers in the feedback section at the end of the chapter.

_____ 1. Junior high social studies students will know the thirteen states of the Confederacy.

_____ 2. First-year math students will understand how to compute cost per unit when given aggregate costs.

_____ 3. Fifth-grade science students will understand the concept of an ecosystem.

_____ 4. First-grade students will understand that they have rights and responsibilities.

_____ 5. Sixth-grade health students will understand how to care for cuts and abrasions.

_____ 6. Senior high civics students will understand the voting system in their city, state, and country.

_____ 7. Junior high health students will know the causes, symptoms, and means of preventing venereal disease.

_____ 8. First-year biology students will know the characteristics of monocotyledons and dicotyledons.

_____ 9. Senior high driver education students will know the driving regulations in their state.

_____ 10. Fifth-grade math students will know how to convert fractions into decimals.

THE THREE DOMAINS

When teachers consider what to teach, the nature of learning must be considered. Learning can be described as a change in behavior that occurs on a regular basis resulting from experience rather than growth. For example, children begin learning early and undertake many physical tasks such as tying shoes, buttoning shirts, holding pencils, and moving their eyes back and forth across a printed page. They learn intellectual tasks such as the names of objects in their home, the alphabet, and the use of mathematical principles. They also learn attitudes and values which influence their feelings and interests such as color preference, confidence in themselves, and reactions to peers.

All the preceding are examples of learning, but they are not all the same kind of learning. Just as goals can be differentiated in terms of their sources, goals can also be described in terms of the type of learning that is intended. In this respect we can describe goals as being primarily concerned with the development of muscular skills and coordination (psychomotor), the growth of attitudes or values (affective), or the transmission of knowlede and intellectual skills (cognitive).

Understanding differences between goals in the different domains helps to clarify teachers' thinking about the goals they're trying to teach. This, then, has implications for planning, implementing, and evaluating. The more clearly teachers understand what they are trying to accomplish, the greater the chance that they will achieve those goals. Other helpful discussions of the three domains and problems encountered in establishing goals in these areas can be found in Bloom, Hastings, and Madaus (1971), and Tanner and Tanner (1980).

Unfortunately for teachers who are trying to separate behaviors, children come to the classroom as whole beings. So as we examine the three domains of learning, we should realize that they do not occur in isolation but rather work together to make up one whole being. Some

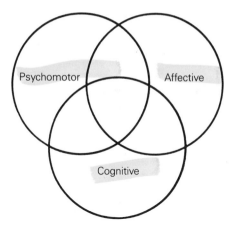

Figure 2.1   The Three Domains

behaviors are easily classifiable into one of the three domains, while others seem to overlap a great deal. When diagrammed, the three domains might appear as pictured in Figure 2.1.

A good example of an integrated behavior that incorporates all three domains of learning in school is handwriting. The child must have the small muscle coordination to make the necessary intricate movements (psychomotor); he must know what movements are used to form the letters (cognitive); and he must want to perform these enough so that proficiency can be developed through practice (affective).

Most tasks taught in schools are more easily separated as to domain, but every teacher should know his domain of primary teaching concentration in order to plan effectively. The importance of knowing the intent of the instruction makes it imperative for the teacher to determine the focus of planned instruction as either affective, psychomotor, or cognitive. Each of these three domains will be described in Chapter 4.

CONTENT IN THE COGNITIVE DOMAIN

Because of the cognitive domain's importance in elementary and secondary curriculums, this section is devoted to a further analysis of the different types of content found within it.

The basic idea presented here is that not all goals within the cognitive domain are of equal worth. Some types of content are more valuable than others in helping students understand the world around them. These ideas are called abstractions.

Abstractions

Abstractions are the *ideas* people use to describe, understand, and simplify the world. They are in a sense the mental currency that we use in our exchange with the environment. To illustrate this notion, imagine a small child beginning to acquire experience in her young life. She encounters an animal her mother or father identifies as a dog. The dog has a set of features such as floppy ears, wagging tail, and scruffy fur that the child reacts to without consciously being aware of it. She then encounters another dog with some similar features, then a third, perhaps a fourth, and ultimately many more. The child, again without realizing, sees a pattern in the features. For instance, even though the dogs vary considerably, they all have four legs, all say "woof-woof," all are hairy, and so on. The pattern in these features common to the dogs result in the child's idea of "dog." This idea is an abstraction. The abstraction is not any particular *example* of dog, nor is it a sort of average of the examples encountered. It is literally an abstracted mental idea of *dog*.

Let's investigate this abstracting process a bit further. We watch or hear the weather forecast over a period of time, and we hear the meteorologist make statements such as, "The barometric pressure is dropping," and at some other point hear, "The rain probability is 50 percent." As we watch or hear these broadcasts, we begin to notice that there is a relationship between low barometric pressure and rain probability. As with the child beginning to acquire an idea of dogs, we see a pattern emerge which could be described as "The lower the barometric pressure, the higher the probability of rain." The child has formed an abstraction and we have formed an abstraction. The difference between the two is that the child found a pattern in the features of different dogs and we found a pattern in the relationship between pressure and rain probability. This abstraction is broader and more encompassing than the one about dogs, but it is a pattern and an abstraction nevertheless.

The power in knowing patterns is enormous. They greatly simplify the world for us because we need only remember the pattern rather than all the individual examples that fit it. For instance, the girl would have to understand or know each example of dog separately if she had no pattern, but with it she has a single idea of dog, into which she fits all the examples she encounters.

As another example of the power of patterning, consider the spelling rule "*i* before *e* except after *c*." (Rules are another form of pattern.) Knowing this rule allows a learner to spell individual words such as

retrieve

believe

conceive

conceit

perceive

Admittedly, the learner must know the pattern's exceptions, but the pattern makes it unnecessary for the learner to know all words individually.

To this point we have suggested that abstractions are formed as a result of seeing patterns in our experiences and have illustrated the importance of these patterns in simplifying our learning. Now let's view this information in the broader context of education.

One way to think of education is to view it as a process in which abstract ideas of a culture are transmitted to the young people of that culture. For example, social studies education is concerned with teaching students to understand the following abstractions:

democracy

socialism

social stratification

The more economically diverse an economy, the more stable it is when economic changes occur.

When supply stays constant, price is directly related to demand.

In a similar manner, science teaching involves the transmission of abstractions such as the following:

ion

magnetism

mass

Acids neutralize bases.

The more recent animal phyla have more complex systems.

English or language arts would incorporate abstractions such as

adverb

metaphor

preposition

When the subject is singular, add an *s* to the verb.

When there are several adjectives modifying a noun, the article goes first.

When there are two adjectives modifying a noun, the one designating size goes before the one designating color.

Similar analyses could be done for each of the subject matter areas. In each case abstractions form the major content or subject matter in that area.

We now turn our attention to the two major types of abstractions taught at the elementary and secondary levels: concepts and generalizations. *Concepts* are classes or categories that share some common characteristic. *Generalizations* are statements relating two or more concepts, typically in a causal or correlational relationship. Each of these types of cognitive goals is described more fully in the paragraphs that follow.

Concepts are ideas that refer to a class or category in which all the members share some common characteristics. For example, *adverb* is a concept that has the characteristic of modifying a verb, an adjective, or another adverb. We use these defining characteristics to decide whether a particular word belongs in the category or not. In addition to the essential or defining characteristics, examples of concepts also contain irrelevant or nonessential characteristics. In the case of the concept *adverb*, the irrelevant characteristics include the length of the word, its sound, and the number of consonants or vowels

Table 2.1   Concepts from Various Disciplines

Language Arts	Science	Mathematics
homonym	nucleus	set
antonym	mitosis	rational number
syllable	evaluation	lowest common denominator
alliteration	mesoderm	quadratic equation
quatrain	metamorphosis	exponent
inference	acid	base
tragedy	base	tangent
gerund	algae	angle
plot	fruit	axiom
prefix	energy	
	plant	

Social Studies	Music	Art
federalism	melody	line
climate	rhythm	texture
tax	syncopation	batik
inflation	harmony	realism
boycott	a cappella	cubism

in it. In other words, these characteristics tell us nothing about whether a word is an adverb or not. In trying to learn a concept, these nonessential characteristics represent noise which the learner must filter out to focus on the essential characteristics. These essential characteristics are important to remember because they comprise the rule for class membership; in other words, they help to determine whether something is a positive or negative example of a concept.

Many of the abstractions that have previously been mentioned are concepts. For example, *dog, adverb, democracy,* and *ion* are all concepts. Typically we think of concepts as being single words which represent ideas. Another way of representing concepts is by a definition; for example, a democracy is a form of government in which the power to make decisions resides in the governed. Some additional examples of concepts from various disciplines are found in Table 2.1.

Let's look again at the idea of patterning. Suppose a learner sees sentences such as:

The boy ran quickly to his locker.

Their conversation was abruptly interrupted.

The material was appropriately analyzed.

Learners recognize on their own, or with the help of the teacher, that in each case the underlined word tells something about the verb. This represents a pattern that is the characteristic of "modifying a verb." The pattern will be expanded to include modification of adjectives and other adverbs, and the result is the concept *adverb.*

Notice as we've discussed abstractions in general and concepts in particular that we've consistently referred to examples. Research consistently supports the value of examples in concept learning (Tennyson & Cocciarella, 1986). Tennyson (1978) and Feldman (1972) in separate studies both found that concept learning depended on the individual being provided with a combination of examples and a definition. We will describe and discuss definitions later in this chapter. The use of nonexamples is also important in learning concepts. By analyzing the positive examples and noting what they have in common, and by contrasting these with negative examples, the learner is often able to figure out these essential characteristics for himself. In addition to providing the student with data from which to extract the important characteristics, examples also provide concrete referents in the world. In a sense, they make abstract ideas less abstract. Bruner, Goodnow, and Austin (1956) investigated the abstraction process, and their work makes interesting reading, both for those interested in the practical and for those interested in the theoretical aspects of this topic.

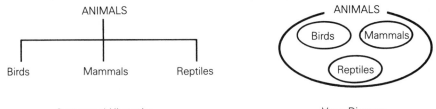

Figure 2.2   Illustrations of Superordinate Relationships

Another way of teaching someone about a concept is by relating it to other concepts. For example, if you were to ask someone what a bird is, a typical reply would be that it's a kind of animal. In a similar way, a social studies teacher might define a democracy as a form of government. In both instances the concept being explained was related to a larger, more inclusive — or *superordinate* — concept. Superordinate relationships can be illustrated either through the use of conceptual hierarchies or through the use of Venn diagrams, as is shown in Figure 2.2.

Knowing that a concept is a member of a larger set or concept is useful because it allows us to apply characteristics of the larger to the smaller. For example, if a person knows a lemur is a mammal, a superordinate concept, then he could infer that lemurs have mammalian characteristics such as having fur, being warm-blooded, giving live birth, and nursing their young. In a similar manner, if someone tells you that salsify is an herb, then you know that it's a plant that is used for seasoning. Superordinate concepts help to make concepts more meaningful by contributing their characteristics to the definition. This is why most dictionaries define concepts in terms of a superordinate one. For example, if you were to look up the term *wok*, you would find it described as a pan for cooking Oriental food dishes. The superordinate concept *pan* allows you to infer that this object is probably made of metal and is meant to be heated.

In addition to allowing us to infer characteristics, superordinate concepts also help to show relationships between concepts. For example, in the case of the concept *birds*, linking this concept to *animals* establishes the fact that birds are related to other concepts like *mammals* or *reptiles*. Linking concepts in our teaching is important so that students learn to see the larger relationships between ideas. One of these relationships is between coordinate concepts.

Coordinate concepts are abstractions that are subsumed by the superordinate concept and that are different from the concept under consideration. In the previous examples with birds, *mammals* and *reptiles* would be coordinate concepts to *birds* because they are types of animals that are different from birds. In addition to using their value to integrate ideas, knowing the coordinate concepts of a given concept is important because it is coordinate concepts that are most easily confused with the concept under study. For example, in a lesson involving the concept *reptiles*, students are most likely to get examples of this concept confused with examples of coordinate concepts such as *amphibians* or *mammals* rather than unrelated concepts like *cars, balls,* or *books.*

A third type of relationship that exists between concepts is a subordinate relationship. A *subordinate concept* is a subset or subcategory of a concept. Subordinate concepts are easy to understand if you understand superordinate concepts, because these are reciprocal relationships. For example, in the case of animals and birds, *animals* is superordinate to *birds,* and *birds* is subordinate to *animals.* In a similar manner, the concept *noun* is superordinate to the subordinate concept *proper noun.*

Superordinate, coordinate, and subordinate concepts are discussed again in Chapter 7 when we describe strategies for teaching concepts. Those wanting to read more about concept teaching in the classroom are referred to the article by Clark (1971) and the books by Klausmeier (1980), and Treman and Markle (1983).

The second major type of abstraction taught in our schools is the form of content called generalizations. Again, generalizations are statements about patterns in the world that are either correlational or suggest a causal relationship. Other terms used to refer to descriptions about these patterns are *rule, principle,* or *law.* For our purposes, we will consider these terms to be synonymous in that they all describe patterns in terms of the ways that objects and events in our environment operate.

Here are some examples of generalizations describing causal relationships:

Smoking causes cancer.

Lack of sunlight makes plants grow tall and spindly.

Heat makes molecules move faster.

These generalizations describe a relationship between concepts in which something causes something else to occur. The other type of generalization describes a relationship between concepts in which a given condition is usually accompanied by a condition. For example, the following generalizations describe situations in which one type of condition is typically followed by or correlated with another:

Children from single-children families have higher IQs than other children.

Lower socioeconomic families have more children than upper socioeconomic families.

More management problems occur during individual student work than in large-group activities.

Note that these generalizations don't imply causality; in other words, being an only child doesn't cause higher IQs but rather is related to a number of other variables like higher socioeconomic status, higher parental educational level, and more contact with adults that may have an influence on IQ. Being an only child in and of itself does not.

As can be seen from the examples presented, generalizations vary in terms of their validity or accuracy, with some being very probabilistic and others, invariant. For example, heat always makes molecules move faster. This would be an invariant relationship in that it always happens. Contrasted with generalizations like this are probabilistic generalizations like children from single-children families having higher IQs than other children. Obviously there are a number of instances in which children from single-child families have lower IQs than children from multiple-child families. But on the whole, this generalization is true.

This brings us to a discussion of how generalizations are formed. People make generalizations by observing the world around them and by trying to see patterns in the things that they observe. As an illustration of this process look at the data in Table 2.2 and see if you can make any general statements about trends or patterns in the data.

Here are several generalizations that could be made by analyzing the data in the table:

The sun rises later each day in the autumn.

The sun sets earlier each day in the autumn.

Days get progressively shorter each day of autumn.

Generalizations like these are formed by people who are observant enough to see patterns in the world around them. In a sense, these patterns can be said to be discovered, in that they have always existed,

Table 2.2 Time for Sunrise and Sunset

Date	Sunrise	Sunset
10/14	7:14	6:42
10/15	7:15	6:41
10/16	7:16	6:40

and one person or a group of persons finally noticed the pattern. One of the major goals of science is to formulate generalizations about the world. What differentiates scientists from other people who form generalizations is that scientists approach this task in a much more systematic fashion than the person on the street. However, all of us form generalizations about the world.

Often generalizations are learned in the same way that they are formed, by observing a number of examples and noticing trends or patterns in them. Generalizations are quite similar to concepts in this regard. The generalizations that you formed from observing the sunrise and sunset data were learned this way. An alternate way of learning generalizations is to have someone tell them to you. This is often quicker, and perhaps it is for this reason that this is the most common way of teaching generalizations in schools today. However, the teaching of generalizations through strictly verbal means has drawbacks. One is related to developmental considerations. The work of Piaget and others who have studied the way children learn shows us the importance of providing children with concrete, tangible experiences in the learning of abstractions. In the absence of such experiences, children learn words and not ideas. A classic example of this was noted by John Dewey.

> John Dewey reports visiting a class in the vicinity of Chicago which was studying the way in which the earth was probably formed. Mr. Dewey asked the students whether, if they were able to dig down to the center of the earth, they would find it hot or cold there. No child could answer. The teacher then said to Mr. Dewey that he had asked the wrong question. She turned to the children and said, "Children, what is the condition at the center of the earth?"
>   The children all replied in chorus, "In a state of igneous fusion."
> (Tyler, 1949, p. 72)

Obviously, the students in that class had learned a string of words rather than a meaningful abstraction. Situations like this occur all too frequently in our schools when teachers forget that concepts and generalizations are meaningful only to the extent that students can relate them to the real world. Forgetting this, teachers teach abstractions as a string of words and are satisfied when students can recall these words without their meanings during class discussion or on a test. The teaching strategies discussed in Chapter 7 describe a number of techniques to ensure that this doesn't happen.

In trying to decide which generalizations should be included in the curriculum, the teacher has several considerations to make. Fraenkel (1980) suggested that the following criteria can be used in trying to decide whether a particular generalization should be included in the curriculum:

To how many varied areas, events, people, ideas, objects, etc., does the generalization apply? (Applicability)

How likely is it that the relationship which the generalization suggests does indeed exist in actuality? (Accuracy)

To what degree does the generalization, as stated, lead on to other insights? (Depth)

To what extent does (do) the relationship(s) that the generalization suggests describe important aspects of human behavior and explain important segments of today's world? (Significance)

How much information does it encompass? (Breadth)

How many powerful (complex) concepts does it include? (Conceptual strength)

The use of these criteria can be illustrated by comparing the following two generalizations:

Tree-ring size is related to the amount of rainfall in that year.

How quickly any change comes about depends not only on the nature of the change itself, but also on the pressures for and against that change.

Obviously, the second is preferable to the first on the basis of a number of the criteria listed.

This concludes our discussion of abstractions. In the following section we describe facts, discuss how facts are different from abstractions, and explore the implications of these differences for teaching. Before that, however, let's focus on two exercises involving abstractions.

EXERCISE 2.2 _____

Read the following teaching anecdotes and answer the questions that follow. Then compare your answers to the ones found in the feedback section at the end of the chapter.

1. Mr. Waters, a fifth-grade teacher, was preparing for his first-period language arts class. His goal for that period was to teach his students transitive verbs. He began his lesson by saying, "I'm going to show you two sentences, and I want you to look at them and tell me how the sentences are different." With this he wrote the following sentences on the board:

> The infielder, bobbling the ball momentarily, threw it in the knick of time.
> They were late again for the start of first period English.

"The first one is longer," said Jim.
"The second one has a plural subject," offered Mary.

''Isn't the verb in the first sentence in the past tense?'' asked Kathy.

''But so is the verb in the second sentence. And we're supposed to be looking for differences,'' corrected Dick.

After writing these ideas on the board, Mr. Waters commented, ''Those are all good ideas. Let me give you another example of the first kind of sentence and see if you can narrow your ideas down.'' To his list he added

The children ate the oatmeal cookies.

''Look at the sentences again,'' directed Mr. Waters, ''and tell me how the first and the third are similar.''

The lesson continued until the students saw that the first and the third both had direct objects. Then Mr. Waters discussed the idea of transitive verbs, relating this idea to the examples the students had used.

a. What abstraction was Mr. Waters trying to teach?

_____

b. What kind of data did the teacher use for examples?

_____

_____

2. Mrs. Jones, another English teacher, was also trying to teach her sixth-grade students about verbs. She started the lesson by saying, ''All of you remember what verbs are. We've been working with them all year. Now we're going to learn about a special kind of verb called the intransitive verbs. Intransitive verbs are verbs that can't take a direct object. Who remembers what a direct object is? Johnny?''

''I think they are words that receive the action of the verb,'' Johnny responded. ''Like, 'He hit me.' *Me* is the direct object.''

''Real fine, Johnny,'' said Mrs. Jones. ''Now remember, intransitive verbs are verbs that can't take a direct object. Some examples of intransitive verbs are different forms of the verb *be,* such as *am, were, was,* and *has been.* I'm going to put a sentence on the board. See if you can tell me whether the verb is intransitive or not.''

He was late.

''Yes,'' offered Sally, ''because it's a form of *be* and can't have a direct object.''
''Good,'' said Mrs. Jones, ''and how about this one?''

The woodsman chopped the tree down.

''That can't be intransitive,'' Rachel said.
''Why not?'' Mrs. Jones asked.
''Because it has a direct object. *Tree* is the direct object.''
''Good, Rachel.''

The lesson continued until Mrs. Jones felt assured that the students understood intransitive verbs.

a. What abstraction was Mrs. Jones trying to teach?

_____

b. What kind of data did the teacher use for examples?

_____

_____

c. How were Mr. Waters's and Mrs. Jones's teaching approaches different? How were they the same?

_____

_____

3. Mr. Black wanted his fourth-grade students to know biodegradable objects so that they would know what kinds of things could be thrown away and not cause litter. He began the lesson by saying, "Today I'm going to teach you about biodegradable objects. Everybody say 'biodegradable objects'." He then put the word on the board. "Orange peels and cigar butts are biodegradable. However, bottles and cigarette filters are not. Neither is aluminum foil or bottle caps. Can you tell me what *biodegradable* means?"

Jerry said, "It must be something to do with plant products."
Chris added, "Or it could be things that are soft."
"Well, let me give you some more information to help you decide."
With that, he took out a container that was filled with moist dirt and other objects. In the container were a number of biodegradable objects like wood chips and paper that had already started to disintegrate, along with other objects like plastic cups and pop tops. As he took each of these objects out of the pail, he labeled them as either biodegradable or not. On the basis of this information the class was able to come up with a definition.

a. What abstraction was Mr. Black trying to teach?

_____

b. What kind of data did the teacher use for examples?

_____

_____

EXERCISE 2.3 _____

Answer the following questions. Note that more than one response may be correct. Compare your answers to the ones found in the feedback section at the end of the chapter.

1. Consider the concept *horse*. Which of the following could be superordinate to the concept?
   a. cow
   b. domestic animal
   c. Shetland
   d. beast of burden
   e. none of the above

2. Consider the concept *radio*. If *electrical instructional tools* is superordinate to *radio*, which of the following is coordinate to *radio*?
   a. encyclopedia
   b. overhead projector
   c. textbook
   d. teacher
   e. none of the above

3. Consider the concept *bread.* Which of the following could be subordinate to the concept?
   a. rye
   b. wheat
   c. meat
   d. white
   e. starch
   f. food

4. Which of the following could be superordinate to *bread?*
   a. banana
   b. rye
   c. food
   d. fruit
   e. vegetable

5. If *fried bacon* and *hot oatmeal* were coordinate to *bread,* which of the following could be superordinate?
   a. banana
   b. food
   c. cooked food
   d. raw food
   e. prunes
   f. none of the above

Facts

Facts are statements about the world that are directly observable and typically singular in occurrence, either in the past or in the present. Some examples of facts are these:

> Johnson was one of Lincoln's vice presidents.
>
> Emil von Behring discovered how to control diphtheria.
>
> The high temperature in Salt Lake City on June 20, 1978, was 87 degrees.
>
> The Japanese bombed Pearl Harbor on December 7, 1941.

Each of these statements is or was directly observable and is singular in occurrence in the past. As such, they are factual reports of what happened at a particular place at a particular time. This differentiates them from abstractions in that abstractions are statements about general patterns. Concepts describe categories and classes which are, in a sense, timeless in that what was an adverb yesterday will be an adverb tomorrow. Generalizations describe patterns that were not only valid in the past but are also valid now and should also be valid in the future.

Facts, on the other hand, occur only once. This characteristic of facts, which we discuss shortly, places severe limitations on their utility to students.

Let's look now at a series of facts and their relationship to patterns. Consider the following:

President Roosevelt was from New York.

President Johnson was from Texas.

President Nixon was from California.

Each of these statements is a fact. Consider also the fact that each state mentioned has a large population. We might then suggest the pattern, "Presidents tend to come from populous states." While there are obvious exceptions to this pattern, it tends to be generally valid. Our point in this example is to illustrate the relationship between facts and abstractions. Abstractions are formed by having learners process facts into recognizable patterns. This is one reason for including facts in the curriculum.

The other major reason for learning facts is that some facts are considered to be valuable to know, in and of themselves, apart from any relationship of abstractions. Examples of these types of facts are

The Declaration of Independence was signed in Philadelphia on July 4, 1776.

Alexander Graham Bell invented the telephone.

Herman Melville wrote *Moby Dick*.

The reason that facts such as these are considered inherently valuable is that they comprise part of the general knowledge store which is shared by most Americans and which is considered to be one of the marks of an educated person. In *Cultural Literacy*, a recent best-seller on the *New York Times* book list, Hirsch (1987) equated cultural literacy with knowledge of a certain number of key facts. However, relative to their utility and importance in the curriculum, facts probably receive an undue amount of emphasis in most classrooms.

Facts and Abstractions: Their Value in the Curriculum

If our biases haven't already crept through in our writing, let us make them explicit. We feel that the major amount of time and effort spent in the classroom on cognitive goals should involve the teaching of abstractions rather than facts. The reason for this is that abstractions can be used to summarize large amounts of information, can be used to predict the future, and can be used to explain phenomena (Martin, 1970). Each of these reasons and its relevance to the classroom is discussed in the paragraphs that follow.

Generalizations serve a summarizing function in that they describe large amounts of information in a statement that is easier to remember than all the individual facts. An example from mathematics helps to illustrate this point. One of the authors was helping his son with his 9s addition facts. The son was having trouble remembering each of the separate facts, so the father taught him the generalization "when you add 9 to any number, your last number is always one less than the original." (For example, in adding 6 and 9, you get 15, the 5 of which is 1 less than the original 6.) By understanding this generalization, the boy was able to bypass the need for memorizing each of the combinations that 9 could make. Instead, he remembered a general pattern that could apply to all instances. The earlier illustration with the spelling rule "*i* before *e* except after *c*" is another example showing the benefits of learning patterns as opposed to isolated facts.

So the first argument against learning many isolated facts is that their sheer number makes them hard to remember, as attested to by anyone who has taken a course that consisted primarily of the rote memorization of facts. Typically in courses like this, students memorize the facts for a test and forget the facts shortly after, since these facts aren't ever used again.

A second reason why abstractions have particular value in the curriculum is that we can use them to make predictions about the future. To illustrate this process, analyze the following facts in Table 2.3 and make a prediction about the tides on June 7.

Three generalizations can be formed from the facts in Table 2.3.

High tides and low tides are six hours apart.

There are 12 hours between occurrences of high tides and 12 hours between occurrences of low tides.

High and low tides occur 45 minutes later each subsequent day.

Table 2.3 High and Low Tides

Date	High Tides	Low Tides
6/4	2:00 A.M.	8:00 A.M.
	2:00 P.M.	8:00 P.M.
6/5	2:45 A.M.	8:45 A.M.
	2:45 P.M.	8:45 P.M.
6/6	3:30 A.M.	9:30 A.M.
	3:30 P.M.	9:30 P.M.

On the basis of these generalizations, we can predict that high tides would occur on June 7 at 4:15 A.M. and P.M. and low tides at 10:15 A.M. and P.M. Note that, on the basis of the facts alone, you could not make this prediction. These facts first needed to be processed into abstractions, and then predictions could be made.

The process of making predictions from abstractions is a common and often unconscious everyday occurrence. For example, what time do you expect it to get dark tonight, and where will the sun be when it sets? Also, how do you expect the temperature this evening to compare to the temperature during the day? Your answers to all of these questions were predictions based on generalizations that you have formed either consciously or unconsciously about the environment. The same type of predictions can be made with concepts, the other major type of abstraction. For example, if you purchase a mystery novel, what do you expect to find in it? Or if you order crepes in a restaurant, how do you expect them to taste? Or if you rent a car, where do you expect the steering wheel, the gas pedal, and the brakes to be? These and other questions like them are fairly easy to answer if we are familiar with the concepts involved. Knowing the characteristics of a concept allows us to apply these characteristics to examples of that concept. Therefore, a mystery novel that we pick up should have some kind of mystery to solve, clues to help solve the mystery, and a resolution by the end of the story. Again, it should be emphasized that facts alone do not allow us to make such predictions.

A third use of abstractions that makes them a valuable component in the curriculum is their abilty to explain phenomena. For example, lower insurance rates for married people and nondrinkers can be explained by the generalizations linking these categories of drivers and accident rates. An additional example from teaching further illustrates this explanatory function. Two elementary teachers taught geometric shapes to their classes. Teacher A pointed out different kinds of circles, squares, rectangles, and triangles around the room, while Teacher B prepared shapes from cardboard and used these as examples. The students in Teacher B's class seemed to learn the concept faster, but on a posttest the students in Teacher A's class did better at identifying shapes that were embedded in complex designs. Both of these results can be explained by referring to generalizations that psychologists have found in their research on concept learning. The fact that Teacher B's class learned the concept more quickly could be explained by the generalization that simplifying examples when initially teaching a concept speeds up the learning process. Because of the simple shapes provided by Teacher B, her class had less difficulty in seeing the characteristics of the concepts in the examples. The fact that Teacher A's class performed better on the embedded figures task can be explained by the generalization that the closer the criterion task is to the learning situation, the better the score on the task. Because Teacher A's class had already had practice in finding shapes embedded in other shapes, they did better on this aspect of the posttest.

Several final comments should be made about the teaching of facts. As already mentioned, one rationale for the inclusion of facts in a curriculum is that some facts constitute a body of knowledge which is generally considered to be a necessity for life in America. A second justification for their inclusion in the curriculum is that they are a means of teaching abstractions by serving as the raw material that students process into abstractions. Unless one of these criteria can be applied to a particular fact, we question its inclusion. All too often, a proliferation of facts in the curriculum indicates that teachers don't know the difference between facts and abstractions and, consequently, treat all content the same. When this is done, students are inundated with minutiae, and their ability to discern and learn the major ideas in a discipline is severely hampered.

Fantini and Weinstein had the following comments to make about the proliferation of facts in the curriculum:

> Considering that so many of the largest problems facing the world and the United States today are predominantly a matter of inadequate human relations and lack of cooperation among different peoples, one wonders why we spend so much time trying to get our young children to memorize such facts as the order of American Presidents, the precise dates on which this or that event occurred, the area in square miles of this or that state (or nation or continent), and the locations of natural resources in the world. We do not deny the importance of knowledge in these areas but we become concerned when schools emphasize these areas to the exclusion of others.
>
> How many of us can remember these facts now? Name even two products of Chile. Can you, right off the top of your head, so to speak, list all the Presidents from Washington through Johnson in perfect order? Can you remember the year in which Texas was admitted to the Union? (1968, pp. 139–40)

More is said on this topic when teaching strategies are discussed in Chapter 7.

EXERCISE 2.4

Now let's see if you understand the difference between facts and abstractions well enough to differentiate between examples of each. (By the way, the ideas of a *fact* and an *abstraction* are both abstractions themselves.) We tried to teach essential characteristics of these ideas and provided you with a number of examples. We now are attempting to determine if you've learned these two abstractions by asking you to classify additional positive and negative examples of them.

Classify the following statements as either fact (f) or abstraction (a). Then compare your answers to the ones found in the feedback section at the end of the chapter.

_____ 1. A geometric figure with four equal sides is called a rhombus.

_____ 2. Extinction is the cessation of responding caused by lack of reinforcement.

_____ 3. The gravitational pull between two bodies is directly related to their mass and inversely related to the square of the distance between two objects.

_____ 4. When asking a question in the English language, the verb comes before the subject.

_____ 5. Pavlov discovered the phenomenon of classical conditioning.

_____ 6. The older a musical piece or composition, the fewer instruments in it.

_____ 7. Questions placed before a text increase learning directly related to the questions but decrease incidental learning (content not directly related to the question).

_____ 8. There are five national parks in Utah.

_____ 9. A novel is a form of literature that narrates a story.

_____ 10. Community helpers are people who perform important jobs in their neighborhoods.

_____ 11. Water boils at a lower temperature at higher elevations.

_____ 12. Sentences that state a fact or give information are called declarative.

_____ 13. Antibodies are body globulins that combine specifically with antigens to neutralize toxins and other harmful substances in the body.

_____ 14. Adagio refers to a way of playing music in an easy, graceful manner.

_____ 15. Ford Motor Company stopped making Edsels after a short time of production.

SUMMARY

This chapter began with a discussion of goals, and you should remember that describing the three orientations to goal setting as mutually exclusive is an oversimplificaton, in that a particular goal could be defended from several perspectives. For example, knowing how to compute the areas of different geometric shapes could have a strictly academic focus or could be presented as a practical law with a number of applications in the real world—knowing how to compute the area of a rectangle could be used to tell how much fertilizer to buy for a garden plot, and knowing how to compute the area of a circle could be used to adjust a pizza dough recipe for a 9-inch diameter pan to an 18-inch pan. (Hint: you don't just double the recipe.) In addition, teaching students about the biological changes that occur during puberty could be defended from all three perspectives. From a student-oriented perspective, this knowledge helps developing adolescents understand and deal with the changes that are occurring in their bodies. From a societal perspective, this information is essential for young people who will soon attempt to assume adult roles in society. And from an academic viewpoint, these changes are interesting in and of themselves as they illustrate the functioning of a number of complex systems within our bodies. Proponents of all three orientations could claim this content area as their own, and a particular goal could have several orientations and could be philosophically defended from a number of perspectives. What is important is that you understand the major sources of teaching goals and that you be able to defend intelligently your choice of goals in terms of a well-thought-out rationale.

The second area of study in this chapter involved a discussion of the three domains. The purpose here was to introduce you to and familiarize you with the psychomotor, affective, and cognitive domains. Additional material is offered in Chapter 4.

Finally, we will summarize our discussion of facts and abstractions by referring to Table 2.4. In our discussion we will treat concepts and generalizations as singular entities, abstractions. In doing so we

Table 2.4 Comparison of Facts and Abstractions

Examples	How Taught	How Measured	Uses
FACTS The closest planet to the sun is Mercury.	Question/Answer S—R	Question/Answer S—R	Can be formed into abstractions.
There were 13 states in the Confederacy.	(The stimulus is the question, and the response is the answer.)	(Either the *S* or *R* is presented, and the student has to provide the missing term.)	(Cannot be used to summarize, explain, or predict.)
ABSTRACTIONS People who exercise regularly have lower pulse rates.	Examples/ Abstractions	S⟍ S—R S⟋	Can be used to summarize, explain, and predict.
The stopping distance of a car is inversely related to its speed.	S⟍ S—R S⟋	(New examples are provided, and students generate correct classification.)	
A herbivore is an animal that eats only plants.		(Abstraction is given and student provides new examples.)	

are emphasizing the similarities between these two content forms which include their formation, the importance of examples in teaching, the measurement of what is learned and their use. Take a second now to glance over this table.

Probably one of the biggest differences between these two types of cognitive content is in terms of how they are taught. Facts can be thought of as stimulus-response connections in which the stimulus is a question and the response is the answer. The major goal of instruction is the strengthening of the S-R bond. A major way of strengthening this bond is through repetition, which can be accomplished by repeating a fact (Now remember, students, there were 13 states in the Confederacy), by asking a question (How many states were there in the Confederacy), or by inducing students to study their notes or reread the text. In contrast to facts, abstractions are learned by presenting a number of different examples which either the teacher or the students analyze for commonalities.

A second major way that facts and abstractions differ is in terms of how they are measured. Facts are typically measured as they were learned, with one part of the fact acting as the stem (e.g., who was the first president of the United States?) and the second part serving as the answer. Abstractions, by contrast, are measured by asking students either to recognize examples of the abstraction (e.g., in the case of the concept *verb*, What do the underlined words have in common?) or to provide new examples (e.g., List three verbs not discussed in class.) In both instances it is important that new examples are used to ensure that the abstraction learned generalizes to new situations. (Note how we did this in the exercises in this chapter.)

REFERENCES

Berliner, D. (1987). Simple views of effective teaching and a simple theory of classroom instruction. In D. Berliner & B. Rosenshine (Eds.), *Talks to teachers* (pp. 93–110). New York: Random House.

Bloom, B., Hastings, J., & Madaus, G. (Eds.) (1971). *Handbook on formative and summative evaluation of student learning.* New York: McGraw-Hill.

Bruner, J., Goodnow, J., & Austin, G. (1956). *A study of thinking.* New York: John Wiley.

Clark, D. (1971). Teaching concepts in the classroom. A set of prescriptions derived from experimental research. *Journal of Educational Psychology, 62,* 253–78.

Fantini, M., & Weinstein, G. (1968). *The disadvantaged: Challenge to education.* New York: Harper & Row.

Fraenkel, J. (1980). *Helping students think and value: Stategies for the social studies* (2nd ed.). Englewood Cliffs, NJ: Prentice-Hall.

Hirsch, E. (1987). *Cultural literacy.* Boston: Houghton-Mifflin.

Klausmeier, H. (1980). *Educational psychology* (4th ed.). New York: Harper & Row.

Mager, R. (1972). *Goal analysis.* Belmont, CA: Fearon.

Raths, L. (1978). *Values and teaching* (2nd ed.). Columbus, OH: Merrill.

Reilly, R., & Lewis, E. (1983). *Educational psychology.* New York: Macmillan.

Tanner, D., & Tanner, L. (1980). *Curriculum development: Theory and practice* (2nd ed.). New York: Macmillan.

Tennyson, R., & Cocciarella, M. (1986). An empirically based instructional design theory for teaching concepts. *Review of Educational Resarch, 56,* 40–71.

Treman, P., & Markle, S. (1983). *A guide to instruction and evaluation* (2nd ed.). Champaign, IL: Stipes.

Tyler, R. (1949). *Basic principles of curriculum and instruction.* Chicago: University of Chicago Press.

EXERCISE FEEDBACK

EXERCISE 2.1

Like previous examples, most of these goals could be defended from several perspectives. However, we believe the *primary* focus of these goals to be the following:

1. (a) Academic.
2. (s) Societal. This would be a skill that would help students shop more economically and use their money more wisely.
3. (a) Academic.
4. (s) Societal. This goal is designed to help students interact in a constructive and positive fashion with other people.
5. (c) Child. A basic knowledge of first aid techniques provides students with the knowledge and skills to care for their bodies when accidents occur.
6. (s) Societal. This information should prove valuable as students become citizens.
7. (c) Child. We consider the primary focus of this goal to be student oriented but consider a societal interpretation to be valid.
8. (a) Academic.
9. (s) Societal. Again, the focus here is on surviving and functioning in a world of other people.
10. (a) Academic.

EXERCISE 2.2

1. a. The abstraction being taught was *transitive verb.*
   b. The data Mr. Waters used to illustrate his abstraction were the sentences with transitive and intransitive verbs.
2. a. The abstraction being taught here was *intransitive verbs.*
   b. The data Mrs. Jones used to illustrate her abstraction were also the sentences.
   c. Mr. Waters and Mrs. Jones both used examples to teach the concepts. Mr. Waters showed the examples first and helped the students discover the con-

cepts, while Mrs. Jones first defined the concept and then had students identify and analyze the examples. We discuss each of these sequences in Chapter 7.
3. a. The abstraction being taught here was the meaning of *biodegradable*.
   b. The data Mr. Black used were the words and the biodegradable and nonbiodegradable objects in the container.

EXERCISE 2.3

1. b and d. A horse is a kind of domestic animal and beast of burden.
2. b. An overhead projector is the only one of these that is an electrical instructional tool.
3. a, b, and d. Rye, wheat, and white are all kinds of bread.
4. c. Bread is a type of food but isn't a subset of any of the others.
5. b and c. Fried bacon, hot oatmeal, and bread are all types of food and cooked food.

EXERCISE 2.4

1. (a) Abstraction. This abstraction defines the concept *rhombus*.
2. (a) Abstraction. Again, this a concept definition.
3. (a) Abstraction. This abstraction is a generalization.
4. (a) Abstraction.
5. (f) Fact. Note how this occurred in the past and was a singular occurrence.
6. (a) Abstraction. Note how you could use this generalization to date the age of a given musical piece.
7. (a) Abstraction.
8. (f) Fact.
9. (a) Abstraction. This is a definition of a concept in which the target concept is defined in terms of the superordinate concept *form of literature.*
10. (a) Abstraction.
11. (a) Abstraction. This is a generalization that can be used to predict why it takes longer to cook vegetables in the mountains, for example.
12. (a) Abstraction.
13. (a) Abstraction. This is a concept.
14. (a) Abstraction.
15. (f) Fact.

3 ‖ Goals and Objectives

INTRODUCTION

In Chapter 1 we introduced the content of this text by presenting a model of teaching described in three interrelated phases. These phases were labeled *planning, implementing,* and *evaluating.* The planning phase begins when a goal is identified, and we discussed sources of goals and domains of instruction in Chapter 2. We are now at the point where we can begin to look at goals in more detail and put them into operational form for instruction. In other words, we are preparing to state goals and use them as guides when we teach. They mark the beginning of the planning process.

The use of goals and objectives is certainly not new. Ralph Tyler (1949), in his classic text *Basic Principles of Curriculum and Instruction,* proposed an instructional model that included objectives as an integral component. Because of his influence, objectives, their form, and the ability to express them have been major components of teacher preparation courses, and much time and energy are devoted to developing preservice teachers' skills in preparing objectives. Tyler suggested that the most useful form for stating objectives "is to express them in terms which identify both the kind of behavior to be developed in the student and the content or area of life in which this behavior is to operate" (p. 46). Thus, behavioral objectives were born.

Another powerful teacher training influence followed Tyler's when Robert Mager published *Preparing Instructional Objectives* in 1962. His highly readable book was popular for years, and literally thousands of teachers have been taught his principles for stating behavioral objectives. His objectives have been criticized as being incomplete, however, and an alternative is called *the goals approach* to preparing objectives or simply *goals objectives,* first proposed by McAshan (1974). This approach combines a goal with an evaluation component into a single statement. In essence, it is the combination of a goal with an objective written according to Mager's principles.

Another alternative and currently a very popular approach to preparing objectives has been suggested by Norman Gronlund (1985). He believes objectives should first be stated in terms of general goals such as "understand," "appreciate," "know," "evaluate," or "apply," which are then followed by observable behaviors specifying evidence that the learner has met the objective. We examine each approach in this chapter.

When objectives first came into widespread use, they were very controversial. The debate raged from state departments of education, through universities, and all the way to the classroom teacher. Many early proponents of objectives implied that because they specifically defined learning outcomes they would be an educational panacea, and the proponents' zeal further fueled the controversy. Opponents were equally adamant; they argued that truly meaningful education could not be broken down into a number of specific objectives.

Although some debate continues today, the issue is insignificant compared to the past, and the use of objectives is widespread in materials such as county curriculum guides, and state-level curriculum frameworks. With the increased emphasis on educational accountability — meaning that teachers are being held responsible for student learning—the use of objectives is becoming even more common. Further, the expanding body of literature on teacher effectiveness suggests the importance of carefully considering specific objectives (Berliner, 1985; Rosenshine & Stevens, 1986). Berliner suggested that the difference between good and effective teachers is that effective teachers, in addition to doing the things good teachers do intuitively, teach directly to precisely stated objectives.

Many textbooks in education and educational psychology use some form of objectives, and most public school texts also use them as learning aids. Our view is that objectives are a part of present reality and are here to stay, so we won't argue the issue further. Our purpose is to acquaint you with a variety of approaches to their use so you will be equipped to use them as effectively as possible.

Let's look now at some different approaches to preparing objectives. We briefly present Mager's approach to behavioral objectives first. This is followed by a detailed discussion of goals objectives. Because goals objectives subsume Mager's approach, the discussion will lead to an understanding of both approaches. This is followed by a presentation of Gronlund's "instructional objectives" and a discussion of how these differ from the other two.

OBJECTIVES

After completing Chapter 3, you should be able to accomplish the following objectives:

1. You will understand the goal statement in a goals objective, so that when given a series of goals, you will identify the learner and learning task in each.
2. You will understand the difference between a goal statement and an evaluation statement, so that when given a series of goals objectives, you will identify the goal statement and evaluation statement in each.
3. You will understand the condition, performance, and criteria, so that when given a series of goals objectives, you will identify the condition, performance, and criteria in each.

4. You will assess the quality of objectives, so that when given a series of goals objectives, you will identify each component that is incorrectly stated.
5. You will understand Gronlund's instructional objectives, so that when given a series of objectives, you will identify which ones are written correctly according to Gronlund's principles.

MAGER'S BEHAVIORAL OBJECTIVES

As we said in the chapter introduction, Robert Mager was enormously influential in his approach to the preparation of objectives. He suggested that an objective ought to describe "what the student will be doing when demonstrating his achievement and how you will know he is doing it" (Mager, 1962, p. 53).

Mager suggests that a good objective has three parts: (1) an observable behavior, (2) the conditions under which the behavior will occur, and (3) criteria for acceptable performance. The following are examples of objectives written according to Mager's format.

1. Given six sentences, fifth graders will identify each that contains a simile.
2. Given 10 addition problems requiring regrouping, second graders will successfully solve 8.
3. Given 15 compounds written with the correct chemical formula, chemistry students will identify the valence of the ions in each.

Mager's system, with its emphasis on final behavior, requires a great deal of specificity. Mager contends that the effort required to achieve this specificity is worthwhile, and he has even gone so far as to suggest that students often can teach themselves if they are given well-stated objectives.

Mager's objectives, sometimes called an *outcomes approach*, can be criticized as being incomplete, however, in that they are only evaluation statements; i.e., they specify the *student outcome* or how students will be evaluated but do not identify the educational intent of the teacher. An alternative that addresses this criticism is called the *Goals Approach to Preparing Objectives*, or more simply *goals objectives*. We turn to a discussion of them now.

GOALS OBJECTIVES

A goals objective can be described as a statement that answers two questions for the teacher:

1. What do I want the learner to know, understand, or appreciate? (or some other educational goal), and
2. How will I know if they know, understand, or appreciate?

Mager's outcomes approach to preparing objectives answers the second question. Answers to both are important, however, particularly if you're a beginning education student developing your understanding of the teaching process. For this reason we have adopted the goals approach in this text. This approach combines Mager's objective, which is an evaluation statement, with a goal. This is how a goals objective subsumes Mager's objectives. Keep in mind that from this point on when we refer to an evaluation statement, it is actually a Mager objective. Let's look now at goal statements within a goals objective.

Goal Statements

An overriding goal for us in writing this text is to help you as readers begin to think like teachers. With this notion in mind, imagine that you are responsible for a class in a certain grade level or subject matter area. You are planning a specific lesson for the next day. Your first step in planning is to ask yourself, What do I want the students to know, understand, or be able to do? All your planning, and ultimately your actual work with the students, derives from the answer to this question. This question is particularly important for people who are now beginning to study and understand education. At this point your understanding is best served by formally and explicitly stating goals in writing. As your thinking and understanding develop, your goals will become less formal and more implicit.

Planning begins with teachers' consideration of what they want their students to accomplish during one or more lessons. This desired result is called an *educational goal*, which is a statement of educational intent that is usually given in general terms. The educational goal answers the question, What do I want the students to know or understand? The following are examples of educational goals.

1. For kindergarteners to know the basic colors
2. For eighth-grade science students to understand Newton's first law
3. Senior trigonometry students will solve written problems involving right triangles.

As we examine the goal statements, we see that they have three common characteristics. First, each identified the particular student population for which it was designed; kindergarteners, eighth-grade science students, and senior trigonometry students, respectively. Sec-

For the elementary school gym student to increase ability to balance, so that . . .

ond, the learning task was identified. The kindergarteners' task is to know colors, the eighth graders' is to understand Newton's first law, and the trigonometry students' is to be able to solve problems with right triangles. Finally the goal's attainment in each case must be inferred rather than observed. We never observe "understanding"; we can only infer it, and it can mean different things to different people. The same is true for "know," "appreciate," and other desired educational goals. When we discuss the evaluation component of goals objectives, we will see how we gather the information needed to infer knowledge, understanding, appreciation, and so forth.

Goal statements should be written as simply and efficiently as possible. They may be simply an introductory phrase, as was the case in the first two examples just cited, or they may be a complete sentence, such as our third example. Let's examine some additional examples.

1. For senior literature students to understand the impact of personal experience on an author's work.
   Learner: senior literature students
   Learning Task: understand the impact of experience on authors' works
2. Sixth-grade science students will understand the concept of density.
   Learner: sixth-grade science students
   Learning Task: understand the concept of density
3. For second graders to understand the rule for adding *-ing* to words
   Learner: second graders
   Learning Task: understand the rule for adding *-ing* to words
4. Eighth-grade algebra students will be able to solve simultaneous equations.
   Learner: eighth-grade algebra students
   Learning Task: solve simultaneous equations
5. Seventh-grade geography students will know the locations of the countries of Europe.
   Learner: seventh-grade geography students
   Learning Task: know the locations of the countries of Europe.

You will note that each of the objectives we've written for this text refers to *you* as a reader and student, and it has been stated in each case. We've done this so our objectives can serve as appropriate models for you as you study. However, if a teacher has the same audience for an extended period of time, it wouldn't be necessary to repeat the learner component in each objective once the learner is clearly established.

Notice also that although the goals are written in nonobservable terms such as *know* and *understand*, they are specific. Goals such as the following are too general to be useful.

For students to understand American literature

Algebra students will be able to solve problems.

Geography students will know about Europe.

These disintegrate into a series of words. Compare the examples you've just read with our first, fourth, and fifth of the preceding examples to see the difference.

EXERCISE 3.1

Identify the learner and the learning task in each of the following goal statements. Then compare your answers with those found in the feedback section at the end of the chapter.

1. For fifth graders to know the parts of the digestive system

   Learner: _____

   Learning Task: _____

   _____

2. American history students will understand Andrew Jackson's philosophy regarding states' rights.

   Learner: _____

   Learning Task: _____

   _____

3. Seventh-grade life science students will know the different types of bacteria.

   Learner: _____

   Learning Task: _____

   _____

4. First graders will like reading.

   Learner: _____

   Learning Task: _____

   _____

5. For kindergarteners to be able to walk a balance beam

   Learner: _____

   Learning Task: _____

   _____

Although each of the goals in Exercise 3.1 appears in a conventional format, remember that the key elements of a properly stated goal are identification of the learner and specification of the learning task. The precise wording of the goal is not critical.

Evaluation Statements

When we introduced goals objectives, we said they provide the answer to two questions:

1. What do I want the learner to know, understand, or appreciate? (or some other educational goal), and
2. How will I know if they know, understand, or appreciate?

The goal statement answers the first question, and we are now prepared to consider the second. The answers can and often do vary, and teachers must make decisions about how they will determine whether or not their students know or understand. Again, we are encouraging you to begin to think like a teacher. For instance, consider the following goal:

For third graders to understand the concept *noun*

This is a simple and straightforward goal. However, when we begin to ask ourselves how we will know if they understand nouns, even this simple goal becomes more complex. The following are some possibilities we might use to determine whether they understand the concept.

1. Have them define *noun* in writing from memory.
2. Have them write a list of nouns that were not used as examples in class.
3. Have them identify examples of nouns from a list of words.
4. Have them identify nouns in a series of sentences.

Even with a concept as simple as *noun* we see that the question requires thought. For instance, if students can define *noun*, does this mean they understand the concept? Probably not. However, you as the teacher are the one who ultimately must answer the question. Now imagine answering the question, How will I determine if students can critically analyze writing? These are questions teachers must answer every day, and this is what it means to "think like a teacher."

Let's look now at the evaluation statement. This statement reflects the teacher's answer to the question, How will I determine if they know, understand, or appreciate? For instance, by stating

For third graders to understand the concept *noun*, so that when given a list of sentences they will underline all the nouns in each,

the teacher has decided that she can infer that the students understand nouns if they can underline all the nouns in a series of sentences she provides.

Let's look carefully now at the entire objective. It contains a specific goal that identifies the learner and the learning task, and it includes an evaluation statement that designates (1) the expected performance, (2) the conditions under which the student is to perform, and (3) the standard for the performance. We first examine the performance.

Specifying Observable Performances.   In one of our examples we see that the students will demonstrate their understanding of nouns by *underlining* the nouns in a series of sentences. The key feature of the performance is that it is *observable* by the teacher. As with all inferences, if we are to conclude that students understand, we must have something observable to base this conclusion on. This observable behavior is the *performance*. When we considered different ways of assessing students' understanding of nouns, the performances were *define, write,* and *identify,* respectively. In addition, verbs such as the following are acceptable for statements of performance.

state	select	list	label
classify	solve	construct	compare
describe	recite	derive	name

Many more could be added to the list, but this gives you a sample of observable performances. Although the approach to writing objectives varies among educators, most adhere to the need for including an observable behavior in the objective's description.

Each objective should contain a single performance. If more than one is desired, a second evaluation statement should be written.

EXERCISE 3.2

This exercise reviews your understanding of goal statements and checks your ability to recognize observable performances. Enclose the goal statement for each of the following goals objectives in parentheses and underline the performance in each. Place an X in front of each objective that *does not* include an observable performance.

_____ 1. For life science students to know the parts of a cell, so that when given a picture of a cell, they will label each part

_____ 2. Physics students will understand the law of conservation of momentum, so that when given a series of problems involving momentum, they will identify all the cases where momentum is conserved.

_____ 3. Second graders will understand how to make plurals for words ending in *y*, so that when given a list of 10 words, they will know the plural for each.

_____ 4. Earth science students will comprehend the importance of topsoil in agriculture, so that when given a series of photographs illustrating erosion, they will appreciate the importance of conservation

_____ 5. Geometry students will understand the construction of circles, so that when given a compass and three points, they will construct a circle through the points.

_____ 6. For kindergarten students to know the letters of the alphabet, so that when shown written letters, they will verbally state the name of each.

Specifying Conditions.   Let's look again at our example with the concept *noun*. The four possibilities we listed for evaluating the goal were

1. Have them define *noun* in writing from memory.
2. Have them write a list of nouns that were not used as examples in class.
3. Have them identify examples of nouns from a list of words.
4. Have them identify nouns in a series of sentences.

Notice that in both examples 3 and 4 the students were asked to *identify nouns*. However, in one case they were asked to identify them from a list of words, and in the other case in a series of sentences. The *conditions* under which the students were to perform the behavior were quite different. The condition specifies the circumstances under which the observable performance will be demonstrated. Some examples of common conditions are

From memory

Without aids

Given a list

Given a compass, volleyball, jumprope, pictures (or other materials needed to demonstrate the performance)

By contrast conditions such as

After instruction,

After exposure to, or

Given experience with

are not acceptable conditions. Rather than specify the conditions under which the performance will be demonstrated, they describe a *learning* condition. Also, conditions such as

Given a test,

Given multiple-choice items, or

When asked

are not appropriate. Although they're technically correct, they don't give us any specific information about the evaluation condition. The learner is always *asked, told,* or *required* to respond. The solution is to specify the form of the test item. For instance, "identify nouns in a list of sentences" accomplishes exactly that. A portion of a test would include a series of sentences, and the student would be asked to identify nouns by circling, underlining, or providing some other indicator. As another example, consider the following objective:

> For American government students to understand different forms of government, so that when given a case study describing a political ideology, they will identify the form of government it represents

The measurement of this objective could be in the form of a multiple-choice item where the stem would illustrate the ideology and choices, such as (a) democracy, (b) monarchy, (c) communism, (d) fascism, would be provided. The objective specifies the form of the item and doesn't merely say, "given a multiple-choice item."

EXERCISE 3.3

For the following objectives enclose the goal statement in parentheses and put a GS over it, enclose the condition in parentheses and put a P over it, and underline the performance.

1. Second graders will be able to subtract with regrouping, so that when given 10 problems requiring regrouping, they will correctly solve 7.

2. Prekindergarteners will know their colors, so that when given individually colored shapes, they will correctly identify the color of each.

3. World history students will know how the Crusades impacted Europe, so that without aids they will list four cultural outcomes resulting from the Crusades.

4. Tenth-grade chemistry students will understand ionization potential, so that when given lists of elements and the periodic table, they will identify the element from each list with the highest ionization potential.

5. Earth science students will know different types of minerals, so that when given mineral specimens and written labels, they will match the labels with the specimens.

Specifying Criteria. As a theme for this chapter, we have been describing the thinking process a teacher must go through when making professional decisions. In asking the question How will I find out whether or not the students know or understand what I have identified in the goal? the performance is critical because different performances tell you very different things about the learner. We've also seen how the condition under which the performance is demonstrated can impact the evaluation.

Let's take the process one step further now. Look again at the first three items in Exercise 3.3

1. Second graders will be able to subtract with regrouping, so that when given 10 problems requiring regrouping they will correctly solve 7.
2. Prekindergarteners will know their colors, so that when given individually colored shapes, they will correctly identify the color of each.
3. World history students will know how the Crusades impacted Europe, so that without aids they will list four cultural outcomes resulting from the Crusades.

We see that in the first example the teacher concluded that solving *7 of 10* correctly was sufficient for students to demonstrate their ability to solve problems with regrouping. However, in the second example the teacher decided that the children should identify the color of *each;* and in the third, students could demonstrate their knowledge by listing *four* outcomes. The teachers specified not only the condition and performance but also how well the students were to perform. This level of performance represents the *criteria*, and it is the final dimension to be considered as you develop your thinking about goals objectives.

As with conditions and performances, criteria vary and depend on the judgement of the teacher. Additional examples of criteria are

With 100% accuracy

With no more than three errors

Within 20 seconds

Four times in 10 seconds

The value of criteria as a tool depends on the topic and activity. For example, consider the objective

For physical education students to demonstrate muscular strength, so that on a horizontal bar they will do 10 pull-ups in 20 seconds.

Here the performance is to do pull-ups, but the objective has little meaning until we specify the criterion. Without it we would immediately ask, How many? and In how much time? On the other hand, look at the objective

For language arts students to understand the concept *hyperbole,* so that when given examples of figurative language, they will identify 80% of the examples of hyperbole

This objective reflects two important teacher decisions: (1) that understanding *hyperbole* is an important goal, and (2) that we will infer that the students understand if they can identify the examples of hyperbole from among a number of cases of figurative language. Specifying the criteria for understanding in advance is less important in this instance than it was for the example in physical education.

In typical classroom practice, teachers rarely set explicit criteria in advance. Instead, they establish grading systems, such as those we've all experienced as students, and the criteria are implicitly incorporated within the system. However, most school districts continue to move toward school accountability through competency testing, and setting criteria is important in these cases. Therefore, an understanding of criteria is important as you develop your thinking about teaching.

EXERCISE 3.4

Identify the four components of goals objectives by enclosing each in parentheses and labeling them GS, C, P, and CT for the goal statement, condition, performance, and criteria, respectively.

1. Vocational technical students will demonstrate carpentry skills, so that when given a saw, square, and 2 X 4s, they will make a 90-degree joint in the boards to within 1 degree.

2. Middle school music students will know the fingerings for the recorder, so that when given an excerpt of music, they will demonstrate the correct fingerings for each note.

3. Elementary physical education students will demonstrate hand-eye coordination, so that when given a basketball, they will dribble it 25 consecutive times in place without losing control.

4. Eleventh-grade oceanography students will know the zones of the ocean floor, so that when given an ocean topographic map, they will label each zone correctly.

5. Physics students will understand components of forces, so that when given the magnitudes and angles of forces on objects, they will calculate the horizontal components of the forces in each case.

EXERCISE 3.5

You are now at the point where you're ready to analyze the quality of goals objectives. Consider each of the following and mark them as follows:

A — Objective is accurate and acceptable as written

GS — Missing or inappropriate goal statement

C — Missing or inappropriate condition

P — Missing or inappropriate performance

CT — Missing or inappropriate criteria

After identifying the problems in the objectives, rewrite each in appropriate form.

_____ 1. Fifth graders will understand the calculation of volume of solids, so that after seeing sample problems, they will solve 9 of 10 similar problems correctly.

_____

_____

_____

_____ 2. For vocational technical students to understand common problems in small gas engines, so that given a stalled lawn mower, they will fix the causes of stalling with 80% accuracy

_____

_____

_____

_____ 3. To demonstrate understanding of figurative language, so that when given a series of statements, students will identify the figure of speech in each case

_____

_____

_____

_____ 4. Prealgebra students will understand order of operations, so that when given problems involving the four operations, they will correctly simplify each.

_____

_____

_____

_____ 5. Seventh-grade geography students will know the geographical location of countries in Europe, so that when given a map and multiple-choice items, they will answer each correctly.

_____

_____

_____

_____ 6. For ninth graders to appreciate the use of verbals, so that when given a series of descriptions, students will know appropriate examples of gerunds, participles, and infinitives for each

_____

_____

_____

_____ 7. American government students will understand the concept of governmental checks and balances, so that on an essay test they will present a written example of check and balance.

_____

_____

_____

_____ 8. Biology students will understand genetics, so that when given case studies with dominant and recessive traits, they will identify the characteristics of each offspring.

_____

_____

_____

GRONLUND'S INSTRUCTIONAL OBJECTIVES

In the last two sections we described Mager's behavioral objectives and the goals approach to preparing objectives. They are very similar in that the goals approach is essentially a Mager objective attached to a goal statement.

We now turn to another alternative, popularized by Norman Gronlund (1985). Let's examine some examples of objectives written according to Gronlund's principles and see how they compare to those we've already illustrated.

Consider the following example taken from elementary school language arts.

General Objective: Knows spelling rules for adding suffixes

Specific behaviors:
1. States rule in his or her own words
2. Distinguishes rule from closely related rule
3. Applies rule to unique example

Now consider a second example taken from algebra.

General Objective: Solves word problems

Specific behaviors:
1. Describes problem
2. Identifies relevant information
3. Specifies variables
4. Writes solution equation
5. Calculates solution

Let's look now at the characteristics of the objectives.

1. Gronlund (1985) has suggested that objectives should be first stated in general terms, such as *know, understand, apply, evaluate,* or *appreciate,* which are then followed by specific behaviors providing evidence that the learner has met the objective. In this regard Gronlund's objectives are similar to the goals approach in that he suggests that a general objective that identifies the instructional intent should be stated first. The general objective is similar to the goal statement in the goals approach. "Knows spelling rules for adding suffixes" and "solves word problems" were the statements of intent in our examples. The specific behaviors listed below each general objective then provide the evidence that the students have met the intent. This approach differs from Mager's in that his objectives specify the evidence but do not include the intent.

2. The objectives are stated in terms of student outcomes rather than teacher performance. For instance, "teach spelling rules for adding suffixes" is a teacher performance and not a student outcome. Virtually all objectives, regardless of the approach, share this characteristic, and both county curriculum guides and state-level curriculum frameworks state objectives in terms of student outcomes.

3. Objectives are not stated in terms of the learning process, such as "students learn spelling rules for adding suffixes." "Learns" is a student process rather than a student outcome, and Gronlund discourages this description. Both Mager's and the goals approach share this characteristic.

4. Objectives are limited to a single performance. Again, this is consistent among the three approaches. We suggested in the last section that a teacher should write two different evaluation statements if more than one performance was involved, and Gronlund would make a similar argument.

5. Gronlund's objectives avoid the specification of subject matter. He stated, "Don't focus on the subject matter topics. (e.g., Student learns the meaning of osmosis, photosynthesis, etc.)" (Gronlund, 1985, p. 11).

Gronlund's approach or a modification of it is probably the most popular one in existence today among curriculum writers. Its primary advantage is one of economy in that his objectives are more inclusive than those written according to the other approaches. Content requiring literally thousands of objectives written according to Mager's approach could be expressed in less than a hundred using Gronlund's.

The compromise Gronlund makes is in terms of specificity. He doesn't identify either the conditions for acceptable performance or the criteria, and he discourages the use of specific subject matter topics. This latter feature is often modified by curriculum writers. They typically include specific topics in their objectives, as we discuss in the next section.

EXERCISE 3.6 _____

Consider each of the following objectives and identify those that are inappropriately stated according to Gronlund's criteria. Rewrite each of the inappropriately stated objectives in acceptable form. We are purposely sidestepping the issue of content specificity, so do not evaluate them on that basis.

1. Learns concepts in chemistry

    1.1 Defines concept in own words

    1.2 Identifies examples of concepts

    _____

    _____

    _____

2. Teach students parts of speech

    2.1 Define parts of speech for students

    2.2 Provide students with examples

    2.3 Have students identify parts of speech in context

    _____

    _____

    _____

3. Understands subtraction with regrouping

    3.1 States rule for borrowing

    3.2 Solves problems requiring regrouping

    _____

    _____

    _____

4. Understands geographical terms

    4.1 States definition in own words and writes definition

    4.2 Identifies examples in paragraphs

    4.3 Identifies examples on maps

_____

_____

_____

5. Understands Newton's second law

   5.1 States the law

   5.2 Writes the law mathematically

   5.3 Solves problems using the law

_____

_____

_____

PERFORMANCE OBJECTIVES— A FURTHER LOOK

Let's look now at what you will likely encounter when you leave the college or university and enter a public school classroom. What role do objectives play there, and how do they appear? For instance, consider the following objectives taken from the *Student Performance Standards of Excellence for Florida Schools* (1984).

STANDARDS

G. The Student Will Acquire Skills To Participate Effectively In A Democratic Society And Apply Problem-Solving Skills To The Democratic Political Process.

SKILLS—The student will

1126. Explain the function of the Cabinet

1127. Relate political elections to processes used to choose leaders in the school and community

1128. Contrast what it means to be a good citizen in the United States with what it means in an authoritarian society

(p. 85)

This excerpt was taken from a state-level document that serves as a guide for instruction. The document was written by teams considering educational goals for the particular state. They have what amounts to a goal statement, which they describe as a *standard*. The evaluation statement is labeled a *skill*.

The following example is based on a county curriculum guide *(Science Curriculum Guide,* 1982). We see here that primary and secondary ideas rather than goals are presented. Understanding these ideas, however, amounts to the goal. The statement they identify as an objective is an *evaluation* statement as we've discussed them in this chapter. Notice in these objectives that a general statement of conditions is written and that an observable performance is specified.

Grade Level: Six   Theme: Matter and Energy

Primary Idea: The interaction of matter involves energy and causes change.

Secondary Ideas	Objectives
All matter can be classified into three general categories: elements (atoms of the same kind), compounds (elements that undergo chemical reactions), and mixtures (solids, liquids, and gases).	Given proper materials and directions, the students will 1. State that all matter is made of tiny parts called atoms. 2. Identify the principal parts of an atom and describe their relationship to one another. 3. Contrast the different states of matter in terms of molecular motion. 4. Describe the conditions under which a mixture may be produced. 5. Compare elements and compounds. 6. State the purpose of chemical symbols and formulas. 7. Compare chemical and physical changes. 8. State the function of group tests. 9. Give examples of how chemistry can affect one's own life.

As the teaching profession continues to move toward holding teachers accountable for student learning, some districts place descriptions of objectives in teachers' hands and require that they specify the date when the objective is taught. For example, consider the following taken from skill sheets for St. Johns County, Florida.

15. _____ Compare fractions using <, >, and =.
16. _____ Add 2 fractions with unlike denominators 2, 3, 4, 6, 8, and 12.
17. _____ Subtract fractions with unlike denominators 2, 3, 4, 6, 8, 12.
18. _____ Read and write decimals in tenths and hundredths.
(Minimum Skills—Fifth Grade)

We have suggested that performance objectives are a way of life in education today, and the examples we've presented support this contention. There are obvious compromises, such as the use of labels and explicit goal statements as opposed to topics lists, but performance objectives are certainly used in the real world of the public schools. They serve as guides and are designed to aid teachers in their instruction.

We are discussing objectives at this point in our text because we want them to serve as guides to aid your thinking. Having you state goals serves this purpose. We believe you will benefit from the process of explicitly considering and writing both goal and evaluation statements at this point in your studies. When you get into the classroom, a topic, as opposed to a goal, may be totally appropriate.

There is one exception to what we've said so far. If you look again at the excerpts, you see that none of the examples we've presented have criteria as described in this chapter. As we've said repeatedly, objectives serve as guides for thinking by requiring you to ask yourself what you want the learner to know or understand, and further, how you will determine this knowledge or understanding. This is common practice. However, the explicit statement of criteria can be difficult to determine and is often quite artificial. The measurement of the objective is most often done with a paper-and-pencil test, and judgements about achievement are based on the test results. If the test items are consistent with the objectives—and they will be if the teacher used objectives as a guide for instruction—we find the practice very acceptable. In other words, we support the practice of not explicitly stating criteria. Our position is that objectives should guide a teacher's thinking but should not restrict it. However, we believe it is worthwhile for you to understand how to specify criteria if it should ever be necessary, and we also recognize that there will be instructors using this text whose position will differ from ours. We are presenting both sides of the issue for this reason.

SUMMARY

The purpose of Chapter 3 has been to help you understand the purpose in preparing objectives and to help you develop your skill in writing them. We have presented three different approaches to their preparation. Of those three we have emphasized the goals approach because of the advantages it provides in developing your thinking about instruction.

A goals objective has two primary parts. First is the goal statement, which is a description of the teacher's intent stated in general, nonobservable terms. It identifies the learner and the learning task.

The evaluation statement, which is identical to an objective written according to Mager's approach to preparing objectives, includes the condition, the performance, and the criteria. The goal statement answers the question, What do I want the learner to know, understand, or be able to do? and the evaluation statement answers the question, How will I determine whether the learner knows or understands?

Gronlund's instructional objectives are similar to goals objectives in that a general statement of intent is first identified, which is followed by specific behaviors providing evidence that the general objective has been met. Gronlund's objectives, however, are much more general than goals objectives.

Examples taken from state and county curriculum materials indicate that although specific procedures for preparing objectives vary, and some of the principles are compromised, objectives play a central role in the "real world" as a guide for instruction.

Objectives are critical to the planning and implementation of instruction. They increase effective communication, aid teachers in developing learning strategies, and encourage thinking about evaluation. The importance of objectives is further illustrated when we study the development of lesson plans in Chapter 5. However, before turning our attention to planning, we want to consider the different levels at which objectives can be written. This is the topic of Chapter 4.

REFERENCES

Berliner, D. (1985, April). *Effective teaching.* Paper presented at the annual meeting of the Florida Educational Research and Development Council, Pensacola, FL.

Gronlund, N. (1985). *Stating objectives for classroom instruction* (2nd ed.). New York: Macmillan.

Mager, R. (1962). *Preparing instructional objectives.* Palo Alto, CA: Fearon.

McAshan, H. (1974). *The goals approach to performance objectives.* Philadelphia: Saunders.

Minimum skills—Fifth-grade mathematics. (1986). St. Augustine, FL: St. Johns County Public Schools.

Rosenshine, B., & Stevens, R. (1986). Teaching functions. In M. Wittrock (Ed.), *Third Handbook of Research on Teaching* (3rd ed.) (pp. 376–391). New York: Macmillan.

Science curriculum guide: Elementary science 1-6. (1982). Jacksonville, FL: Duval County Public Schools.

Student performance standards of excellence for Florida schools. 1984–85 through 1988–89. Tallahassee, FL: Division of Public Schools, Florida Department of Education.

Tyler, R. (1949). *Basic principles of curriculum and instruction.* Chicago: University of Chicago Press.

EXERCISE FEEDBACK

EXERCISE 3.1

1. *Learner:* fifth graders
   Learning Task: know parts of the digestive system
2. *Learner:* American history students
   Learning Task: understand Jackson's philosophy regarding states' rights
3. *Learner:* seventh-grade life science students
   Learning Task: know different types of bacteria
4. *Learner:* first graders
   Learning Task: like reading
5. *Learner:* kindergarteners
   Learning Task: walk a balance beam

EXERCISE 3.2

_____ 1. (For life science students to know the parts of a cell), so that when given a picture of a cell, they will <u>label</u> each part.

_____ 2. (Physics students will understand the law of conservation of momentum), so that when given a series of problems involving momentum they will <u>identify</u> all the cases where momentum is conserved.

__X__ 3. (Second graders will understand how to make plurals for words ending in *y*), so that when given a list of 10 words, they will know the plural for each.
   The goal in this case is for students to understand the rule for forming plurals. "Knowing" the plural for each is not an observable performance. It puts us right back where we started, and again we must ask, How will I determine if they "know" the plural for each?

__X__ 4. (Earth science students will comprehend the importance of topsoil in agriculture), so that when given a series of photographs illustrating erosion, they will appreciate the importance of conservation.
   Again, "appreciating" the importance of conservation is not observable, and we must have some observable indicator to help us determine whether the students understand the importance of erosion to agriculture.

_____ 5. (Geometry students will understand the construction of circles), so that when given a compass and three points, they will <u>construct</u> a circle through the points.

_____ 6. (For kindergarten students to know the letters of the alphabet), so that when shown written letters, they will verbally <u>state</u> the name of each.

EXERCISE 3.3

1. (Second graders will be able to subtract with regrouping),[GS] so that (when given 10 problems requiring regrouping)[P] they will correctly <u>solve</u> 7.

2. (Prekindergarteners will know their colors),[GS] so that (when given individually colored shapes)[P] they will correctly <u>identify</u> the color of each.[P]

3. (World history students will know how the Crusades impacted Europe), so that
(without aids) they will <u>list</u> four cultural outcomes resulting from the Crusades.

4. (Tenth-grade chemistry students will understand ionization potential), so that
(when given lists of elements and the periodic table) they will <u>identify</u> the element
from each list with the highest ionization potential.

5. (Earth science students will know different types of minerals), so that (when given
mineral specimens and written labels) they will <u>match</u> the labels with the
specimens.

EXERCISE 3.4

1. (Vocational technical students will demonstrate carpentry skills), so that (when
given a saw, square, and 2 × 4s), they will (make) a 90-degree joint (in the boards
to within 1 degree).

2. (Middle school music students will know the fingerings for the recorder), so that
(when given an excerpt of music), they will (demonstrate) the (correct fingerings
for each) note.

3. (Elementary physical education students will demonstrate hand-eye coordination),
so that when (given a basketball), they will (dribble) it (25 consecutive times
in place without losing control).

4. (Eleventh-grade oceanography students will know the zones of the ocean floor), so
that (when given an ocean topographic map), they will (label) (each zone correctly).

5. (Physics students will understand components of forces), so that (when given the
magnitudes and angles of forces on objects), they will (calculate) the horizontal
components of the forces in (each) case.

EXERCISE 3.5

In each case of an inaccurately written objective, we've presented an appropriate
alternative. As you rewrite the objectives, they may look a bit different from ours and
still be acceptable. If you're uncertain, discuss your objectives with your instructor.

__C__ 1. "After seeing sample problems" is a learning condition rather than an
evaluation condition. A better objective would be

Fifth graders will understand the calculation of volume of solids, so
that when given 10 pictures of solids with their dimensions, they will
correctly determine the volume of 9.

__CT__ 2. To fix the causes of stalling ''with 80% accuracy'' doesn't make sense. The engine still won't start. The objective would be appropriately written as follows:

> For vocational technical students to understand common problems in small gas engines, so that when given a stalled lawn mower, they will eliminate all the causes of stalling

__GS__ 3. The learner is not identified in the goal statement. An improved description would be

> For sixth-grade English students to understand figurative language, so that when given a series of statements, they will identify the figure of speech in each case

__A__ 4. This objective is accurate and appropriate as written.

__C__ 5. ''Given . . . multiple-choice items'' is an inappropriate condition. A more precise description would be

> Seventh-grade geography students will know the geographical location of countries in Europe, so that when given a map with numbered locations and lists of countries, they will identify the appropriate country for each number.

This objective is a bit lengthy, but we've presented it purposely to illustrate one way that multiple-choice items can be specified in an objective. The students would be given a map with each country numbered. The ''lists of countries'' would be the four or five choices that would go with each number. There are other appropriate ways to write the objective, of course.

__P__ 6. ''Will know'' is not an observable performance. A better objective would be

> For ninth graders to appreciate the use of verbals, so that when given a series of descriptions, students will identify all those that are gerunds, participles, or infinitives

__C__ 7. ''On an essay test'' is an inappropriate condition. An objective with an appropriate alternative would be

> American government students will understand the concept of governmental checks and balances, so that without aids they will present a written example of check and balance.

__GS__ 8. ''Will understand genetics'' is a goal statement that is so broad that it is no longer meaningful. An improved objective would be

Biology students will understand dominant and recessive patterns, so that when given case studies with dominant and recessive traits, they will identify the characteristics of each offspring.

EXERCISE 3.6

1. "Learns . . ." is a learning process rather than a student outcome. The subobjectives are properly stated according to Gronlund. An acceptable general objective would be

   Understands concepts in chemistry.

2. Both the general objective and the subobjectives are stated in terms of teacher performance rather than student performance. An improved objective could be stated as follows:

   Understands parts of speech
   2.1 Defines parts of speech in own words
   2.2 Generates examples
   2.3 Identifies parts of speech in context

3. This objective is properly stated. Gronlund would be critical of specifying content, but as we noted, we have set this issue aside.
4. Subobjective 4.1 identifies two performances. Otherwise, the objective is properly stated. The subobjective could be written as two objectives and could appear as follows:

   States definition in own words
   Writes definition

5. The objective is properly stated.

4 ‖ The Affective, Psychomotor, and Cognitive Domains

INTRODUCTION

As we emphasize throughout the book, it is crucial for teachers to vary the academic challenge, methods, and materials employed in the classroom. In doing so, they can more readily meet the individual needs of their students. The three domains lend themselves to this effort not only in the area of formulating objectives, as discussed in Chapter 2, but also in the development of questions. For example, a goal statement might call for the students to increase their knowledge of trees. In implementing this goal, the teacher might ask any of the following questions:

What are the names of three trees found in this geographical area?

Can you think of an example of a deciduous tree?

What is one major difference between a pine tree and an oak tree?

Look at these pictures of trees. What do they all have in common?

What is one way in which we economically utilize trees in this area?

Which tree does not belong on this list?

Can you devise a plan which will make better use of trees in this area that are cut for lumber?

How do you feel about the lumber industry in this area?

As you will see in this chapter, the preceding questions employ various levels of the domains and promote a wide range of student activity. It is also important to note at the onset that teachers can learn to use the three domains in a relatively short time and that the use of them in the classroom causes a significant difference in the types of responses students give (Sund & Carin, 1978).

A further consideration is found regarding the emphasis educators are placing upon the promotion of critical thinking. A major concern here is that an overabundance of the memorization of information delimits the quantity and quality of activities that require the processing of material. Additionally, students who memorize material may not retain it as effectively as those who incorporate material in other ways (Coomber, 1986).

Finally, there can be little doubt that questions (as well as objectives) that require more than simple recall are essential for exercising or stimulating thinking (Beyer, 1987). The domain that impacts the most upon the critical-thinking issue is the cognitive domain, but it is important to note that critical thinking also has ramifications for both the affective domain and the psychomotor domain. Therefore, we believe a general knowledge of the affective and psychomotor domains is worth your consideration. The cognitive domain will be presented in depth because the trend across the country is to emphasize the academic subjects as exemplified by Secretary of Education William J. Bennett's *James Madison High School* (Bennett, 1988). Furthermore, the cognitive domain dominates the academic subjects with few exceptions. However, we urge some caution here. The cognitive domain should not be the end-all and be-all in the curriculum. All three domains must be employed if we are to meet the commonly held goal of maximizing student potential.

OBJECTIVES

After completing Chapter 4, you should be able to accomplish the following objectives:

1. For you as a pre/inservice teacher to become aware of the different activities found in the affective domain so that, given a topic, you will write a goals objective in this domain
2. For you as a pre/inservice teacher to become aware of the different activities of the psychomotor domain so that, given a topic, you will write a goals objective in this domain
3. For you as a pre/inservice teacher to become aware of the levels of the cognitive domain so that, when given examples of cognitive objectives or questions, you will be able to identify whether each item is a low-level or a high-level behavior
4. For you as a pre/inservice teacher to become familiar with the cognitive domain so that, given a topic, you will be able to write a goals objective for both the low and high levels of this domain

THE AFFECTIVE DOMAIN

Probably the most pervasive, in terms of implicit inclusion in the curriculum, is the affective domain. This domain is primarily concerned with the development of attitudes and values, and deals with feelings, likes, and dislikes. By *implicit*, we mean that virtually all teachers want their students to go away from their classes with a more positive attitude toward the subject, themselves, and others. However affective goals like these are seldom made explicit and then consciously translated into teaching procedures. More is said about this later.

The primary focus of the affective domain is the development of two major attributes: attitudes and values. *Attitudes* are feelings of like or dislike toward objects, people, or ideas in our environment (Reilly & Lewis, 1983). We can have attitudes about educationally unimportant things like spinach and baseball or more educationally important things like minority groups and the environment. Like most aspects of human behavior, attitudes are learned and result from experiences. For example, students typically develop some type of attitude toward school. If their experiences with school have been pleasurable, with opportunities for growth and reward, then their attitudes will be positive. On the other hand, if they constantly encounter boredom and frustration in school, then their attitudes about school will tend to be negative. A significant finding from recent classroom research is that positive attitudes toward school are related to achievement and success; when students learn more, they feel better about themselves and school (Berliner, 1987).

The fact that attitudes are formed through experiences is good in the sense that it allows teachers to influence positively the attitudes of their students, but, on the other hand, it places a burden of responsibility on teachers not to contribute to the development of negative attitudes toward various aspects of schooling. An excellent discussion of the problems involved in influencing students' attitudes in the schools can be found in Mager (1968).

One word should be mentioned about how attitudes are measured. Attitudes are what psychologists call theoretical constructs. This means that we don't really believe that there is a place in a person's body where a particular attitude, knowledge, or skill actually exists. Instead, we infer the existence of an attitude or skill by the person's behavior or performance on some task. For example, we would infer that a person has the skill of converting ounces to pounds if he or she is able to do this on a test. In a similar way we would infer the existence of a negative attitude toward school by behaviors such as truancy, tardiness, and eagerness to leave school as quickly as possible. So one of the major ways that we infer the existence of positive and negative attitudes toward something is by observing behaviors. To use a mundane example, it makes sense that if a girl has a positive attitude toward ice cream, this positive attitude will be reflected in the way she acts around ice cream.

An alternate and more systematic way of measuring peoples' attitudes is through the use of some type of formal instrument. Probably the most common type of instrument used in this regard is a Likert scale, named after the person who developed the technique. Anyone who has attended college for any length of time will be familiar with Likert-type formats, as these are often used to evaluate students' attitudes toward a particular course or instructor. The key elements in a Likert item are (1) some type of statement to which students are asked to react and (2) a response scale that typically varies from "strongly agree" to "strongly disagree." For example, an item measuring students' attitudes toward a course's textbook might look like this:

The text was appropriate for the content and objectives of the course.

1	2	3	4	5
Strongly disagree	Disagree	Agree and disagree	Agree	Strongly agree

While fairly easy to prepare, the intent of items like this is fairly apparent, and students who are either eager to please or displease an instructor can influence their responses in spite of their true attitudes. In this respect, other less obtrusive measures such as student comments and willingness to read the book might give a teacher a more valid indicator of the students' true feelings. Readers wanting to pursue this topic further are referred to Mager (1973) and Webb, Campbell, Schwartz, and Sechrest (1972).

A second major goal in the affective domain is the development of values. *Values* differ from attitudes in that they are more global, referring not to specific objects such as school or ice cream or a textbook, but instead to aims of existence or ways of leading a life. Some typical values taught in our schools are honesty, cleanliness, wisdom, self-respect, and broad-mindedness. Each of these is an abstract idea about how people ought to act or lead their lives rather than a feeling about specific things or objects.

In addition to being broader in terms of focus, values also differ from attitudes in terms of how they are measured. We don't typically think of values as being accepted or rejected but rather in terms of their relative importance to an individual. For example, it would be hard to find students in our schools who would outwardly reject values such as self-respect or broad-mindedness. To some, however, these qualities would be of less significance than to others. Try the following exercise yourself.

Rank the following values in terms of their relative importance to you by placing a 1 in front of the most important value, a 2 in front of the second most important value, and so on down the list:

_____ Pleasure
_____ Honesty
_____ Self-respect
_____ Social recognition
_____ An exciting life
_____ A sense of accomplishment

If you're like other people who have completed similar exercises, you probably had to think a while before ranking these. This is because many, if not all, of these values are important to most people. The difficulty results in having to prioritize these in terms of your own life. One of the values of an exercise like this, in addition to the information it can provide to the teacher, is the value it can provide to students in helping to clarify their own value structures.

One way that a teacher can use information like this is by noting the relative importance students place on different values. For example, teachers who note that students rank pleasure, social recognition, and an exciting life above other values such as honesty, self-respect, and a sense of accomplishment, gain insight into the minds of their students and are in a better position to do something about this if they choose to do so.

This brings us to a final comment about the place of the affective domain in teaching. As mentioned previously, probably every teacher at every grade level in every subject matter area deals with affective goals either implicitly or explicitly. Every teacher wants students to exit from his class with at least as positive an attitude toward that subject as when they entered. All the teachers that we've met would like to develop values in their students including honesty, open-mindedness, and ambition; but few teachers make affective goals an explicit part of their curriculum, preferring instead to keep these implicit. Part of the reason for this is that many educators aren't quite sure about the appropriateness of affective goals in the curriculum. Some critics of these goals contend that they have no place in schools and that teachers ought to be spending their time teaching students to think rather than feel. Other critics point to the subjectiveness of these goals and raise the question of whether teachers should impose their own attitudes and values on students. These same critics contend that this is a role best left to other institutions such as the family or the church. Responses to these critics typically focus on the fact that schools can't help but teach attitudes and values and that, unless these attitudes and values are critically examined and made explicit, we may be teaching students undesirable things or teaching desirable things improperly. Like other issues covered in this book, this is a topic all teachers should think about, hopefully adopting a position consistent with their own personal values. Students interested in reading more about the place of the affective domain in the curriculum are referred to *Perceiving, Behaving, Becoming: A New Focus for Education* (1962) and Raths, Harmin, and Simon (1960).

The Levels of the Affective Domain

Receiving. The key feature at this level is that of students exhibiting a degree of open-mindedness, for without this trait they may not be willing to "receive" the information under study. It is important to note that although the students may be aware of the material being presented and willing to listen to a presentation, it is not implied here that the material will provide a behavior change or be absorbed in a positive way. The critical factor here is that the students are merely attending to the ongoing activity.

Responding.   The significant difference between *responding* and *receiving* is that the former assumes a somewhat positive attitude whereas the latter implies neutrality. At this level students are exhibiting some interest, involvement, or even commitment. Again, there is the matter of degree, for students may be willing to undertake an activity but not actually have bought into it. However, it is hoped that the students will perceive the experience positively and to some degree enjoy what they are doing even though they did not initiate the objective.

Valuing.   This level of the affective domain implies that the students perceive an attitude, value, or belief as having worth and that their behavior has been internalized and reflected on a continual basis. A major difference between valuing and the two levels of the affective domain previously discussed is that a behavior is not initiated by the teacher but is offered by the student who is committed to a particular position and is willing to openly discuss and support that position.

Organization.   The organization level builds upon the valuing level in that the latter is singular and the former implies a system. In other words, valuing implies a commitment to a specific belief or position, but in most cases, a value does not exist as a separate entity. As defined here, organization requires the student to justify, accept, or reject other values that may impact upon a given abstraction and thereby adopt a more complex point of view.

Characterization by a Value or Value Complex.   The previous levels of the affective domain have made it possible for the student to group complex objectives and operate at the characterization level, which allows the students to develop personal yet global views about such things as the nature of the universe or a philosophy of life. At this level, students have arrived at and exhibited a large group of attitudes and, more importantly, have incorporated them on a consistent basis and reflected them as an integral part of their character.

THE PSYCHOMOTOR DOMAIN

Developing muscular strength and coordination is the primary focus of goals within the psychomotor domain. This domain probably re-

ceives the least emphasis of the three, but the accuracy of this generalization will vary with the subject and age level of students taught.

Probably the most obvious exception to this generalization is in
the area of physical education, where the primary focus is on the
psychomotor domain. (It should be mentioned, though, that cognitive
and affective goals do form an important part of the physical education curriculum. For example, students must know how to perform a
certain skill before they can properly execute it and must understand
the rules of a game before they can play it; both of these are cognitive
goals. Also, a major affective goal of the physical education curriculum
is to develop positive attitudes and values about the importance of
keeping our bodies physically fit.) Examples of psychomotor goals
within the physical education curriculum include the following:

> Physical education students will serve a volleyball with speed and
> accuracy.
>
> Health students will develop cardiovascular strength and endur-
> ance.
>
> Physical education students will know how to swim using the
> breast stroke.
>
> Physical education students will do a forward roll in gymnastics.

As can be seen from these examples, the psychomotor domain involves
not only the development of strength and endurance but also the teaching of skills and the development of coordination.

Another area of the curriculum where psychomotor goals are
emphasized is in the area of vocational-technical education. Here goals
like learning to type, operate a wood lathe, and splice two wires all involve the development of manipulative skills and abilities. A third area
of the curriculum emphasizing psychomotor goals is the area of music.
Here students are training different parts of their bodies to perform in
the proper way at the proper time. In the music curriculum these goals
vary from being able to keep time with the music to learning how to
place the fingers on the keyboard in different piano pieces to forming
the lips and breathing properly while playing wind and brass instruments.

The three groups of examples from different subject matter areas
illustrate how the content being taught influences the relative emphasis placed on the psychomotor domain. Grade level also influences this
emphasis, with relatively greater emphasis being given to psychomotor goals at lower levels. For example, most early childhood curriculums have as goals the development of sensorimotor skills and
eye-hand coordination. Activities aimed at accomplishing these goals
include skipping, walking on a balance beam, and playing catch with

beanbags. Later on, students are taught additional psychomotor skills like printing, writing, and coloring. At an even later time in the curriculum, psychomotor skills don't receive as much explicit attention because teachers assume that skills such as handwriting have already been mastered. Harrow (1969) and Jewett and Mullan (1977) have developed a system to sequence learnings within this domain. Readers interested in this topic may wish to consult these sources.

The Levels of the Psychomotor Domain*

Classification Level 1—Reflex Movements. Reflex movements or actions are elicited in response to some stimulus without conscious volition on the part of the learner. They are not voluntary movements but may be considered as an essential base for movement behavior.

Though educators or curriculum developers will not be concerned with writing behavioral objectives for this particular classification level, it is included in the taxonomy for classifying behaviors in the psychomotor domain because reflex movements are actually prerequisites to development in the following classification levels.

Classification Level 2—Basic-Fundamental Movements. Basic-fundamental movement patterns occur in the learner during his first year of life. He builds upon the reflex movements inherent within his body. The common basic movement behavior, such as visually tracking an object, reaching, grasping, and manipulating an object with the hands, and progressing through the developmental stages of crawling, creeping, and walking, emerge in the learner in a highly patterned and predictable way. All of these basic-fundamental movement patterns are built upon the foundation of reflex movements listed in the first classification level of this model. Many of these basic-fundamental movement patterns, which develop early in the learner's life, literally unfold from within rather than being taught.

Classification Level 3—Perceptual Abilities. Though classification level 3 appears to suggest cognitive as well as psychomotor behaviors, it is included in the psychomotor domain because many investigators claim that perceptual and motor functions are inseparable, and enriched movement experiences usually enhance a child's abilities to structure and perceive more efficiently the many events to which she is exposed.

Efficiently functioning perceptual abilities are essential to development of the learner in the affective, the cognitive, and the psychomotor domains. These abilities assist the learner in interpreting stimuli, thus enabling her to make necessary adjustments to her environment. Present-day society places high premiums on cognitive excellence and superior performance in psychomotor activities; both depend upon the development of perceptual abilities. It should be obvious that the learner should have maximum opportunities to engage early in sensory stimulating activities and to explore a variety of movement tasks to facilitate the development of these essential perceptual abilities.

Classification Level 4—Physical Abilities.   Physical abilities are essential to the efficient functioning of the learner in the psychomotor domain. Proper functioning of the various systems of the body enable the learner to meet the demands placed upon him by his environment. *These physical abilities are in fact an essential part of the foundation for the development of skilled movements.*

This fourth classification level, Physical Abilities, incorporates the following characteristics: endurance, strength, flexibility, and agility.

Classification Level 5—Skilled Movements.   The term *skill* has been defined by several authors. Munn (1946) defines skill as proficiency in performing a task; Laban and Lawrence (1947) state that skill is the economy of effort a learner displays while perfecting a complex movement; they call skill the final state of perfection. Mohr (1960) defines skill as a progress toward better performance; while Seashore (1940) contends that skill is a degree of efficiency in performing a complex movement. Cratty (1964) states that skill denotes that an integration of learner behavior regarding a specific task has occurred. In other words, he is calling skill a degree of efficiency in performance of a specific, reasonably complex movement behavior. The reader should note that all the authors appear to be selecting, in essence, the same unique characteristic, a degree of efficiency in performing a complex movement task.

Classification Level 6—Nondiscursive Communication.   Movement communication is obvious in everyday life and is an important aspect of the learner's movement behaviors. Each learner develops a style of moving which communicates her feelings about her affective self to the perceptive observer. Accurately interpreting communicative movement behaviors of a learner heightens an educator's perceptions of the learner's feelings, needs, and interest, thereby enabling the educator to make more meaningful selections of learning strategies for that particular learner.

This completes our discussion of the affective and psychomotor domains. Now take a few moments to complete the exercise that follows, which is designed to see if you can differentiate between goals in these two domains.

EXERCISE 4.1 _____

Examine the following goals and determine whether their focus is primarily affective (a) or psychomotor (p). When you're through, you can compare your answers to the ones found in the feedback section at the end of the chapter.

_____ 1. Third-grade students will learn respect for the American flag.

_____ 2. First-grade students will print the letters of the alphabet in upper- and lowercase.

_____ 3. High school literature students will develop an appreciation for poetry.

_____ 4. Physical education students will improve their putting ability.

_____ 5. Fourth-grade health students will become convinced of the importance of proper eating and sleeping habits.

_____ 6. Kindergarten students will develop their scissor-cutting skills.

_____ 7. Advanced shorthand students will be able to take dictation at the rate of 120 words per minute.

_____ 8. Driver education students will develop an appreciation for safe driving habits.

_____ 9. Preschool children will be willing to share toys in a free-play situation.

_____ 10. Elementary music students will be able to clap with their hands to simple rhythm found in songs.

THE COGNITIVE DOMAIN

Probably the most common types of instructional goals found in our schools today are cognitive. This is because the cognitive domain focuses on the transmission of knowledge and skills, which is the most prevalent view of the role of the school both today and in the past. We would estimate that anywhere from 80 to 90% of the average elementary and secondary student's school time is devoted to the achievement of cognitive goals. This emphasis can be seen in the goals teachers have, in their teaching strategies, and in the kinds of tests that teachers give. Virtually all of the items of both teacher-made and standardized tests are devoted to the measurement of cognitive goals. This will, of course, vary with the grade level and with individual courses, but we believe that, on the whole, our estimates are accurate.

However, because schools focus on the cognitive domain doesn't suggest that we believe the affective domain is not important. In fact, when parents send their children to school initially, they most often ask the child upon returning, "How was your teacher? Is she nice?" Rarely do parents ask, "Well, what did you learn on the first day of school?" While this is only one small example, it indicates that parents are concerned about their children's learning, but they are also concerned with how the children are treated. Probably, if forced to choose, they would prefer good treatment to optimal learning. Furthermore, at the high school level, a recent study sponsored by the National Association of Secondary School Principals involving 1,500 public and private school students showed a teacher's caring attitude toward students to be more important than a vast knowledge of the subject (Cromer, 1984).

These are all issues open to debate, of course. While the *explicit* emphasis is clearly on the cognitive domain, the affective domain is enormously important, and *implicit* affective goals undergird much of our educational concern. We discuss this relationship between cognitive and affective emphasis in Chapters 6 and 7.

The cognitive domain is often confused with the affective domain. One way of differentiating the two is to think of the cognitive domain as involving rational and analytical thinking processes, whereas the affective domain deals with feelings and likes or dislikes. Metaphorically, we can think of the focus of the cognitive domain as being in the mind, whereas the focus of the affective domain is in the heart. Another way of differentiating between the two domains is by asking these questions: (1) Does the person know how to do it? and (2) Will the person do it freely, without any type of coercion? The first question implies a cognitive answer, whereas the second implies an affective answer. For example, when students fail to follow a school rule or policy, these two questions could be asked to determine the cause of the problem. If students are unaware of the rules, then the solution to the problem is cognitive, involving teaching or informing students of the rules. However, if students know what the rules are but choose to ignore them, then the problem is affective and involves their willingness to follow these rules. Here is a clear example of how understanding the difference between the cognitive and affective goals can help to make teaching more effective. For example, lecturing, which implies a cognitive goal, is a fairly inefficient way of changing people's attitudes, which is an affective goal. Consequently, lecturing students who have chosen to disregard a particular rule is a fairly ineffective way to change their behavior. A teacher who understands these distinctions can more readily analyze a problem situation and select a teaching strategy that is appropriate for the task at hand.

The cognitive domain includes a large number of diverse goals, but its primary focus is on intellectual development. Within the domain, goals can be divided into two major areas: (1) knowlege and (2) the processing and manipulation of information. Knowledge goals in the cognitive domain involve the learning and remembering of basic facts, concepts, generalizations, and theories, whereas processing goals involve using or applying this knowledge in some type of problem-solving situation. The examples in Table 4.1 are designed to illustrate the relationships between these two areas.

Table 4.1   Knowledge-Level Goals and Their Related Processing Activities

Knowledge	Related Processing Activity
Knowing the formula for the area of a rectangle	Being able to apply the formula in a problem-solving situation
Knowing the definition of a noun	Being able to identify nouns in a sentence
Knowing the definition of a controlled variable	Being able to design an experiment with a controlled variable in it
Knowing the terms *rhythm, meter, personification,* and *alliteration*	Using these terms to analyze a poem

EXERCISE 4.2

Examine the following goals and determine whether they are primarily cognitive (c), affective (a), or psychomotor (p) in their orientation. When you're through, you can compare your answers to the ones found in the feedback section at the end of the chapter.

_____ 1. In an unsupervised setting, third-grade students will follow traffic rules on foot, on bicycle, or on another conveyance.

_____ 2. Junior high social studies students will recite the Gettysburg Address.

_____ 3. The intermediate school student will, during a classroom discussion, listen to another's ideas, evidencing this by using the other's ideas in his comments.

_____ 4. The first-year history student will be able to paraphrase the definition of *constitutional monarchy.*

_____ 5. Senior high driver education students will be able to parallel park.

_____ 6. Senior high driver education students will know the major traffic signs.

_____ 7. The reader will understand the differences among the cognitive, affective, and psychomotor domains.

_____ 8. Seventh-grade students will behave properly in the cafeteria.

_____ 9. Beginning secretarial skills students will type at a minimum of 45 words per minute.

_____ 10. Auto mechanics students will know how to read a schematic diagram of a diesel engine.

_____ 11. Advanced algebra students will construct a proof to prove the commutative property of real numbers.

_____ 12. Middle school students will listen to students who disagree with their points of view.

_____ 13. Advanced American literature students will spend at least one hour a week reading unrequired American literature classics.

_____ 14. Second-grade students will follow classroom rules as prescribed by the teacher.

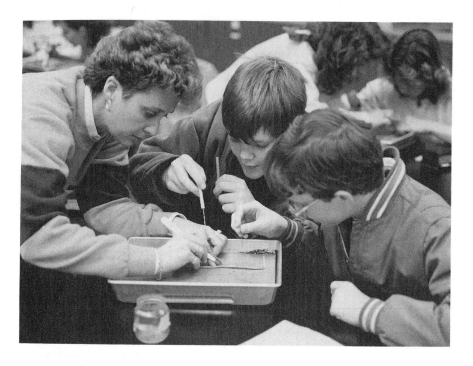

Teachers should employ the taxonomy in order to vary the intellectual experiences in the classroom.

The Levels of the Cognitive Domain

Knowledge. As noted earlier in the chapter, knowledge is one of two major areas of the cognitive domain. This area is also referred to as *low level* because it does not call for the processing or manipulation of information. Simply stated, knowledge is defined here as merely recalling memorized material. The range of material can be quite broad and commonly includes such things as (Bloom et al., 1956)

> Knowledge of specifics
>
> Knowledge of terminology
>
> Knowledge of specific facts
>
> Knowledge of trends and sequences
>
> Knowledge of classifications and categories
>
> Knowledge of universals
>
> Knowledge of principles and generalizations
>
> Knowledge of theories

The most common vehicles that provide the material to be memorized are reading of printed words and listening to teachers who disseminate information. Then, at the appropriate time, the learner recalls material when provided with a cue.

For example, most of us were told that George Washington was the first president of the United States, and we have stored this information. When confronted with a verbal cue (e.g., Who was the first president of the United States?), we *retrieve* the information and respond accordingly. It is important to note that everything we have learned has been stored in our brains, but sometimes it can be very difficult to retrieve the information. For instance, who was the 21st president of the United States? Most of us have learned this isolated fact at one time or another, and most of us simply cannot call it up. This is particularly so when information is disseminated on a singular basis. In other words, the less use we make of information learned, the less likely we are to recall that information.

Knowledge is the only low-level area of the cognitive domain, because the act of retrieving types of information—facts, for example—does not require us to do anything with the data. The other area of the cognitive domain requires us to alter or employ information in one form or another and is considered to be a high level of behavior. Table 4.2 contains a depiction of this arrangement.

Although knowledge may imply very little in the form of intellectual activity, the memorization of such things as trends, classifications, principles, and theories can be very difficult and can require a great amount of practice (Loftus & Loftus, 1976; Wickelgren, 1977). Furthermore, if the student does not have a sound foundation of retrievable information, utilizing the higher levels of the domain may become an almost impossible task.

Examples of knowledge-level behavioral objectives are as follows:

Given a picture of a chair previously studied in class, the student will name one characteristic of the chair.

Table 4.2 The Two Areas of the Cognitive Domain

AREA 1 (Low Level):	Knowledge
AREA 2 (High Level):	Comprehension
	Application
	Analysis
	Synthesis
	Evaluation

Without aid, the student will orally identify the author of the *Iliad*.

Given a list of formulas, the student will circle the one used to solve the area of a rectangle.

Without aid, the student will recite Newton's third law.

Given a list of historical dates, the student will circle the date of Columbus's first voyage to the New World.

EXERCISE 4.3

Read the following behavioral objectives and place a (k) in front of all those written at the knowledge level. Then compare your answers to the ones in the feedback section at the end of the chapter.

_____ 1. Given a list of historical dates, the student will organize them in correct chronological order.

_____ 2. Given a variety of art materials, the student will draw a rabbit that has two long ears and four short legs.

_____ 3. From memory, the student will name the last three presidents of the United States.

_____ 4. Given a list of plays, the student will circle all those authored by Shakespeare.

EXERCISE 4.4

Write a knowledge-level behavioral objective for each of the following concepts. When you finish, compare your statements to the ones found in the feedback section at the end of the chapter.

Mammals: _____

_____

_____

Presidents: _____

_____

_____

Comprehension. As shown in Table 4.2, comprehension is positioned as the least complex of the high levels. This is so because it is generally assumed that as we progress from comprehension to evaluation, the objectives or questions require increased amounts of manipulation. The following examples depict the minimum amount of manipulation required at the comprehension level.

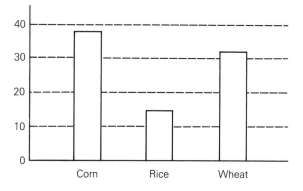

Figure 4.1   Bar Graph Handout

OBJECTIVE: Given a bar graph representing the major crops grown in the United States (see Figure 4.1), the students will orally name the most widely produced crop.

In this case the students are not asked to give a memorized answer, because at no point prior to the activity did the teacher state that more corn is produced in the United States than any other crop. The students therefore must interpret the data in the graph. We surely would agree that the task is relatively simple. Nevertheless, in order to arrive at the desired response, the students had to process information, and this function represents a high-level behavior.

Restating information in one's own words is another form of comprehension. For example, Mr. Johns defined the concept *war* for his students by saying, "War is an armed hostile conflict between opposed forces which is accompanied by death and destruction and which usually involves an economic factor." Mr. Johns then asked the class to consider their own definitions in light of his observation. Georgianne replied, "War occurs when one country wants something another country has and is willing to kill and destroy to get it." Georgianne has redefined the concept of war in her own terms and, in doing so, has manipulated or processed information. Again, this might not be a very difficult task, but it is surely one that would not involve memorization.

Translation is another form of comprehension. Used here, the activity requires a change in format so that the information can be presented in a different way. Students regularly accomplish this task when taking arithmetic problems in the form of words and changing them into numerical symbols. What we find here is a conceptualization not found at the low level of the cognitive domain.

You will find in the following list some examples of comprehension *questions:*

Look at this pie chart. Which piece of the federal budget consumes the most taxpayer dollars?

Glance around the room. Can you find an example of a circle?

In your own words, can you tell me what *genocide* means?

John's mother gave him a dime, which he added to the 20 cents he had in a box. He decided he would buy three pieces of penny candy and give his little brother the nickel he owed him. Later he counted his money. How much did he have left?

Keep in mind that when working at the comprehension level, the students will not have prior knowledge of the desired outcome and will in some way have to alter the material with which they are confronted.

Exercise 4.5

Read the following behavioral objectives and place a (c) in front of all those written at the comprehension level. Then compare your answers to the ones in the feedback section at the end of the chapter.

_____ 1. Without aid, the student will recite, in order, the 10 original amendments in the Bill of Rights.

_____ 2. Given a number of objects they have not previously seen, the student will identify all those that are squares.

_____ 3. Given a number of objects they have not previously seen, the students will point to their favorite one.

_____ 4. When shown five pictures of furniture, the student will identify all those that are chairs.

Exercise 4.6

Write a comprehension-level behavioral objective for each of the following concepts. When you finish, compare your statements to the ones found in the feedback section at the end of the chapter.

Mammals: _____

_____

_____

Presidents: _____

_____

_____

Application. This high level of the cognitive domain requires problem solving. There are two critical features to be noted regarding the application level. The first is that the situation confronting the students should be one which has not been lectured about or practiced during the unit of instruction. Otherwise, the students probably would simply recall the desired answer or solution.

The second feature is that the students must select the appropriate tool which in turn is *applied* to the problem at hand. The following example shows how these two features work hand-in-hand.

> OBJECTIVE: Given a drawing of a house and yard (see Figure 4.2), the student will correctly determine the area of the back yard.

The first thing the students have to do is determine the shape of the problem. Then they have to recall the appropriate formula and *apply* it to the data in order to solve the problem. Again, it is assumed that the students have not been confronted with this specific problem prior to its implementation.

The following are some examples of application-level behavioral objectives:

> Given a swimming pool with a diameter of 16 feet and a depth of 30 inches and the instructions from a bottle of chlorine, the student will determine the appropriate amount of chlorine to be poured into the pool.

> Given the appropriate tools and a specific set of instructions, the wood-shop student will build a coffee table that clearly reflects the specifications.

> Given the necessary culinary equipment, all or some of which may be used, the student will make three crepes that will fold without breaking and hold a cottage cheese mixture.

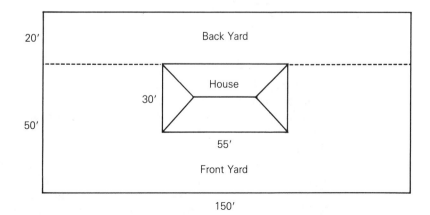

Figure 4.2 House/Yard Handout

In each case, the students must produce an answer or a finished product. It is important to note at this point that although the students are solving problems, they are not doing anything that is new or unique. To do so would place the students at a more complex level, as discussed shortly.

EXERCISE 4.7 _____

Read the following behavioral objectives and place an (ap) in front of all those written at the application level. Then compare your answers to the ones in the feedback section at the end of the chapter.

_____ 1. Given an amount of energy consumed and the rate per consumed unit, the student will correctly determine the total amount due on an electric bill.

_____ 2. Given five written passages, the student will determine all those that represent propaganda.

_____ 3. Without aid, the student will define *generalization* as described in class.

_____ 4. Given 20 subtraction problems, the student will solve 80% of them correctly.

EXERCISE 4.8 _____

Write an application-level behavioral objective for each of the following concepts. When you finish, compare your statements to the ones found in the feedback section at the end of the chapter.

Mammals: _____

_____

_____

Presidents: _____

_____

_____

Analysis. In its simpliest form, analysis involves taking a *whole* and breaking it down into its separate parts or determining its particular characteristics. A common laboratory technique involving analysis occurs when a student is provided with a substance and is asked to determine its elements. This might involve weighing, dissolving, splitting, flaming, and so forth. However, in most academic situations it is more common to analyze the printed or electronic word in the form of essays, speeches, editorials, poems, and the many forms of books. In working at the analysis level, there are a number of "buzz" words you might consider, such as assumptions

implications

fallacies

central themes

persuasion

consistency

For example, let us say that the students are assigned the task of reading selected editorials from the local newspaper. Obviously, the columnist is using persuasive techniques, such as the presenting of factual information or data. If the students basically accept the position presented, they might then be directed to identify or discuss implications in light of possible future events.

Pinpointing a central theme is a very common analysis-level operation and often can present quite a challenge. For instance, the student might be asked to read Plato's *Republic* and ascertain the role of the individual in a perfect state.

Employing a wide range of visuals also promotes analysis behavior. Let us say Ms. Fry was teaching a third-grade science class. She showed them pictures of three groups of animals and asked the students to figure out which group did not belong. Drawings of animals in the pictures included:

1. horse	2. pig	3. chicken
cow	goat	wolf
sheep	bull	colt

The students then began the process of comparing the animals and eventually concluded that picture 3 does not belong because

1. Of all the animals, only a colt is a *baby* animal

2. Of all the animals, only the chicken has feathers

3. Of all the animals, only the chicken is not a mammal

4. Of all the animals, only the wolf is a meat eater

You will find additional examples of analysis behaviors written in the form of *questions,* as follows

How many facts do you find in this passage?

What is the main ingredient in this mixture?

On what assumption has the author based his position?

Read the page carefully. Do you find anything that is incorrect?

What is the major difference between Gina's point of view and Mike's point of view?

Look at these two paintings. Compare at least two characteristics of the artists' styles.

EXERCISE 4.9

Read the following behavioral objectives and place an (an) in front of all those written at the analysis level. Then compare your answers to the ones in the feedback section at the end of the chapter.

_____ 1. Given a list of 50 automobiles, the students will circle their favorite one.

_____ 2. When given a concept and superordinate concept in diagram fashion, the student will write one coordinate concept.

_____ 3. Without aid, the student will determine one assumption upon which Darwin's theories are based.

_____ 4. Given 10 pictures, the student will identify all those that are farm animals.

EXERCISE 4.10

Write an analysis-level behavioral objective for each of the following concepts. When you finish, compare your statements to the ones found in the feedback section at the end of the chapter.

Mammals: _____

_____

_____

Presidents: _____

_____

_____

_____

Synthesis. Synthesis is more or less the opposite of analysis. Whereas analysis requires us to take something apart, synthesis involves putting things together to produce a new and unique whole. There are two critical considerations when assigning students synthesis-level behaviors. The first is that the finished product must be new and unique unto the student, not the world. In other words, if

Marsala solved the problem depicted in Figure 4.2 on page 93 without any prior knowledge of the applicable formula, she would be working at the synthesis level. It makes no difference that the "world" has known this formula for quite some time.

The second point is that a criterion must be present in order to allow us, to some degree, to apply a standard of success. For example, the criterion for Marsala's problem might be that she simply derives the correct answer. Let us look at two additional examples to clarify this point.

> OBJECTIVE: Given the use of any materials of their choice, the wood-shop students will design and build an original boat that will be at least 14 feet in length, will accommodate up to four adults, and will be capable of handling a small electric engine.

The fact that the finished product may resemble other boats is immaterial; the students designed it, and it is theirs. In that it is a creative exercise, there is room for subjective evaluation regarding excellence, but a clearcut criterion is used to determine whether or not the task has been accomplished successfully. The same holds true for the following objective:

> OBJECTIVE: Without aid, the language arts student will create one haiku poem that contains the correct number of syllables and deals with nature.

EXERCISE 4.11 _____

Read the following behavioral objectives and place an (s) in front of all those written at the synthesis level. Then compare your answers to the ones in the feedback section at the end of the chapter.

_____ 1. Given any materials of their choice, the homemaking student will create a dress that is sleeveless and below knee length and that contains at least two different kinds of material.

_____ 2. Given appropriate materials, the student will construct a model of an airplane that clearly reflects a set of preexisting specifications.

_____ 3. Given a variety of art materials, the student will develop an original design that incorporates a single geometrical shape.

_____ 4. Without aid, the student will list two characteristics of informal balance.

EXERCISE 4.12 _____

Write a synthesis-level behavioral objective for each of the following concepts. When you finish, compare your statements to the ones found in the feedback section at the end of the chapter.

Mammals: _____

_____

_____

Presidents: _____

_____

_____

Evaluation. This complex level of the cognitive domain requires the student to make a judgement; however, the judgement in and of itself is insufficient. For example, let us say Mr. Grimaldi asked his children the following question: "What is the best dog?" The children responded excitedly with examples such as Labrador, boxer, cocker spaniel, and poodle. At this point the children were merely expressing a feeling or opinion and therefore were operating in the affective domain. Although making a judgement is critical, when considering the evaluative level we need something else — a criterion. Let us continue our example and see how this is accomplished.

After the children had provided examples, Mr. Grimaldi then asked them to be very specific when thinking about the characteristics a "best" dog might need. After Mr. Grimaldi facilitated the experience, the list was as follows:

1. The best dog should be under 50 pounds, or it will cost too much to feed.
2. The best dog should have a gentle disposition.
3. The best dog should be short-haired if in a warm climate.
4. The best dog should be short-eared because of a moist climate that would promote ear infections.

Having established a *criterion*, Mr. Grimaldi then directed the children to *apply* the criterion to the list of four dogs. The children then concluded that the boxer was the best dog, even though it weighed more than 50 pounds.

This example clearly illustrates that a criterion must be employed if the students are working at the evaluative level. Now let us examine a few additional examples.

Given a list of famous 20th-century figures, the student will select the one he or she believes had the greatest impact on the 1900s and document the choice by citing two of that person's major achievements that impacted upon the world's population.

Given five paintings completed by grand masters, the students will select the one they consider to be the most outstanding and support the selection by discussing (1) the style of the artist's work and (2) the contemporary value of the artist's work.

Given geographical and geological information regarding a mountain river, the student will determine the most logical place to erect a dam and will cite data on soil composition, terrain, and water pressure in support of the selection.

EXERCISE 4.13

Read the following behavioral objectives and place an (e) in front of all those written at the evaluation level. Then compare your answers to the ones in the feedback section at the end of the chapter.

_____ 1. Given a list of computer models, the students will select the one they consider to be the best.

_____ 2. Given specifications and road tests of five major automobiles, the students will select the one they consider to be most efficient and will support their choice by discussing cost, maintenance, gas consumption, and road handling.

_____ 3. Without aid, the student will name three Native American reservations found in the southwestern United States.

_____ 4. Given any art materials of their choice, the students will create an oil painting using no more than three colors.

_____ 5. Given a list of 10 books, the students will select the one they would most like to read.

EXERCISE 4.14

Write an evaluation-level behavioral objective for each of the following concepts. When you finish, compare your statements to the ones found in the feedback section at the end of the chapter.

Mammals: _____

_____

_____

Presidents: _____

_____

_____

SUMMARY

In Chapter 4 we have thoroughly familiarized you with the three domains, with a heavy emphasis upon the cognitive domain. This was not because we believe that domain to be the most important but because it is the focus in so many educational programs. Although objectives involving the affective domain are fewer in number, we are convinced that they should play a critical role in the development of youngsters. This is particularly true at the primary level, where socialization is such an important factor.

Regarding the psychomotor domain, pediatricians throughout the country have become increasingly disturbed with the cardiovascular development in children who are not engaged in a constant, sequential physical education program. In addition, the drive toward academics in the upper grade levels has clearly limited the amount of time spent in physical activities.

As stated early in the chapter, we believe all three domains have to come into play to promote the healthy growth of children, and even though we have presented only a brief overview of the affective and psychomotor domains, we urge you to incorporate them in your curriculum whenever possible.

Whether or not the cognitive domain is the most critical source of objectives and questions is immaterial, for this domain is surely the most commonly employed in schools; and that provides the rationale for our treatment in this chapter. We have clearly delineated low- and high-level behavior because we take the position that the low-level area, knowledge, often dominates the curriculum and that we need to shift our emphasis to the higher levels which are crucial to the promotion of critical thinking. Whether or not we can teach critical thinking is a controversial point, but we believe there is general agreement that if we fail to provide a learning environment which requires the processing of information, we will be doing our students a major disservice.

Finally, we believe we have covered two of the three domains in terms of their impact upon you. The affective and psychomotor domains have been presented with the hope that we have impressed upon you the importance and utility of employing various levels of these domains and that you will be *willing* to do so in your classroom. In terms of the cognitive domain, we have supplied you with the tools to employ the material at least at the synthesis level for you are now able to produce original objectives and questions for your unit and lesson plans, which are discussed in Chapter 5.

REFERENCES

Bennett, W. J. (1988). James Madison High School: A curriculum for American students. *Education Week, 7* (15–16), 1, 26.

Beyer, B. K. (1987). *Practical strategies for the teaching of thinking.* Boston: Allyn & Bacon.

Bloom, B., Englehart, M., Furst, E., Hill, W., & Krathwohl, D. (1956). *Taxonomy of educational objectives. Handbook 1: Cognitive domain.* New York: David McKay.

Coomber, J. E. et al. (1986). Elaboration in vocabulary learning: A comparison of three rehearsal methods. *Research in Teaching of English, 20,* 281–293.

Cromer, J. (1984). *The mood of American youth.* Washington, DC: National Association of Secondary School Principals.

Cratty, B.J. (1964). *Movement behavior and motor learning.* Philadelphia: Lea & Febiger.

Harrow, A. (1972). *A taxonomy of the psychomotor domain: A guide for developing behavioral objectives.* New York: David McKay.

Jewett, A., & Mullan, M. (1977). Movement process categories in physical education in teaching-learning. *Curriculum design: Purposes and procedures in physical education teaching-learning.* Washington, DC: American Alliance for Health, Physical Education and Recreation.

Krathwohl, D., Bloom, B., & Masia, B. (1964). *Taxonomy of educational objectives—The classification of educational goals. Handbook II: Affective domain.* New York: David McKay.

Laban, R., & Lawrence, F.C. (1947). *Effort.* London: McDonald & Evans.

Loftus, G., & Loftus, E. (1976). *Human memory, the processing of information.* Hillsdale, NJ: Lawrence Erlbaum.

Mager, R. (1968). *Developing attitudes toward learning.* Belmont, CA.: Fearon.

Mager, R. (1973). *Measuring instructional interest.* Belmont, CA.: Fearon.

Martin, J. (1979). Effects of teacher higher-order questions on student process and product variables in a single classroom study. *Journal of Educational Research, 72,* 183–187.

Mohr, D.R. (1960). "The contributions of physical activity to skill learning." *American Association for Health, Physical Education, and Recreation Research Quarterly, 31.*

Munn, N. L. (1946). *Psychology.* Boston: Houghton Mifflin.

Perceiving, behaving, becoming: A new focus for education. (1962). Washington, DC: Association for Supervision and Curriculum Development.

Poole, R. (1971). Characteristics of the "Taxonomy of educational objectives: Cognitive domain." *Psychology in the Schools, 8,* 379–385.

Poole, R. (1972). Characteristics of the "Taxonomy of educational objectives: Cognitive domain"—A replication. *Psychology in the Schools, 9,* 83–88.

Raths, L., Harmin, M., & Simon, S. (1966). *Values and teaching.* Columbus, OH: Merrill.

Seddon, G. (1978). The properties of Bloom's taxonomy of educational objectives for the cognitive domain. *Review of Educational Research, 48,* 303–323.

Seashore, R. (1940). "An experimental and theoretical analysis of five motor skills." *American Journal of Psychology, 53.*

Stoker, H., & Kropp, R. (1964). Measurement of cognitive processes. *Journal of Educational Measurement, 1,* 39–42.

Webb, E., Campbell, D., Schwartz, R., & Sechrest, L. (1972). *Unobtrusive measures: Nonreactive research in the social sciences.* Chicago: Rand McNally.

Wickelgren, W. (1977). *Learning and memory.* Englewood Cliffs, NJ: Prentice-Hall.

EXERCISE FEEDBACK

EXERCISE 4.1

1. (a) Affective
2. (p) Psychomotor. In interpreting this goal in this way, we are placing primary emphasis on students' ability to form letters, which assumes that they already know how to form the letters. This latter component is a cognitive skill which is discussed in the next section.
3. (a) Affective
4. (p) Psychomotor
5. (a) Affective. Here the teacher is trying to develop positive attitudes toward good health habits.
6. (p) Psychomotor
7. (p) Psychomotor
8. (a) Affective
9. (a) Affective
10. (p) Psychomotor

EXERCISE 4.2

1. (a) Affective. The key word here is *unsupervised.* Note how this goal assumes that students already know these rules, the cognitive component.
2. (c) Cognitive
3. (a) Affective
4. (c) Cognitive
5. (p) Psychomotor. Note, too, how this goal assumes that students know the proper procedure for parking, again, the cognitive component.
6. (c) Cognitive
7. (c) Cognitive
8. (a) Affective. Again, note how an affective goal assumes the necessary prerequisite cognitive knowledge.
9. (p) Psychomotor
10. (c) Cognitive. This goal would probably be a prerequisite to the goal of actually applying this knowledge to work on an engine, which has psychomotor components.
11. (c) Cognitive
12. (a) Affective. This goal is probably related to the value of open-mindedness.
13. (a) Affective. This goal is aimed at developing positive student attitudes toward American literature.
14. (a) Affective

EXERCISE 4.3

1. _____ This material was probably not memorized.
2. _____ Although the student may recall characteristics, the drawing will be high level.
3. _(k)_ The key phrase here is "from memory," which identifies this behavior as recall.
4. _(k)_ This material was probably memorized.

EXERCISE 4.4

Mammals: Given a list of animals, the student will circle all those that are mammals.
Presidents: Without aid, the student will name, in order, the first three presidents of the United States.

EXERCISE 4.5

1. _____ The fact that the student will recite implies memorization.
2. _(c)_ Pointing out *examples* is a comprehension task.
3. _____ Affective objective
4. _____ This would be a knowledge objective *if* the students had prior access to the pictures.

EXERCISE 4.6

Mammals: Given a bar graph of mammals living in Africa, the student will determine the mammal group having the largest population.
Presidents: Given a variety of materials, the student will summarize the current president's first two years in office by including areas of domestic policy, defense, and foreign affairs.

EXERCISE 4.7

1. _(ap)_ This is assumed to be a new problem. The student will have to take into account the data and then solve the problem.
2. _____ This behavior goes beyond problem solving.
3. _____ Recall
4. _(ap)_ If the students have not seen these problems before and make a tool selection, they are working at the application level.

EXERCISE 4.8

Mammals: Given the characteristics of a specific mammal and the characteristics of a specific environment, the student will determine three physiological changes that would have to occur for the mammal to survive.
Presidents: Given economic data on trade, foreign markets, and world currency applicable for the current presidential administration, the student will determine the amount of trade deficit for the coming year.

EXERCISE 4.9

1. _____ Affective objective

2. __(an)__ The student would have to determine the characteristics of the superordinate concept and the concept in order to generate a coordinate concept.
3. __(an)__ This is clearly an analysis-level task.
4. _____ This is a knowledge objective if the student had prior contact with the specific pictures.

EXERCISE 4.10

Mammals: Given materials on Darwin's theories, the student will project two implications for human beings living in the 21st century.
Presidents: Given a wide range of printed and mediated materials, the student will pose two probable motives behind John F. Kennedy's response to the Cuban missile crisis.

EXERCISE 4.11

1. __(s)__ The student is not creating a predetermined dress.
2. _____ This is a predetermined product and therefore involves application at best.
3. __(s)__ Once again, this involves an original creation with a criterion.
4. _____ Recall

EXERCISE 4.12

Mammals: Given the properties of an alien environment, the student will design a life-support system for humans that will deal specifically with the problems of air, food, and shelter.
Presidents: Given a wide range of material regarding the current administration, the student will develop a Mideast peace plan that will address the issues of borders, settlements, and peoples.

EXERCISE 4.13

1. _____ There is no criterion, and therefore the student may be working at the affective level.
2. __(e)__ A judgement is accompanied by a criterion.
3. _____ This involves memorization and therefore a knowledge-level behavior.
4. _____ A synthesis-level objective.
5. _____ Again, a criterion is not present and therefore this is not evaluation, by definition.

EXERCISE 4.14

Mammals: When supplied information on a given physical environment and a list of 10 mammals, the student will determine which mammal would be most likely to survive based upon diet, reproductive capability, and physical features.
Presidents: Given a choice of materials and a list of the five most recent presidents of the United States, the student will select the one that has been most successful based upon achievements in the areas of domestic and foreign policy and technological advancement.

5 ‖ Unit and Lesson Planning

INTRODUCTION

Can you imagine a surgeon beginning an operation without having studied tests or X-rays? Can you imagine a construction superintendent building a bridge without blueprints? Does a pilot go into the air without consulting weather reports, charts, and maps? In each case, the result would be, at the least, inefficient and often disastrous. So it is with effective teaching in the classroom. To be a successful teacher, one who assists students in the mastery of content, you must plan thoroughly.

Perhaps the most important value in learning to plan lessons is that it provides a way to help teachers learn to think about what they are doing. One of the themes of this text is the development of teachers as conscious decision makers. As such, teachers think carefully about what goes on in their classrooms, know reasons for doing certain things, and employ a variety of ways of teaching children. We want to help teachers avoid the pitfalls of blindly following a textbook, constantly giving fact level tests, and mechanically teaching classes. While learning to construct unit and lesson plans doesn't automatically ensure creative, insightful, and sensitive teachers, it is one step toward helping them become conscious decision makers. Clark and Peterson (1986) found that planning plays a major role in the decisions teachers make when they work with students.

A second important reason for planning is emotional. McCutcheon (1982) found that careful planning provided a source of security and confidence for teachers, and Neale, Pace, and Case (1983) found that beginning teachers tend to be quite extensive with their written plans. Even veteran teachers take extra care in planning when they face content with which they're not totally secure or content that is difficult for students. These findings have important implications for us all: we should plan with extra care when we are inexperienced, uncertain, or insecure. The extra effort will pay dividends in our effectiveness as we work with students. Because of these factors we are devoting this chapter to a discussion of planning.

The purpose of this chapter is to introduce you to unit and lesson planning. A daily lesson plan is a complete outline of the objectives, content, and procedures for a one-period instructional segment. A unit plan is a detailed outline for a series of connected lesson plans on a selected topic of study which lasts a week or two. Both time estimates are approximations; sometimes lessons planned for one period spill over into the next, and some units may extend for many weeks. As you become more experienced in the classroom, you'll become more accurate when gauging time frames for your teaching.

In this chapter we will discuss planning on a daily basis as well as planning for longer periods. Daily lesson plans are important because they provide the teacher with a means of thinking about and providing for meaningful learning experiences within a given class period. But good teaching is more than individual lesson plans tacked together. Here we see the importance of thoughtful unit planning. A good unit plan ties the individual lesson plans into a meaningful whole. The idea here is that a successful unit plan is more than the sum of the individual lessons. We will discuss planning units in the next section.

As a final note before beginning our study, let us impress upon you two critical initial considerations. The first, as stated briefly in Chapter 2, is that it is important for you to establish a positive learning environment at the very onset of the school year. You will want your students to view you as sincere and supportive. We suggest you discuss, in general, your academic plans and the rules and regulations to be followed in your classroom. You should clearly communicate to your students that you are there to promote their learning and growth.

A second important initial step is becoming familiar with any learning objectives, curriculum guides, required materials, and rules and regulations that may have been established by the school system in which you are teaching. Only when this has been accomplished are you ready to consider unit, and more specifically, lesson plans.

OBJECTIVES

After completing Chapter 5, you should be able to accomplish the following objectives:

1. For you as a pre/inservice teacher to acquire proficiency in unit planning so that given a unit topic you will develop a unit summary and topical outline appropriate for the topic
2. For you as a pre/inservice teacher to increase your knowledge of lesson planning so that, given the three-stage model as applied to lesson planning, you will be able to list all of the seven subcomponents
3. For you as a pre/inservice teacher to understand the parts of a lesson plan so that, given a series of goals, you will describe units that fit the topics described in the goals
4. For you as a pre/inservice teacher to understand the parts of a lesson plan so that, given a series of goals, you will describe a rationale appropriate for each goal
5. For you as a pre/inservice teacher to understand the parts of a lesson plan so that, given a series of goals, you will describe evaluations appropriate for each goal
6. For you as a pre/inservice teacher to acquire a proficiency in lesson planning so that, given a topic, you will develop an origi-

nal single-concept lesson plan using any materials of your choice. You plan must include all seven of the subcomponents.

7. For you as a pre/inservice teacher to increase your knowledge of lesson planning so that, without aid, you will describe each of the seven steps of the Madeline Hunter planning model.

UNIT PLANNING

Unit planning begins with the selection of a unit topic; a starting point for this process could be examination of the chapter headings in the students' text. The chapter divisions in texts are usually organized to correspond to approximate unit lengths. This does not mean that the teacher must mechanically adhere to chapter topics as unit headings. In some of the best-planned units teachers have disregarded the text completely or dealt with segments of chapters in unique ways. However, chapter topics do provide one readily available source for unit identification. Some sample unit topics in various disciplines can be seen in Table 5.1.

Having identified the unit topic, the teacher is now ready to consider the overall goal or purpose of the unit. One way of doing this is to summarize in several sentences the major outcomes that the teacher hopes will occur. This statement should include some description of the content to be covered as well as what students will do with this content. Some examples of these statements follow:

Second-Grade Unit on Word Endings
The purpose in this unit is to help students understand the rules for adding suffixes to words. This will provide them with the basis for better understanding the word meanings, spelling, and pronunciation.

Table 5.1   Sample Unit Topics

Language Arts	Social Studies
Nouns	The Civil War
Punctuation	The Colonial Era
Short Stories	Capitalism and Socialism
Paragraph Writing	Industrial Movement in America
Health	*Science*
Respiratory System	Reptiles
Drugs	Plants
Nutrition	Electricity
Exercise	Nuclear Energy

Seventh-Grade Life Science Unit on Plants
The unit will introduce life science students to plants and seeds. Students will understand the parts of plants and seeds, as well as the necessary conditions for healthy plants. This unit will also teach them how to make new plants from seeds, roots, and cuttings.

Eighth-Grade Unit on the Civil War
This unit is designed for eighth-grade American history students to learn causes, events, and results of the Civil War. General themes of slavery, states' rights, tariffs, and compromises will be stressed. Songs of the Civil War, a few major battles, the type of warfare employed, and many of the famous people who sacrificed and defended their beliefs at all costs will also be emphasized.

High School Home Economics Unit on Milk and Dairy Products
At the completion of this unit on milk and dairy products, students should understand the history of milk production, milk's nutritional composition, milk processing, the variety of dairy products that come from milk, forms of milk, storage of milk, and uses of milk in the six areas of menu planning.

The statement of purpose serves two functions. One is to communicate to students the nature and substance of the unit they will encounter. The second is as a planning tool for the teacher. In wrestling with this statement of purpose teachers prepare themselves for the next two planning tasks: organizing content and writing and sequencing objectives.

Having wrestled with the general purpose and scope of the unit, the teacher is now ready to outline the major concepts or ideas in the unit. Outlining helps the teacher organize the content to be taught, which is helpful when sequencing instruction and writing objectives.

Another use for this outline is as a teaching aid. In introducing the unit, the teacher can provide the outline as a type of advanced organizer to help students understand where the unit is going. In addition, as daily lessons are introduced, the teacher can refer back to the outline to help students understand the relationship of that lesson to previous and future ones.

Two ways of outlining the content of two previously discussed units are illustrated in Figures 5.1 and 5.2. The format that you choose will depend on your own preferences as well as the particular content being considered.

Using the outline as a planning guide, the teacher is now ready to consider specific objectives for the unit. The task at this phase of the planning process is to translate content topics into measurable goals objectives. In addition, once constructed, these objectives need to be sequenced in terms of Bloom's taxonomy. This provides a suggested

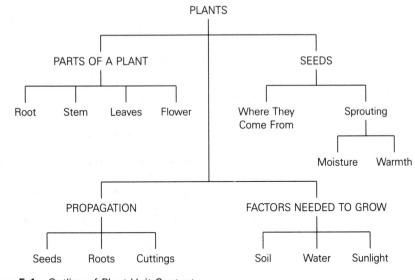

Figure 5.1 Outline of Plant Unit Content

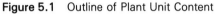

MILK AND DAIRY PRODUCTS

    I. History
   II. Nutritional Composition of Milk
      A. Fats, proteins, carbohydrates
      B. Vitamins
      C. Minerals
  III. Processing of Milk
      A. Pasteurization
      B. Homogenization
  IV. Variety of Milk Products
      A. Milk
          1. Whole
          2. Skim
          3. Cream
          4. Half and half
          5. Buttermilk
      B. Butter
      C. Yogurt
      D. Cheese
      E. Sour Cream
      F. Ice Cream
   V. Storage and Care of Milk and Milk Products
  VI. Uses of Milk in Menu Planning

Figure 5.2 Outline of Dairy Product Unit Content

order for teaching as well as helping to clarify the kinds of behaviors expected of students. An example of this process applied to one segment of the plant unit is shown below.

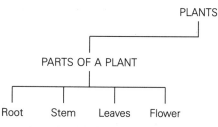

1. Third-grade science students will know the parts of a plant, so that when given a description of the part, they will be able to supply the correct term. (Knowledge).

2. Students will be able to identify the parts of a plant, so that when given an unlabeled picture of a plant, not encountered previously, they can label the parts of the plant with 100% accuracy. (Comprehension).

3. Students will know the functions of each of the parts of a plant, so that when presented with a problem in which one of the parts is damaged or destroyed, the students will be able to explain in their own words the effect this injury will have on plant functions. (Comprehension).

This process of constructing and sequencing objectives continues until all of the major topics in the content outline are addressed. When this is completed, the teacher is then ready to consider the next task, lesson planning, in which objectives are translated into instructional strategies.

EXERCISE 5.1 _____

Look at the following series of goals, each of which provides a topic for a lesson plan. For each, identify a possible unit that may fit the topic. Then compare your answers to the ones found in the feedback section at the end of the chapter.

1. You want your language arts students to understand homonyms.

_____

2. You want your American history students to know the causes of the Civil War.

_____

3. You want your kindergarteners to know the difference between a square and a rectangle.

_____

4. You want your science students to understand the structure of a paramecium.

_____

5. You want your carpentry students to understand factors affecting wood strength.

_____

EXERCISE 5.2 _____

For the following unit topic, develop a unit summary and topical outline. A kindergarten teacher is beginning to plan for a unit on parts of the body. What might the unit summary and topical outline look like?

UNIT SUMMARY: _____

_____

_____

_____

_____

_____

TOPICAL OUTLINE:

_____

LESSON PLANNING

In this phase of the planning process the teacher is thinking about the single class period rather than a longer period of time. The task here is to think through and plan for a meaningful segment of instruction lasting anywhere from 20 minutes to an hour. The format that we recommend has seven components: unit, goals objective, rationale, content, procedures, materials, and evaluation. Each of these components relates to an important part of the lesson-planning process. After we have described each of these seven components we will discuss alternate ways of thinking about the planning process.

Stage 1: Planning

Unit Component. In constructing daily lesson plans the teacher should continually keep in mind the relationship of individual lessons to the larger content of the unit. One way of reminding the teacher of these connections is to identify the unit at the top of the lesson plan. Describing or identifying the larger unit to which a particular lesson belongs affords the opportunity to think about how a particular lesson plan fits in with the others. Seldom do we as teachers teach isolated lessons. Rather, we try to sequence learning experiences that are logically organized. The unit statement reminds us of the context into which the individual lesson is placed. For example, a lesson on the parts of a flower would fit into the context of the overall unit on plants. A lesson on the rule for adding *-ing* to words would fit into the overall unit on adding suffixes, and identifying the reasons that the South lost the war would be one lesson from a unit on the Civil War.

Goals Objective Component.   In this component of the lesson plan, the teacher's major objectives for the lesson at hand are listed. Since these have already been constructed during unit planning, the major task is to decide upon the number of objectives to be covered in the lesson. This is difficult for beginning teachers because they lack experience in judging how much work students are capable of doing. Also, individual classes react differently. What works well with one may nearly fail with another. Further, contingencies, such as assemblies, help make each day unique.

Despite these problems, it is necessary to have a concrete number of goals in mind when planning a lesson. The advantages of goals objectives to you and the student in lesson planning are as follows:

1. Objectives identify the end product and help the teacher remain focused on the lesson. Brophy (1982) found that teachers play a key role in determining the curriculum students actually receive, even when clear curriculum guidelines and materials are in place. Objectives help teachers emphasize the content that is most important for the learners.
2. Objectives enable the teacher to plan precisely the steps leading to the end behavior.
3. Objectives help the teacher and the student assess performance because the objectives specify these performances in clear and exact terms.

4. Objectives allow students to direct better their own efforts in the learning process because they know precisely what is expected of them.

A rule of thumb in planning the number of objectives is, *When in doubt, err on the side of too many.* You have nothing to lose. If you've planned more content than you can cover, you have less planning to do for the following lesson. On the other hand, a lesson completed when half the period remains can lead to uncertainty, classroom management problems, and even embarrassment. This is one of the more challenging tasks for interns and beginning teachers.

Rationale Component.   As we noted in the introduction to this chapter, the lesson plan serves as a way of helping teachers think about their teaching, as opposed to going through daily activities in a rather mechanical way. Because of this theme, the *rationale* is perhaps the most important part of a lesson plan. In a word, the rationale explains *why* you've decided to teach this lesson, something that should be critical to any teacher. If a rationale cannot be given, perhaps the lesson should not be taught. All too often the fact that it has always been taught is the only rationale that can be given for teaching a particular lesson. This is not much of a reason! With this in mind, let's discuss the rationale.

Imagine a visitor to your classroom asking, "Why are you teaching this to them at this time?" The rationale would be your response. Typically it involves some type of philosophical reason for teaching the content of the lesson.

Rationales for the sample lessons on adding *-ing* to words, knowing the parts of a flower, and the reasons the South lost the Civil War could be the following:

1. Understanding the rules for adding *-ing* to words is important in understanding the spelling and pronunciation of general classes of words.
2. Understanding the parts of a flower is important in understanding plant reproduction and the origin of the fruits we commonly eat.
3. Understanding the reasons the South lost the Civil War helps students understand the interrelationships between the way of life, geography, politics, agriculture, and industrial strength of the South and North and how these factors impact the outcome. This in turn helps students understand factors affecting wars and their outcomes in general.

In addition to philosophical reasons, the rationale helps us get at one of the most popular and often-used terms in education today —

relevance. When establishing a rationale, you are also considering the utility or applicability of the work under study. It should be obvious that the more applicable the work, the more relevant it may be for the students.

However, when all is said and done, the rationale should be considered as a defense for teaching the content in the lesson. As noted earlier, if you feel you might not be able to defend the lesson, either to yourself or to your students, you should rethink the objectives for that particular plan.

EXERCISE 5.3

For each of the goals in Exercise 5.1, provide a possible rationale. Then compare your answers to the ones found in the feedback section at the end of the chapter.

1. _____

_____

_____

2. _____

_____

_____

3. _____

_____

_____

4. _____

_____

_____

5. _____

_____

_____

Stage 2: Implementing

Content Component.   The content component is simply *what* you plan to teach. In some cases this is simple. If the lesson focuses on a concept, the content is simply a definition of the concept and a series of examples. In the case of a generalization, it's a statement of the generalization and illustrations of it. For example, in the lesson on adding *-ing* to words, the content is simply the rule with some examples, and it could be stated as follows:

> When adding *-ing* to a word, you double the final letter if it's a consonant preceded by a short vowel sound, but you do not if it's preceded by another consonant or involves a long vowel sound.

flop	flopping	sing	singing
trip	tripping	jump	jumping
fly	flying	play	playing
read	reading		

On the other hand, if the lesson involves a more complex concept, such as the parts of a flower, the content may exist in outline form. A sample outline might appear as follows:

Pistil (female)
    Stigma
    Style
    Ovary (ripened ovary becomes fruit)
    Ovules (later become seeds)

Stamen (male)
    Anther
    Filament

Petals (add color and attract birds and insects)

Sepals (protect reproductive organs)

The outline serves as a guide for teachers and helps remind them of what is to be covered. They may refer to it as the lesson progresses to be certain that they haven't forgotten anything, and they may even check off the items as those are covered. The outline also allows teachers to emphasize the parts of the lesson that are most important or those parts that may present problems for the students.

How much should you put in the content section of the lesson plan? The answer depends upon your individual needs. Many teachers need a point-by-point outline, whereas a few key words or phrases might suffice for others. The most critical factor here is to organize the presentation of the material.

Finally, one way of thinking about the content of a lesson is this. If someone were to walk into the room and ask you, "What are you teaching?" you would respond by describing the content section of the lesson plan.

Procedures Component. In the content section, you list *what* you intend to teach. In this section, you state *how* you intend to teach it. At this point, you may not have a wide range of strategies available other than the lecture technique you have experienced for a number of years. Much of the content of education courses should be devoted to providing you with a variety of alternatives so that you may select appropriate teaching strategies.

The procedures section can be viewed as a set of directions or instructions on how to present the lesson. If you were absent from school on a particular day, the substitute who came in should have enough information in the procedures section to teach the lesson just as you had planned. Accordingly, the procedures should be as specific as possible and will usually be longer and more detailed than the content section.

A technique that is often helpful is to write the procedure as a series of steps or directions for the teacher. For example, a procedures component for the lesson on the parts of a flower might appear as follows:

1. Display a transparency showing the parts of a flower.
2. Write the name of each part on the display.
3. Describe the function of each part.
4. Show the students an actual strawberry flower.
5. Ask individuals to identify verbally the different parts of the flower.
6. After each part is identified, have the students describe the function of the identified part.
7. Give the students a colored drawing of a flower. Have them independently identify in writing the parts on the drawing.

Notice how the content and procedures portions of the lesson plan relate. We see that the content is the *what* of the lesson, and the procedures are the *how*. In our example with the flower, when the procedure calls for identifying each part, the content outline provides a reference for the specific parts. The same is true for each element of the content and procedures components.

Materials Component.   This area should include a list of any *special* materials needed to teach the lesson. By special we mean materials other than chalk, chalkboard, textbook, and similar items. Although they're technically materials, listing them in a lesson plan isn't necessary because they're always available. On the other hand, materials such as the transparency showing the parts of the flower and the actual strawberry flower would be listed in the materials section for the lesson plan on flowers. They are unique to the particular lesson and are therefore special. Other examples would include audiotapes, videotapes, records, slides, models, realia, resource books, magazines, and newspapers.

Teachers should carefully consider the procedures and materials that will most effectively facilitate an objective.

In considering the goals for Exercise 5.1 (page 111), materials for the rectangle and the square might be cardboard or wooden cutouts of the shapes. For the paramecium lesson, materials might be prepared slides of the animals. Actual wood samples may be the materials in the case of the carpentry class.

A written description of the materials provides the teacher with a quick reference prior to the lesson. Although you will often remember what materials are necessary, having a written reference helps remove some of the mental clutter and simplifies the planning process. In a sense, it's analogous to preparing lists for those routine things we have to do each day, professionally, personally, and socially. As with materials, we often remember what we have to do, but having a handy list simplifies our busy lives.

As a final note, the effective teacher is often one who scrounges for a wide variety of materials. Be sure to check with librarians, content supervisors, and media specialists who can provide invaluable information as to the many sources of learning materials.

Stage 3: Evaluating

The Evaluation Component.   The evaluation component of the lesson plan encourages the teacher to consider, before the lesson actually takes place, how to evaluate the student learning. Actually, this can be quite a simple process if the goals objective is complete and includes an evaluation statement.

When planning your lesson, try to be as specific as possible in describing your evaluation procedures. Don't just say, "I'll evaluate on the basis of student responses." Of course you will, but what student responses will you be looking for? Thinking about this will help you form a concept of what will be acceptable and nonacceptable performances when you teach your lesson.

Don't confuse this component of the lesson plan with a critique, which is your evaluation of your own teaching performance. Although the critique is not actually one of the components of a lesson plan, as presented, it should be considered an important step upon the conclusion of actually teaching the lesson. In the critique you might consider questions like these:

1. Was my objective appropriate for my students?
2. Were my instructional procedures effective?
3. Could I have done anything differently or better?
4. Were the materials I used appropriate for the content?

Again, don't confuse the evaluation component, which aims at *student* performance with a critique, which gets at *teacher* performance.

As examples, consider the following objectives and evaluation components.

Objective:
Second graders will understand the rule for adding *-ing* to words, so that when given a list of words, they will correctly add the suffix in each case.

Evaluation:
Write a series of words on the chalkboard. Have the students write each word with an *-ing* ending on it.

Objective:
Seventh-grade life science students will know the parts of a flower, so that when given a drawing showing the structure of a flower, they will correctly label each part.

Evaluation:
Give the students a handout with a drawing showing the structure of a flower. Direct them to label each part identified with an arrow.

The critical point here is that the evaluation must be consistent with the goals objective. If the goal statement called for a listing behavior, it would be inappropriate to call for a discussion in the evaluation. A detailed discussion of the preparation of items to measure students' attainment of goals is presented in Chapter 11.

EXERCISE 5.4

For each of the goals in Exercise 5.1, (page 111), provide the evaluation component of the lesson plan. Then compare your answers to those found in the feedback section at the end of the chapter.

1. _____
   _____
   _____

2. _____
   _____
   _____

3. _____
   _____
   _____

4. _____
   _____
   _____

5. _____
   _____
   _____

The Total Lesson Plan

We have already mentioned that the amount of information placed in a lesson plan depends upon your individual needs in addition to other factors such as administrative requirements. However, an effective lesson plan must take into consideration the three-stage model, and we suggest to you that the seven components are all critical features worth your consideration. A simple way of organizing this material is presented in Figure 5.3

UNIT: Social Classes in America

GOALS OBJECTIVE: For the high school history student to understand social stratification in America, so that when given a list of characteristics of a certain family, the students will choose one of the three classes that best represents the family, giving at least three examples as proof

RATIONALE: It is necessary for a history student to understand that America's social stratification is a fluid division of people. It is part of this country's social makeup to have little classification of people, although there are noticeable differences in this country's people.

CONTENT	PROCEDURE

I. Upper Class
  A. Income
  B. Education
  C. Occupation
  D. Political affiliation
  E. Residence
II. Middle Class
  A. Income
  B. Education
  C. Occupation
  D. Political affiliation
  E. Residence
III. Lower Class
  A. Income
  B. Education
  C. Occupation
  D. Political affiliation
  E. Residence
	1. Identify characteristics of upper class.
	2. Discuss relationship of characteristics with each other. Ask "How are education and income related? How about education and occupation?"
	3. Ask "What characteristics separate them most from other classes?"
	4. Repeat steps 1, 2, and 3 for middle and lower classes.
	5. Present case study 1 on overhead. Have class try to identify class in terms of characteristics discussed above.
	6. Present case study 2 on overhead. Discuss characteristics.
	7. If time permits, present case study 3 as a quiz. If there is not enough time, have students prepare for a quiz tomorrow.

MATERIALS: Dittos of characteristics for each student.

EVALUATION: Students should be able, in short essay form, to describe why a certain family could fit into one of the social classes studied, giving reasons why and characteristics of that class.

Figure 5.3 Sample Lesson Plan

EXERCISE 5.5

At this point, you should be able to list all the steps of a lesson plan as discussed in this chapter. In the space below, list them according to the stage they facilitate. Then compare your answers with the ones given in the feedback section at the end of the chapter.

PLANNING:

_____

_____

_____

_____

IMPLEMENTING:

_____

_____

_____

_____

_____

EVALUATING:

_____

_____

_____

EXERCISE 5.6

Using the format on this page, develop a lesson plan for the topic "Mammals." Then compare your ideas to the ones given in the feedback section at the end of the chapter.

UNIT:

GOALS OBJECTIVE:

RATIONALE:

CONTENT:

PROCEDURES:

MATERIALS:

EVALUATION:

Notice that in Exercise 5.6 we listed the procedures below the content, whereas in Figure 5.3 they're listed side by side. This arrangement is a matter of personal preference, and one is no more correct than the other. For this reason we've presented the arrangement both ways.

THE MADELINE HUNTER PLANNING MODEL

Madeline Hunter (1982) has developed an enormously popular approach to instructional effectiveness. Her principles, largely derived from educational psychology, have served as a framework for a tremendous amount of public school staff development across the nation and in schools around the world.

Her work also has implications for planning. Figure 5.4 contains an illustration of the planning steps based on Hunter's work. From Figure 5.4 we see that Hunter's model is consistent with the one we've presented in this chapter but provides for additional elements. Her objective and purpose parallel our goals objective and rationale, *input* compares to the *content* component, and *modeling* is similar to procedures. In addition, Hunter's model indicates specific plans for attracting students' attention (anticipatory set), checking for understanding, and two kinds of practice. For example, with our lesson on plants, a teacher might display an apple and an orange and ask the students to try and explain where they come from. This would be a form of anticipatory set. Hunter has also suggested that we consciously plan for a

Component	Function
1. Anticipatory Set	How will students' attention be focused?
2. Objective and Purpose	What will students learn and why?
3. Input	What new information will be discussed?
4. Modeling	How can the teacher illustrate the new skill or content?
5. Checking for Understanding	How can the teacher ascertain whether students are learning the new material?
6. Guided Practice	What opportunities are students given to practice the new materials in class?
7. Independent Practice	How can assignments and homework be used for long-term retention?

Figure 5.4   Madeline Hunter's Elements of Lesson Design

way to *check students' understanding* of the content as we deliver it. One way of accomplishing this is through questioning, which we discuss in detail in the next chapter. Practice, both guided and independent, can be accomplished by preparing additional examples and having the students work with the examples. For instance, look again at the sample procedure we presented for the lesson on plants. In step 5 the procedure called for having the students verbally identify different parts of the strawberry flower and identify the function of each part. This process is a form of *guided practice.* This was followed by *independent practice* in step 7, where the procedure provided for the teacher giving the students a colored drawing of a flower and having them independently identify the parts in writing on the drawing.

ADOPTING LESSON PLANNING FOR EVERYDAY USE

Both the format we've presented here and the Hunter planning model are probably more detailed than formats you will encounter in the schools. Experienced teachers typically use an abridged format that looks something like this:

	Monday	Tuesday	Wednesday	Thursday	Friday
Period 1					
Period 2					
Period 3					
Period 4					
Period 5					
Period 6					
Period 7					

Planning books blocked out in terms of days and periods are useful tools for keeping track of the week's activities. Because of the lack of space in these books, teachers usually list only the major activities or topics of the period. Accordingly, a sample cell might look like this:

Monday

Period 1

> Hand back quiz
> Introduce new unit
> Give reading assignment
> Individual project conference

On that day a quick glance at the page tells the teacher the major activities for the period of that day. This is often helpful after a long weekend or as a means of keeping track on a particularly hectic day.

The brevity of this format and the ease with which it can be completed are potentially misleading. Writing down major activities is not a substitute for thorough planning. Every lesson that a teacher teaches should be thoughtfully planned for in terms of the criteria we've discussed in this chapter. The fact that this thought isn't evident in the shortened plan format of experienced teachers does not mean the planning has not occurred. Professional teachers should always know their objectives and rationale for a lesson, the relationship between that lesson and others, the content they will teach, the procedures and materials they will use, and the way they will evaluate the students. In short, while abbreviated formats are helpful as supplements, they are no substitute for thoughtful lesson planning.

SUMMARY

In this chapter we discussed ways of planning for daily lessons and longer spans of instruction called units. We began with unit planning and emphasized the need for thinking about instruction in broader terms than the daily lesson. The organization of the unit and the interconnection of the lessons may be as important as the lessons themselves.

Lesson planning was described in terms of the three-phase model of teaching. In the planning phase teachers consider the connection of the daily lesson to the unit, select goals objectives, and construct a rationale for the lesson. In the implementing phase they formulate the content and procedures and plan for the material aids. Finally in the evaluation state, they design means of evaluating student progress.

The Hunter planning model includes anticipatory set, checking for student understanding, and two forms of practice in addition to the components described in the format presented in the chapter.

This chapter concludes the planning stage of the three-stage model for teaching. In Unit 2 and Unit 3 we discuss implementing and evaluating respectively. We hope that Unit 1 has provided you with critical skills that will enable you to effectively plan instruction and establish a sound foundation for successful implementation and evaluation.

REFERENCES

Brophy, J. (1982). How teachers influence what is taught and learned in classrooms. *Elementary School Journal, 83,* 1–14.

Clark, C., & Peterson, P. (1986). *Teacher simulated recall of interactive decisions* [Research report]. Palo Alto, CA: Stanford Center for Research and Development, Stanford University. (ERIC Document Reproduction Service No. ED 124 555)

Hunter, M. (1982). *Mastery teaching.* El Segundo, CA: TIP Publications.

McCutcheon, G. (1982). How do elementary school teachers plan? The nature of planning and influences on it. In W. Doyle, & T. Good (Eds.), *Focus on Teaching* (pp. 260–279). Chicago: University of Chicago Press.

Neale, D., Pace, A., & Case, A. (1983, April). *The influence of training, experience, and organizational environment on teachers' use of the systematic planning model.* Paper presented at the annual meeting of the American Educational Research Association.

EXERCISE FEEDBACK

EXERCISE 5.1

Listed below are possible units for the topics in the exercise. Remember there are a number of ways to organize content; therefore, there could be a number of units. The identification of the unit helps insure that organization. The important thing is that the teacher thinks about organizing the material. The key is teaching in an organized rather than unorganized fashion, not the particular form of organization.

1. The unit could be "Word Pairs." Another possibility would be "Basic Vocabulary."
2. The unit could simply be "The Civil War."
3. "Basic Shapes" might be the unit here. Other possibilities would be "Visual Discrimination" or "Reading Readiness."
4. A probable unit here could be "Protozoans."
5. "Building Materials" might be the unit in this example.

EXERCISE 5.2

Your unit summary and the topical outline for the kindergarten unit on body parts might look like this:

UNIT SUMMARY: The purpose of this unit is to acquaint kindergarten students with the names and functions of the major body parts. At the completion of this unit, students should be able to identify the major body parts and match these with their functions.

TOPICAL OUTLINE:

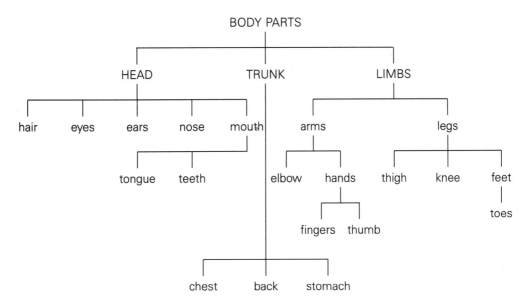

EXERCISE 5.3

As with the unit, the rationale may vary. The important thing is that the rationale exists, showing that the teacher has thought about the lesson. Possible rationales are as follows:

1. Homonyms are important as basic building blocks in vocabulary. It is important that students understand that words that sound alike and are spelled alike don't have the same meaning.
2. The causes of the Civil War are important to a total perspective on the war. Also, an understanding of the Civil War causes may lead to an understanding of the causes of other wars.
3. Visual discrimination is a critical reading readiness skill. The ability to discriminate shapes is an indication of visual discrimination ability.
4. Paramecia are common and widely known protozoans, and understanding a protozoan is the foundation for understanding the animal kingdom.
5. Understanding wood strength allows a carpenter to select the proper materials for a job at the most reasonable cost.

EXERCISE 5.4

As with the other components, evaluations may vary and we are providing only possible ones.

1. Present the students with word pairs and have them identify the homonyms.
2. List a number of factors causing wars. From this list have the students identify those related to the Civil War.
3. Give the children a sheet with shapes drawn on it. Have them color the squares red and the rectangles blue.
4. Have the students draw a paramecium and label all its parts.
5. Show the students a series of three wood samples. Have them order the three from strongest to weakest.

EXERCISE 5.5

PLANNING:	Unit
	Goals Objective
	Rationale
IMPLEMENTING:	Content
	Procedures
	Materials
EVALUATING:	Evaluation

EXERCISE 5.6

Although your responses will differ from those that follow, here is what the content of the lesson plan might look like:

UNIT: Warm-Blooded Animals

GOALS OBJECTIVE: For first-grade students studying science to increase their awareness of animals so that, when given 10 pictures of animals, each will be able to identify all those that are mammals.

RATIONALE: In that the children are mammals themselves, this lesson will serve as one of the many that will provide the child with body awareness and hopefully awaken an interest in human physiology.

CONTENT: Mammals are warm-blooded animals that have hair, suckle their young, and give live birth. Some examples are cows, horses, people, wolves, seals, whales, and tigers.

PROCEDURES:
   Show the students a picture of a cow with a calf.
   Ask them to describe the picture.
   Show them a picture of an eagle sitting on a nest of eggs.
   Ask students to compare the pictures.
   Show the students a picture of a tiger.
   Ask the students to compare all of the pictures.
   Continue showing pictures of mammals and other animals.
   Prompt students to classify the mammals.

Call for a definition of mammals based on the characteristics shown in the pictures.

MATERIALS:
Pictures of mammals and nonmammals
Slides of mammals and nonmammals

EVALUATION: Students will take out a piece of paper and number from 1 to 10. Show 10 pictures of animals (mammals and nonmammals). Next to the appropriate number, the student will write yes if the picture is a mammal and no if it is not.

IMPLEMENTING

6 ‖ Questioning Skills

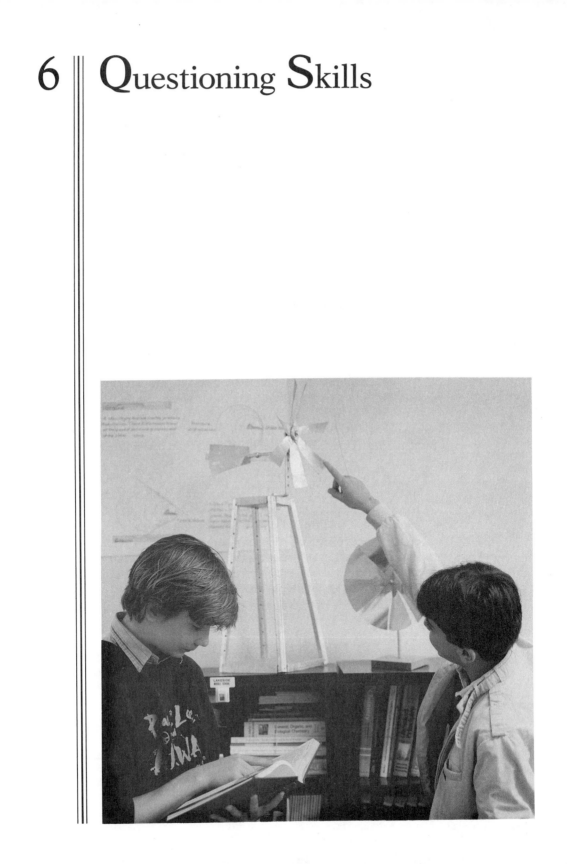

INTRODUCTION

Education as it is currently practiced in this country is a combination of art and science. While research tells us in a systematic way about effective compared to less effective teacher behavior (the science of teaching), individuals must practice and apply what is known according to their own personality and to a certain extent their own intuition (the art of teaching). There is no one best way to teach, no *super strategy*. No program of instruction or curriculum is any better or any worse than the individual doing the teaching.

This chapter and the ones to follow are based on this foundation. We are now beginning the second phase, *implementation*, of our three-step model. You may want to review Chapter 1 briefly to refresh your understanding of implementation. Simply stated, you have identified one or more objectives, and you are now prepared to help learners to reach the objective(s). The specific experiences and behaviors you design for students to reach or master an objective are called implementation. In a simple phrase, implementation is *how you teach*.

A cornerstone of any effective teaching technique is classroom questioning. It is a critical skill that can be used with virtually any subject matter area, grade level, or teacher personality. It promotes involvement, enhances learning, requires little effort, and motivates students (Good, 1983; Gall, 1984). The use of questioning helps a teacher become and remain flexible and responsive to students, a critical characteristic of effective teaching (O'Keefe, 1986). It helps promote a student-centered learning environment while maintaining a teacher-led activity. Because of these factors, we discuss questioning specifically in this chapter and then describe how questioning skills can be incorporated into complete teaching procedures in Chapter 7. Hopefully, after completing this chapter and Chapter 7, you will have the background to begin forming a personal teaching style. Such development is an evolving process where the skills presented here are practiced, internalized, and incorporated into the strategies that follow. Finally, as the strategies are rehearsed and modified, the style develops.

We will begin our discussion with a description of question level followed by direction and will close the chapter with illustrations of questioning techniques.

OBJECTIVES

After completing Chapter 6, you should be able to accomplish the following objectives:

1. For you as a pre/inservice teacher to increase your understanding of low- and high-level questions, so that when given a case study, you will identify each
2. For you as a pre/inservice teacher to understand convergent and divergent questions, so that when given a scenario, you will identify each of these questions
3. For you as a pre/inservice teacher to understand questioning technique (redirection, prompting, probing), so that when given a case study, you will identify each

QUESTION LEVELS

To be employed most effectively, questions must be adjusted to fit the needs of the students (Duffy, Roehler, Meloth, & Vavrus, 1985). Gall (1984), in examining research on questioning, found that different types of questions are effective at different times, depending on the characteristics of the learner and the topic being taught. At certain times, questions that require mere recall are important, whereas at others considerable thought is elicited. For instance, consider the questions:

What is 9×6?

What present-day significance does studying the play *Julius Caesar* have for us?

The demands on the learner are obviously much different, but for an elementary teacher whose goal is for students to know their multiplication facts, the first question is valid and important, as is the second one for a secondary literature teacher who wants students to analyze moral dilemmas.

The key to effective questioning is to ask questions that allow you to reach your goal most efficiently. Berliner (1985) states that the difference between good and effective teachers is that in addition to doing all the things good teachers have always done, effective teachers direct their instruction at a clear and specific goal. This will require different levels, directions, and techniques as teachers use their questioning skills. We address these topics in the sections that follow.

Low-Level Questions

In our discussion of the cognitive domain in Chapter 4, we said that the lowest, or knowledge, level requires students to recall information that has been memorized and stored. Low-level questions tap this knowledge. The following are examples:

What are the three most common tools in a metal shop?

How much is 5 + 5?

What is the Pythagorean theorem?

Who was the pacifist leader of India after World War II?

How do you spell *anonymous?*

What is one animal that survived the prehistoric age?

Again, the simplest key to follow is that anytime you ask a student to do no more than recall information such as terms, facts, names, and events, you have framed a low-level question.

High-Level Questions

We have suggested that low-level questions require a student merely to *recall* information. For certain goals they are important and valuable, but for others we must help students give more complete responses and expand their thinking. This leads us to a discussion of *high-level questions.* As discussed in Chapter 4, the characteristic which separates a low- from a high-level question is that the latter requires a degree of intellectual processing on the part of the student, whereas the former is limited to memorization with the information being recalled upon demand.

We further pointed out that, regarding the cognitive domain, only the knowledge level is considered to be of a low nature. The remaining five levels (comprehension, application, analysis, synthesis, and evaluation) are all considered to be high level.

Simply stated, we are defining a high-level question as any question that requires the student to do more than recall previously learned information. Obviously, high-level questions will vary in difficulty and demands placed on the student, but the key characteristic they possess is that they require more than mere recall. Researchers will vary to a certain extent in their definitions of high and low level. If you wish to read further on this topic, we refer you to Dunkin and Biddle (1974). The primary issue, however, is not to be rigid in defining question level but rather to ask questions at a level appropriate for the learner and learning activity. Both low- and high-level questions are important.

Let's look now at an example.

A teacher begins, "In looking at balance of power arrangements through history, we have seen most such arrangements rarely last more than a few decades. Why do you suppose these arrangements collapse?" (pause) "Bob?"

"I think the foreign policies of many countries are changing rapidly, and, as their goals change, the nations have to seek new alliances."

"How does the United States seek out these alliances? Wanda?"

"We try to find out who agrees with our position. This would include not only countries who would support us but also those in need of our support."

By asking students questions beginning with phrases such as "why do you suppose" and "how does the United States seek," the teacher pushes the student beyond a rote memory exercise. Both students had to manipulate prior information and were therefore working at a high level.

Consider the statement "Give me an example, that we haven't previously discussed, of a simile." A student responding to this question must generate, on the basis of previous examples, a new example of the concept *simile*. This is an excellent and commonly asked high-level question.

Another important high-level question involves the ability to state an idea or definition in the student's own terms. An example is the question "Tell me in your own words what we mean by the statement, 'literature reflects the time and society of the authors.' " The answer to this question would likely be followed by the teacher asking for an example of an author, his or her work, and the characteristics of the society—another high-level question.

A valuable discussion question of high level is the consideration of author motive, perspective, or reference frame, as in this example: "We've read the column by William F. Buckley (a noted journalist). Where do you suppose Buckley is coming from in the column?" The discussion would involve consideration of his conservative orientation, probable motives, and basic philsophical stance.

An important additional high-level question is one that requires the solution to a problem, such as "An item originally selling for $20.00 is marked 20% off. What is the sale price?" The solution to the problem requires a high-level response. There is one caution we should mention, however. It is a quite common practice in math texts to include a series of problems identical to each other in form. The students solve each like they solved the first, and the level of the task after the first problem is no longer high but, in fact, is merely recall of process. While this occurs more often in assigned work than in a questioning situation, it can occur in both, and teachers think they are getting a high-level response when the opposite is actually occurring. The solution is simple. Mix up the types of problems, and students will be required to give high-level responses in each case.

There are two other forms of high-level questions that are easy to ask, quite easy to answer, and excellent for promoting student involvement. These are called *description* questions and *comparison* questions. The first type asks the learners to observe and describe an object or event such as an illustration, demonstration, map, graph, table, or statement. The description is initiated by the teacher making a directive such as the following:

1. "What do you notice here?"
2. "Tell me about this."
3. "What do you see?"
4. "Describe the object in front of you."

This type of question offers an effective technique for promoting involvement, success, and depth of response. While it requires a simple and seemingly low-level response, it calls into play the learner's experience, perception, and senses. It requires more than a mere recall, and we therefore define it as a high-level question.

The second type, comparison questions, requires the learner to look at two or more objects, statements, illustrations, or demonstrations and identify similarities or differences between them. As students identify similarities, they are moving toward the establishment of a pattern that ultimately results in a concept or generalization. For example, suppose students are shown the following three sentences:

1. He is quiet as a mouse.
2. He was as large as a mountain.
3. They ran as fast as the wind.

The question, "What is similar about the sentences?" requires the learners to identify patterns that ultimately specify the characteristics of the concept *simile*. For instance, the word *as* appears in each, and a nonliteral comparison between two objects or ideas occurs in each.

Comparison questions are very effective high-level questions in that they encourage students to process information. We refer to description and comparison questions in greater depth in the following sections as well as in Chapter 7.

EXERCISE 6.1

Read the following scenario and identify each teacher statement as being either a low- (l) or a high-level (h) question. Then check your answers with the ones given in the feedback section at the end of the chapter.

_____ 1. "On the board are three lists of words I'd like for you to analyze for a minute." (pause) "What is special about the first two lists? Amy?"

"All the words are alike."

_____ 2. "Could you explain what you mean by 'are alike'?"

"Well, they're all words that I would use to mean something good about somebody."

_____ 3. "That's right. Does anyone notice anything else about these words? Bob?"

"You could use one of them to mean the other."

_____ 4. "Can you give me an example of this?"

"I could say, 'You are a very *competent* teacher,' or I could say, 'You are a very *skillful* teacher,' and, either way, I'd mean the same thing."

_____ 5. "Good, Bob. So the terms in column 1 are more or less interchangeable with those in column 2, right?"

There is general agreement shown by tumultuous applause.

_____ 6. "What term do you use to designate this type of relationship?" There is no response.

_____ 7. "O.K. Think back to your study of prefixes, suffixes, and root words. Can anybody remember the prefix that means *same?* Sally?"

"*Syn-*"

_____ 8. "Right. How about the one for *name?*"

"*-Onym-*"

_____ 9. "So, Sally, when you put them together you get . . ."

"*Synonym.*"

_____ 10. "Very good. Can you find some relationship between the words in column 1 and those in column 2? Bob?"

"Those in column 2 are synonyms of those in column 1."

Amy adds, "And those in column 1 are synonyms of those in column 2."

_____ 11. "Yes. Now look at column 3." (pause) "How do these words relate to those in the first two columns?" Amy doesn't response.

_____ 12. "O.K. Does *odious* mean the same thing as *pleasant?*"

"No."

_____ 13. "Does it mean the same thing as *agreeable?*"

"No, it's the opposite of *agreeable.*"

_____ 14. "O.K., Amy. Now, Bob, can you see another set of words in the column that has a similar relationship?"

"Yes, *ugly* means just the opposite of *pretty* and *attractive,* and *mean* is just the opposite of *kind.*"

_____ 15. "So can someone state the relationship between the first two columns and the third? Sally?"

"Those in column 3 are opposites of those in columns 1 and 2."

_____ 16. "Good. Do you recall the word that expresses this relationship, Sally?"

"*Antonym.*"

QUESTION DIRECTION

Convergent Questions

Convergent questions are those that require *one correct answer*. In general, they are questions of fact or recall and are often of a low level, as described in the previous section. For example, the following are convergent questions:

1. What is 6×9?
2. What part of speech modifies a noun or pronoun?
3. A turtle is in what animal class?
4. What is the chemical formula for table salt?
5. What is the most populous country in the world?

Note in each of these that there is only one correct answer for each question and the answer requires recall of previously learned information.

An exception to this pattern would involve solutions for problems requiring application, analysis, or synthesis. For example, if you ask, "I have four hundred feet of fence and I want to enclose the maximum area in a four-sided figure. What should the dimensions be?" this is a very high-level question but is still convergent in that only one answer to the problem is correct.

Divergent Questions

While convergent questions require one correct answer, divergent questions are just the opposite in that many different answers are appropriate. For instance, consider the following questions:

1. How are the beans alike?
2. Give me an example of a first-class lever.
3. Give me one of the most significant dates in world history.

Notice that each of the questions can be answered in several ways. For example, in the first case, responses would be:

1. "All are sort of fat."
2. "They have seeds in them."
3. "Round."
4. "They have lines on them."

In the second example:

1. "Screwdriver prying open a paint can lid."
2. "Crowbar prying up a rock."
3. "Scissors."

And the third:

1. "1588—The defeat of the Spanish Armada."
2. "1215—The signing of the Magna Carta."
3. "1066—The Battle of Hastings."
4. "1776—The American Declaration of Independence."

Obviously, many more answers could be given in each case, but the illustrations show how divergent questions can be used to promote student involvement by allowing a number of students to respond to the same question. Notice also that the level of divergent questions is high.

EXERCISE 6.2

Return to the scenario offered in Exercise 6.1 (pages 138–139). Decide whether each of the 16 teacher statements is convergent (c) or divergent (d). Then check your answers with the ones given in the feedback section at the end of the chapter.

_____ 1.	_____ 5.	_____ 9.	_____ 13.
_____ 2.	_____ 6.	_____ 10.	_____ 14.
_____ 3.	_____ 7.	_____ 11.	_____ 15.
_____ 4.	_____ 8.	_____ 12.	_____ 16.

EXERCISE 6.3

As a review for both the level and the direction of questions, label the following statements as low level/divergent (l/d), low level/convergent (l/c), high level/divergent (h/d), or high level/convergent (h/c). Then compare your answers with the ones given in the feedback section at the end of the chapter.

_____ 1. How is architecture influenced by culture?

_____ 2. What were some of the possible economic motives of the U.S. that added to its conflict with Japan prior to World War II?

_____ 3. What assumptions can you make about a novel that is referred to as a classic?

_____ 4. Name the major organs of the digestive system.

_____ 5. What may have caused Achilles to choose youth and fame over long life?

_____ 6. What are the two elements found in salt?

_____ 7. Put into your own words what effect the philosophies of Aristotle and Plato had upon the generations that followed them.

_____ 8. What would be the implications of an average world rate of 5.1 births per woman?

_____ 9. Giving all points discussed in the readings equal weight, what was the main argument favoring separatism?

_____ 10. You want to get from Jacksonville to Miami, which is 360 miles. The speed limit is 55 mph. If you stay within the speed limit and drive at a steady speed, what is the minimum amount of time the trip will take?

_____ 11. Can anyone give us an example of *iambic pentameter*?

_____ 12. What fallacies appeared in the theory that the earth was the center of the universe?

_____ 13. List the steps involved in operating a lathe.

_____ 14. What do you think JFK meant by the "new frontier"?

_____ 15. In Orwell's *Animal Farm* what techniques are used to persuade the animals to devote their all to the farm?

QUESTIONING TECHNIQUES

Redirection

The first step toward developing effective questioning techniques is to increase the amount of student participation. Typically, interaction patterns involve a teacher asking a question and a student volunteering a response to the question. As the activity proceeds those desiring to respond continue to be involved, and those not desiring to participate drift away from the activity. The patterns can be well established, with those volunteering being the primary participators and the others rarely responding and often not even attending to the activity. As a result, a teacher often only has a portion of the class paying attention which, in turn, means only that portion is learning.

In general, teachers do not direct questions to particular students. Further, when questions are asked of individuals, the perceived high achievers are called on much more often than the perceived low achievers. (Good & Brophy, 1987). An interesting and somewhat ironic aspect of both these phenomena is that teachers are quite unaware of the patterns and will, sometimes, deny their existence, even to an observer who has pointed them out to the teachers immediately after a lesson.

It is very important that teachers break these patterns. When different patterns are established, powerful results can occur. Kerman (1979) describes a project, one component of which involved training teachers to call on *all* students in a class approximately equally. The results of the project were very impressive. Not only did student achievement increase but both discipline referrals and absenteeism decreased.

Redirection can be a useful questioning technique to help establish positive patterns and high levels of interaction in a classroom. This technique involves the framing of a single question for which there are many possible responses and the receiving of responses from several students. The following is an example of how you might accomplish this task:

> "Having completed our overview of the presidents, who do you think was the greatest American chief executive? Tom?"
> "Abraham Lincoln."
> "Sally?"
> "Woodrow Wilson."
> "Joe, another one?"
> "George Washington."

You will notice the teacher does not respond to or discuss the students' replies. She simply redirects the original question and, in doing so, eliminates any possible domination of the discussion and increases the frequency of questions and student participation, both of which are related to increased student achievement (Brophy & Evertson, 1976; Denham & Lieberman, 1980, Soar, 1973).

In the next sequence, pay close attention to the ways in which the teacher redirects the question.

> "Some of you mentioned the presidents you believe to have been great. Why do you think they were great men? Yes, Betty."
> "I think Lincoln was great because he was able to hold the country together, and Washington was great because he got the country started."
> "Do you have something, David?"
> "I think Wilson was great because he was a man of peace and could see the problems beyond his time."
> "Mark, can you add anything else?"
> "They were all great men because they were strong and had the courage to fight for what they believed in."

It is important to note that, although the three students may not have been dealing with the same individual, they were all responding to a single question posed by the teacher.

Notice first in the preceding example that all the redirected questions were divergent. This, of course, is an obvious requirement. It is impossible to redirect a convergent question in any sensible way.

Second, you see that the questions were also high level. This further illustrates the value of redirecting. Not only is it a powerful technique in promoting interaction, but it is also a convenient means for helping the teacher ask high-level questions.

Questions that are very easy to redirect are those that require description and comparison. For example, using the illustration of the concept *simile* provided earlier, the teacher could present the sentence, "He is quiet as a mouse," and direct different individuals to describe the sentence, requesting that each say something different about it. The interaction pattern could appear as follows:

Teacher: What do you notice about the sentence? . . . Tim?

Tim: It has six words in it.

Teacher: What else, Sue?

Sue: He is the subject.

Teacher: And what else, Steve?

Steve: It's about a boy.

This process can go on as long as the teacher desires or until it looks as if the class is ready to move on.

A sensible following step would be for the teacher to present a second example and ask for comparisons. For instance, the students may now have displayed before them the sentences: "He is quiet as a mouse" and "She was a rock of strength." The teacher could then ask, "What is the same or different about the two sentences?" The responses would vary, and the question could be redirected to several students.

In summary, we have defined redirecton as any question that is divergent and asked of several different individuals. It is a powerful technique in promoting involvement. Finally, teaching effectiveness research (Wright & Nuthall, 1970) found that redirection is significantly related to achievement. For these reasons, redirection is one of the most effective questioning techniques a teacher can employ.

EXERCISE 6.4

Read the following anecdote and identify the teacher's questions that are examples of redirection by marking them with an X. Then check your answers with the ones given in the feedback section at the end of the chapter.

_____ 1. "We've been discussing immigration this week, and I want to see if we can tie things together at this point. Just for review, thousands of people came to America during the late 1800s. Name some of the countries they came from." (pause) "Bob?"
"Ireland."

_____ 2. "Paul, another one?"
"Germany."

_____ 3. "Do you have one, Pam?"
"Italy?"

_____ 4. "Fine. All good answers. Now let's use these countries as representative examples. What can we say about the people from these countries? Jim?"
Jim doesn't respond.

_____ 5. "Well, let's take a close look, Jim. Do you think they have the same religious structure?"
"No."

_____ 6. "Anything else, Jim?"

"Their languages are different."

_____ 7. "Right. That's a good one. Anybody want to add another one? Pam?"

"Oh . . . I can think of a lot of things like clothes, food, economic factors, political structure, and attitudes."

_____ 8. "Fine, fine. What is the obvious point we can draw from this, Bob?"

"That American immigrants were different."

_____ 9. "Different from what, Bob?"

"From each other."

_____ 10. "Good, now let's break off for just a second. How did the book define immigration?" (pause) "Nancy?"

"People who leave their country immigrate from their homes."

_____ 11. "O.K., let's look at the word closely. Does immigration make you think of _in_ or _out_? Nancy?"

"In."

_____ 12. "So a person who is an immigrant . . .?"

"Comes into a country," Nancy finishes.

_____ 13. "And to emigrate . . .?"

"Is to leave a country."

_____ 14. "Very good, Nancy!"

Prompting

What happens when we ask a student a question, and he either fails to reply or he responds incorrectly? Generally, teachers move on to another student in order to maintain interest and momentum. By doing so, the student who was unable to respond often becomes confused and psychologically removed from the discussion. We have stressed desirability of total involvement, but how can we deal with students who cannot answer questions or whose responses are wrong? The following sequence between a teacher and one student deals with this problem:

> "Regarding our discussion on international power patterns, which pattern does this equal arms scale demonstrate?" (pause) "Pat?"
>
> Pat seems to be confused and doesn't respond.
>
> "Any idea?"
>
> "I don't know."
>
> "O.K., let's take another look at the scale. If this object is two ounces and the one on the other tray is two ounces, they are said to be . . .?"

"Equal."

"Right. Equal in what?"

"Weight."

The teacher nods. "Now, if we have these equal weights, one on each tray, what happens?"

"They balance each other."

"Fine. Let's suppose each weight represents three countries and that the groups are basically opposed to each other. If they are equal in strength or power they would be . . .?"

"Balanced."

"Great! Then this demonstration represents what pattern of power?"

"The balance of power pattern."

"Now you've got it!!"

The preceding example demonstrates the technique referred to as *prompting* and involves the use of hints or clues which are used to aid the student in responding successfully. This method can also be employed when a response is incorrect. Note the following example between a teacher and one student:

"To be specific, the pattern of power called *balance* is one in which two or more nation-states form a coalition in order to protect themselves from a specific enemy. Coalitions of equal power oppose each other; they are in balance and peace is preserved. However, once the balance is broken and one coalition tips the power scale in its favor; the likelihood of war is increased. As with our scale, if too much weight is added to one side, the other side will be overpowered. Now, let's apply the example. Does the United Nations represent a balance of power arrangement?" (pause) "Mary?"

"I think it does."

"Let's analyze it and find out. Mary, does the UN aid and support any group member attacked by an enemy?"

"It's supposed to."

"O.K. Is the UN a coalition of two or more nations?"

"Yes."

"Is the UN pledged against a specific enemy?"

"I'm not sure."

"Is there another organization of equal size and power with which the UN is locked in mortal combat?"

"No."

"Then what do you conclude?"

"The United Nations is not an example of balance of power."

"Very good."

The effectiveness of prompting is supported by research. Anderson, Everston, and Brophy (1979) and Stallings, Needels, and Stayrook (1979) found that students benefited most, after giving an incorrect response, when the teacher asked a series of simple questions and gave clues to help them arrive at the correct answer. Merely giving the correct answer and moving to another student or asking another student to help immediately after the incorrect response were less effective than prompting.

Consider now one more example. In the previous section we used the sentence, "He is quiet as a mouse," and "She was a rock of strength." The teacher presumably wants the students to identify the first as a simile and the second as a metaphor. She probably has asked a series of divergent questions—descriptions and comparisons—which have been redirected to several individuals. However, let's assume that the students don't recognize the sentences as examples of the respective concepts. The effective teacher now prompts the students to arrive at the correct answer. The dialogue might appear as follows:

Teacher: What do you notice about *she* and *rock* in the second sentence?

Student: It says she is a rock.

Teacher: Does the sentence mean she really is a rock?

Student: No, not really.

Teacher: So we say the comparison is what?

Student: (Pause)

Teacher: Literal or nonliteral?

Student: Nonliteral.

Teacher: Okay. Good. We have a nonliteral comparison between two ideas. The same is true about the first sentence, but there is a special word in it. What word?

Student: As.

Teacher: Yes. The word *as* is added. Otherwise, the two sentences are similar. What are they called?

Student: The first is a simile and the second is a metaphor.

Teacher: Excellent. We have identified the sentences.

As the research literature indicates, prompting is a very important technique employed by effective teachers. However, our experience in working with teachers suggests that it is difficult for them and isn't employed as often as would be desirable. The reason for the difficulty probably is that prompting requires *thinking on your feet.* While many other teaching procedures and skills can be planned and practiced in advance, prompting can only be practiced in the context of an actual lesson, and a prompting question is formed and asked *on the spot,* following a student response. This can be difficult and requires practice. However, research indicates that it can be learned (Kerman, 1979; Rowe, 1986). This technique can be enormously rewarding and frankly, it is enjoyable to help learners provide responses they previously could not provide. For these reasons we encourage you to persevere. With practice you will become skilled and will reap the intrinsic rewards of feeling that you have had a positive, direct, and tangible influence on student learning.

Careful preparation can be an aid that will help your prompting efforts. For instance, if a teacher knows in advance that she wants the students to identify "nonliteral comparison without *as* or *like*" as the key characteristic of metaphor and "nonliteral comparison using *as* or *like*" for simile helps her to *think on her feet* because she knows what she wants from the students. She can then ask whatever questions it takes to get them to the idea.

As a reader you might ask, "How do you get them to supply the words *simile* and *metaphor* respectively?" The simple answer is, *you don't!* The teacher prompts the students to identify *characteristics*, and if the students are unable to supply the label, the teacher supplies it for them. Remember, labels are items of fact learning and serve the purpose of communicating concepts, so telling the students the label is perfectly appropriate.

EXERCISE 6.5

Turn back to Exercise 6.4 (pages 144–145) and identify all of the teacher's statements that are prompts by marking their numbers here with an X. Then compare your answers with the ones given in the feedback section at the end of the chapter.

_____ 1.   _____ 4.   _____ 7.   _____ 10.   _____ 13.
_____ 2.   _____ 5.   _____ 8.   _____ 11.   _____ 14.
_____ 3.   _____ 6.   _____ 9.   _____ 12.

EXERCISE 6.6

Read the following anecdote and identify all of the teacher's statements that are either redirections (r) or prompts (p).

_____ 1. "Today we're considering the properties of numbers. Here is a list of some numbers." The teacher points to a list on the board. "From the list show me a prime number. Bob?"
"Three."

_____ 2. "Another, Paul?"
"Two."

_____ 3. "Another one, Lynn?"
"Five."

_____ 4. 'Now, give me a number that is not prime. Paul?"
"Six."

_____ 5. "Another one, Rudy?"
"Eight."

_____ 6. "O.K. Let's try something we haven't done yet. Six can be reduced to the product of two prime numbers. What are they, Bob?"
Bob doesn't respond.

_____ 7. "Let me help you, Bob. Now remember your times tables. What times what equal six?"
"Oh, three times two."

_____ 8. "O.K., good. Now, from this list, select a number that is a perfect square."
Bob adds, "Nine."

_____ 9. "Good, Bob. Another one, Lynne?"
"Sixteen."

_____ 10. "O.K. Another one? Ralph?"
"Twenty-four."

_____ 11. "Let's check this one. First let's back up a step. A perfect square is some number that can be broken down into the product of another number times itself. What number did we say times itself equals nine?"
"Three."

_____ 12. "Good, Ralph. Let me continue to help you with this. What number times itself equals sixteen?"
"Four."

_____ 13. "Now, does any number times itself equal twenty-four?"
"Hmmm. No, twenty-four isn't a perfect square."

_____ 14. "O.K. Then can you name a perfect square from this list."
"Twenty-five?"

_____ 15. "That's the way!!"

Probing

At this point, you have identified the redirection and the prompting techniques. The former involves increased numbers of students, and the latter deals with incorrect responses. An additional situation arises when the student's reply is correct but insufficient because it lacks depth. In such a case, it is important for the teacher to have the student supply additional information in order to have better, more inclusive answers. This technique is called *probing*. Let's take a close look at this technque in action:

> The teacher begins, "Do you think trees are important to the land?" (pause) "Carmelina?"
> "Yes."

Asking the student for additional information is a very useful questioning technique.

"Why, Carmelina?"
"Because they help hold things together."
"What do you mean by that?"
"Well, the roots and all go down into the ground and help the ground stay in one place."
"That's very good, Carmelina, and as we learned yesterday, when the earth begins to move away to a different place, it's called *erosion.*"

It is important to note that no new ideas have been introduced. The purpose here is to get students to justify or further explain their responses, thereby increasing the depth of the discussion. It also helps to move students away from surface responses. All too often, we don't take our students beyond the simple yes or no or correct answer response. We need to provide our students with increased opportunities to process information, to deal with the *why*, the *how*, and the *based upon what*. By doing so, the student not only gains experience in dealing with higher-level tasks but also experiences a greater feeling of success.

EXERCISE 6.7

Read the following anecdote and identify the teacher's questions that are redirections (r), prompts (pt), and probes (pb). Remember, not all questions will be one of these three types. After completing the exercise, check your answers with the ones found in the feedback section at the end of the chapter.

_____ 1. "In front of each of you are two containers, each with a different substance. Look at the substances carefully and try to make some comparisons between them. What comparison would you make. Jim?"

"Well, they're both whitish colored."

_____ 2. "O.K., good. Nancy?"

"They look sort of grainy. They both look sort of grainy."

_____ 3. "Could you explain what you mean by _grainy_?"

"Well . . ."

_____ 4. "Would you say they're chunky or powdery, Nancy?"

"Chunky."

_____ 5. "What do you call these chunks? Anyone?"

Manny answers, "Crystals."

_____ 6. "Good. They're both made of crystals. What else can we say about the two as a comparison? Tom."

Tom doesn't respond.

_____ 7. "Tom, what could we do with the substances besides look at them?"

"Well, we could rub them in our hands."

_____ 8. "Okay, try that. Here." The teacher passes Tom the containers. "How do they feel?"

"This one is finer grained," Tom says as he holds one up.

_____ 9. "Fine. How could you relate that to what we said about crystals?"

"The crystals of this one are smaller."

_____ 10. "O.K., good, Tom. Now, Jake, what else could we do with the substances to make comparisons?"

"I'm not sure."

_____ 11. "Well, we've looked at them, and we've rubbed them in our hands to utilize the senses of touch and sight. What other senses could we use to extend our observations?"

Jake answers, "We could smell them."

_____ 12. "O.K., try that." The teacher lets Jake smell the crystals. "What do you smell?"

"I don't smell anything."

_____ 13. "What do you suppose we should try next? Anyone?"

"We could taste them," Murray replies.

_____ 14. "Your idea is good, but remember I've said that for safety you should never put anything into your mouth until you're sure it's harmless. However, these are harmless substances, so, Jim, you taste this one, and Peter, you taste the other. How do they taste?"

Jim speaks first. "This one tastes like it would be isotonic with the body fluids."

Peter follows quickly with, "This one tastes just the opposite."

_____ 15. "Whoa! Could you clarify that statement Jim?"

"O.K. It tastes like salt."

_____ 16. "How about yours, Peter?"
"It must be sugar."

_____ 17. "O.K. What is the formula for salt, Jim?"
Jim doesn't answer.

_____ 18. "Let's try this, Jim. What is salt composed of?"
"Sodium and chloride, I think."

_____ 19. "That's right. What might the formula be then?"
"NaCl?"

_____ 20. "Right, good! Now, anyone, what is sugar composed of?"
Murray says, "There's carbon in it."

_____ 21. "Yes. What else? Nancy?"
Nancy looks confused.

_____ 22. "What is there a lot of in the atmosphere?"
Nancy mumbles, "Oxygen?"

_____ 23. "Right! Do you suppose there might be some oxygen in sugar, Nancy?"
Hesitantly she says, "Yes."

_____ 24. "You're right; there is. What else, Johnnie?"
"Maybe hydrogen?"

_____ 25. "Right. Now, would anyone guess at the formula for sugar?"
A girl answers, "CHO?"

_____ 26. "Good thought, Helene. It's consistent with what we said about salt. Suppose though that there are twice as many atoms of hydrogen as there are carbon or oxygen in sugar. What might the formula be then, Helene?"
"CH_2O."

_____ 27. "Right. This is an empirical formula for sugar. Now suppose that the molecular weight of sugar is 180. What would the formula be? Take a minute and figure it out." (pause) "Anyone?"
There is no response.

_____ 28. "What is the weight of the empirical formula? Tom?"
"Hmmm . . . 30?"

_____ 29. "Right! Now what would the molecular formula be if CH_2O has a weight of 30 and the molecular weight is 180? Tom?"
Tom answers after a short pause, "$C_6H_{12}O_6$."

_____ 30. "Good! How did you get that?"
"Well, 180 is 6 times greater than 30, so the formula should be 6 times CH_2O."

_____ 31. "Very good."

Wait-Time

An additional technique that is conceptually simple but powerful in its effect is called *wait-time*. Based on the work of Mary Budd Rowe (1974, 1986), it is simply the amount of time teachers wait after asking a question until they intervene by prompting or redirecting the question to another student. Rowe found that teachers typically wait one second or less for students to answer. Think about that for a moment. Suppose you as a student studying this book were asked in a class discussion, "Under what conditions would it be inappropriate to use redirection as a skill?" and your instructor gave you less than one second to answer before asking another question or turning the question to someone else? This is the situation students are usually put in. By contrast, if they are given a bit more time to think, the quality of their answers will improve. These are the results Rowe found in examining the effects of increased "think time." She found that when teachers waited approximately three seconds or longer that the quality of student responses improved, and this simple process of giving them more time to answer increased achievement.

The implications of this research are obvious. As we question students, we should make an effort to wait a few seconds for them to answer. At first a period of silence may seem awkward, but both you and the students will quickly get used to it.

However, as with the others, this technique should be implemented with judgement and sensitivity. Earlier in the chapter in citing the work of O'Keefe (1986), we said that teachers need to be responsive to their students. Imagine, for example, that you call on a student and he appears to draw a blank. As you wait, he panics. In this case you wouldn't wait as long as you would in another where the student appears to be "really thinking" about the answer. Also, in asking low-level, convergent questions, such as, "What is 4 × 7?" or "What city is at the tip of Lake Michigan?" you wouldn't wait as long as you would in asking a question such as, "Why do you suppose Chicago developed into such a major city?"

Our primary goal in this discussion is to make you aware of the value of wait-time, so you will make an effort to practice it when you teach. None of us employs the technique perfectly, and we aren't suggesting that you silently count after every question you ask. However, with effort you will increase the amount of time you give your students and will add another dimension to your questioning skills.

MOTIVATING STUDENTS

We have to this point presented specific and separate discussions of the different question levels, direction, and techniques and have illustrated how they can be applied in various teaching situations. However, when they are synthesized and systematically applied to classroom activities, they can also become powerful techniques in motivating students. We turn now to this discussion.

"Skill in motivating students to learn is obviously basic to teacher effectiveness" (Good & Brophy, 1987). Interestingly, however, it has only been within the last few years that motivation has received systematic attention from educators. Prior to that time many teachers felt that it was their job to teach and that they couldn't also be expected to motivate reluctant learners. In other cases motivation was a haphazard bag of tricks. Now, all that has changed. Concern about alienated youth, the high dropout rate, and kids spending much of their days with their heads down on desks has contributed to this renewed focus.

Although there is certainly more to motivation than questioning, a skilled teacher can do much to enhance student attention and interest through classroom interaction. We have observed teachers achieve striking results with systematic application of the skills described in this chapter. How can this be accomplished?

Conceptually, the process is actually quite simple, although putting it into practice requires diligence and effort. Essentially, we want to establish two expectations in the students.

First, we want to put them in a position where *they know with certainty that they each will be called on during the course of a learning activity.* Earlier in the chapter we noted that Kerman (1979) found impressive results when teachers were trained to call on all students equally. Also, Gage and Berliner (1984) have stated that volunteers should be called on only 10 to 15% of the time in a learning activity. This means that much of the time you will be calling on students who don't have their hands raised. This can be accomplished by extensively using the skill of redirection. It can be particularly effective when redirection is combined with divergent questions calling for description or comparison. The type of question, however, is not as important as putting students in a position where they know they will be called on. When they know *for certain* that they will be called on at some point in the process, their attention improves markedly.

"I can't do that," some people might argue. "I put the kids on the spot, and they're worse off than they were before." This bring us to the second expectation: *when students are called on, they know that you will arrange the question so they can give an acceptable answer.* Notice carefully that we said *an acceptable answer.* We didn't say that they will give you *the answer* you want to the original question, but they will give you an answer that you can acknowledge as acceptable. As an illustration, consider the following dialogue taken from a lesson on adverbs.

Mrs. Wu is involved in an exercise where the students are supposed to identify adverbs in sentences. She went through a series of examples, calling on the students to analyze the sentences. She continued by writing the following on the board:

Steve quickly jumped over the hedge to get out of sight.

She then continued, "What is the adverb in this sentence, Tim?"
" . . . I don't know."
"What did Steve do?"
"He jumped over the hedge."
"Yes indeed! He certainly did! Very Good, Tim."

At this point, Tim has given *an acceptable* answer. He admittedly didn't identify the adverb in the sentence, but his answer was nevertheless appropriate and also gave the teacher a chance to praise him. Mrs. Wu could then continue prompting and probing by asking Tim, "How did he jump?" or she could "let him off the hook" and continue the process with another student. Either way, Tim has had a successful and positive experience.

For students who are rarely called on and who even more rarely give a correct answer, this simple process is very positive. As a result, they will be less uncomfortable the next time they are called on, and they will be more inclined to try and answer. Wlodkowski (1984) stated that an emotionally safe learning environment is critical to student motivation, and Mrs. Wu helped create a safe environment for Tim.

Obviously, you won't turn a hostile or seriously unmotivated student around immediatley with these techniques. However, if the pattern in the classroom becomes one in which all the students are called on — *and* when they are, they are able to answer — in time you can markedly improve their attention and their inclination to respond. Consider also the kind of classroom climate you're establishing with this process. You're communicating to the students that they all are capable of learning, you expect them to be able to answer, and you're there to help them. This climate, together with using the skills of redirection and prompting to help you involve your students and promote success, can do much to enhance their motivation.

SUMMARY

We began Chapter 6 by saying that questioning skills are the cornerstone of effective teaching. The different levels, direction, and techniques contribute to teachers' overall repertoire of skills. At times high-level questions are most desirable, whereas at others low levels are preferable. You will ask some questions that are convergent and some that are divergent. The levels and direction of your questions will be determined by the goal for the lesson.

Redirection, prompting, probing, and wait-time are all techniques that can be used to promote student involvement, enhance success, and promote a positive and emotionally safe learning environment. As with the levels and direction of your questions, the techniques are employed to help you reach the goals of your lesson. However, you have an additional goal for every lesson, which is to involve and motivate your students. When systematically integrated, the specific techniques can help you reach this goal.

REFERENCES

Berliner, D. (1985, April). *Effective teaching*. Paper presented at the annual meeting of the Florida Educational Research and Development Council, Pensacola, FL.

Brophy, J., & Evertson, C. (1976). *Learning from teaching: A developmental perspective*. Boston: Allyn & Bacon.

Denham, C., & Lieberman, A. (1980). *Time to learn*. Washington, D.C.: National Institute of Education.

Duffy, G., Roehler, L., Meloth, M., & Vavrus, L. (1985). *Conceptualizing instructional explanation*. Chicago: American Educational Research Association.

Gage, N., & Berliner, D. (1987). *Educational psychology* (4th ed.). Boston: Houghton Mifflin.

Gall, M. (1984). Synthesis of research on teachers' questioning. *Educational Leadership, 41*, 40–47.

Good, T. (1983). Research on classrom teaching. In L. Shulman & G. Sykes (Eds.), *Handbook of teaching and policy* (pp. 42–80). New York: Longman.

Good, T., & Brophy, J. (1987). *Looking in classrooms* (4th ed.). New York: Harper & Row.

Kerman, S. (1979). Teacher expectatons and student achievement. *Phi Delta Kappan, 60*, 716–718.

O'Keefe, P., & Johnston, M. (1987). *Teachers' abilities to understand the perspectives of students: A case study of two teachers*. Washington, DC: American Educational Research Association.

Rowe, M. (1974). Wait-time and rewards as instructional variables, their influence on language, logic, and fate control: Part one—Wait-time. *Journal of Research in Science Teaching, 11*, 81–94.

Rowe, M. (1986, January/February). Wait-time: Slowing down may be a way of speeding up. *Journal of Teacher Education*, 43–50.

Soar, R. (1973). *Follow-through classroom process measurement and pupil growth, 1970–1971: Final report*. Gainesville, FL: University of Florida.

Wlodkowski, R. (1984). *Motivation and teaching: A practical guide* (2nd ed.). Washington, DC: National Education Association.

EXERCISE FEEDBACK

EXERCISE 6.1

1. (h) High. The teacher has asked an analysis-level question.
2. (h) High. This asks for clarification.
3. (h) High. This again involves clarification.
4. (h) High. This is a comprehensive question.
5. (l) Low. The teacher has probably led the students.
6. (l) Low. This is a memorization recall task.
7. (l) Low. This is, once again, recall.
8. (l) Low. This, too, is recall.
9. (l) Low. This is a prompt leading to a right answer.
10. (h) High. Finding relationships is definitely not a recall situation.
11. (h) High. Again, making comparisons is not a recall situation.
12. (l) Low. This is a comparison of memorized definitions.
13. (l) Low. This, too, is a memorized comparison.
14. (h) High. Searching for similarities is not recall.
15. (h) High. Again, this is finding a relationship.
16. (l) Low. This is a recall task.

EXERCISE 6.2

1. (d) Divergent. There may be other things than likeness.
2. (d) Divergent. Self-expression would be varied.
3. (d) Divergent. There is still a range of possibilities.
4. (d) Divergent. Examples would vary.
5. (c) Convergent. The teacher leads the students to only one conclusion.
6. (c) Convergent. The answer is a specific term.
7. (c) Convergent. This is a question with only one answer.
8. (c) Convergent. This is recall also.
9. (c) Convergent. The teacher is leading to a single answer.
10. (d) Divergent. There might be more than one relationship.
11. (d) Divergent. Again, there might be several relationships.
12. (c) Convergent. This is recall of definitions.
13. (c) Convergent. There is only one answer.
14. (d) Divergent. This is assuming there is more than one set. The question is convergent if there is only one.
15. (d) Divergent. There may be more than one possible relationship.
16. (c) Convergent. A single response is correct.

EXERCISE 6.3

1. (h/d) High level/Divergent
2. (h/d) High level/Divergent
3. (h/d) High level/Divergent
4. (l/c) Low level/Convergent. There is only one correct list of major organs.
5. (h/d) High level/Divergent
6. (l/c) Low level/Convergent

7. (h/d) High level/Divergent
8. (h/d) High level/Divergent
9. (h/c) High level/Convergent
10. (h/c) High level/Convergent
11. (h/d) High level/Divergent
12. (h/d) High level/Divergent
13. (l/c) Low level/Convergent
14. (h/d) High level/Divergent
15. (h/c) High level/Convergent

EXERCISE 6.4

1. No X
2. X. After Bob had answered, "Ireland," the teacher posed the same question to Paul.
3. X. After Paul's response, the teacher once again posed the original question to Pam.
4. No X
5. No X
6. No X
7. X. After Jim's response the teacher asked if anybody wanted to generate additional examples for the question posed.
8. No X
9. No X
10. No X
11. No X
12. No X
13. No X
14. No X

  Note that in each case of redirecton the teacher is getting more than one student to respond to a question. Once the teacher poses a new question, the redirection technique is no longer being used unless that new question is then redirected.

EXERCISE 6.5

1. No X
2. No X. Redirection.
3. No X. Redirection.
4. No X
5. X. After Jim could not respond, the teacher gave him a leading question for consideration.
6. X. In this same sequence, the teacher is urging Jim to think of other examples.
7. No X. Redirection.
8. No X
9. No X
10. No X
11. X. Although Nancy has already defined *immigration*, the teacher is beginning a sequence where she is given hints so she can use the two terms appropriately.
12. X. An unfinished question is considered prompting.

13. X. Nancy is prompted to define a term she may not already have known.
14. No X

EXERCISE 6.6

1. Neither
2. (r) Redirection
3. (r) Redirection
4. Neither
5. (r) Redirection
6. Neither
7. (p) Prompt. The teacher is getting Bob to recall his times tables so that he can generate an appropriate answer.
8. Neither
9. (r) Redirection
10. (r) Redirection
11. (p) Prompt. Statements 11 through 14 represent a prompt sequence. The teacher begins by providing additional information and helping the student to respond with appropriate examples.
12. (p) Prompt.
13. (p) Prompt
14. (p) Prompt
15. Neither

EXERCISE 6.7

1. None
2. (r) Redirection
3. (pb) Probe
4. (pt) Prompt
5. None
6. (r) Redirection
7. (pt) Prompt
8. (pt) Prompt
9. (pt) Prompt
10. (r) Redirection
11. (pt) Prompt
12. (pt) Prompt
13. (r) Redirection
14. None
15. (pb) Probe
16. (r) Redirection
17. None
18. (pt) Prompt
19. (pt) Prompt
20. None
21. (r) Redirection
22. (pt) Prompt
23. (pt) Prompt
24. (r) Redirection

25. None
26. (pt) Prompt
27. None
28. (pt) Prompt
29. (pt) Prompt
30. (pb) Probe
31. None

7 ‖ Teaching Strategies

INTRODUCTION

We are now to the implementation phase of the general teaching model where different strategies are used in helping students reach the objectives that teachers prepare in the planning phase of instruction. In this chapter we incorporate the questioning skills described in Chapter 6 and show how the skills are directly applied within the strategies. The specific strategies discussed are *expository, guided discovery, discussion,* and *inquiry* techniques, which are illustrated with examples from different disciplines. Similarities exist among the strategies, of course, and they aren't exclusive of each other. As a teacher, you will probably incorporate features from more than one as you teach. This is desirable as you develop a personal style. However, we discuss them in separate and distinct presentations for the sake of clarity and the development of your initial understanding. As your thinking develops and your teaching evolves, you should make adjustments in the strategies to fit your personality, style, and students' needs.

Because expository and discovery are closely related in terms of goals, content, and procedures, we present an overview of the two together in the first section before they are separately described in greater detail.

OBJECTIVES

After completing Chaper 7, you should be able to accomplish the following objectives:

1. For you as a pre/inservice teacher to understand the difference between expository and discovery teaching techniques, so that when provided with a description of a teaching episode, you will be able to identify it as discovery or expository and explain your choice.
2. For you as a pre/inservice teacher to understand the planning and implementing of expository lessons, so that when given a description of a teaching episode involving expository teaching, you will be able to identify all of the major steps.
3. For you as a pre/inservice teacher to understand the importance of examples in expository and discovery lessons, so that given a series of examples on different topics, you will write an analysis of their effectiveness for teaching the abstraction.
4. For you as a pre/inservice teacher to understand the planning and implementing of discovery lessons, so that when given a description of a discovery teaching episode, you will identify all of the steps.

5. For you as a pre/inservice teacher to understand the planning and implementing of inquiry lessons, so that when given a description of an inquiry teaching episode, you will identify all of the major steps.

6. For you as a pre/inservice teacher to understand the planning and implementing of discussions, so that when given a description of a discussion episode, you will identify the important features illustrated in it.

EXPOSITORY AND DISCOVERY TEACHING

An Overview

As an introduction to these two teaching strategies let's look at a math teacher working with her fifth-grade class.

> Ms. Morton had been working with her class for the past few weeks on different geometric shapes. Today her lesson focused on circles. To begin the lesson, she gave the students rulers, string, and a handout containing a number of circles like the one shown in Figure 7.1.
>
> In addition to the handout containing the circles, she passed out a sheet that looked like Table 7.1.
>
> She began her lesson by saying, "Look at the circles you have on the handout I've given you. What do you notice about them? Suzy?"
>
> "There's a line with an *A* and a *B* and a *C* on it."
>
> "Yes indeed," Ms. Morton smiled. "And what do we call that line? Kevin?"
>
> "... The radius?" Kevin responded hesitantly.
>
> "Does this line go all the way across the circle or only halfway across, Kevin?"
>
> "All the way across."
>
> "Yes, good. And what do we call that?"
>
> "Oh, yes! I've got it. It's the diameter. I remember you told us that *diameter* sort of sounds like *dime*, and it goes all the way across the dime."

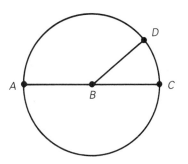

Figure 7.1 Circles Handout

Table 7.1   Chart Handout

Circle	Radius	Diameter	Circumference
A			
B			
C			
D			
E			
F			

"Yes, very good memory, Kevin. What else do you notice about the circles? Juan?"

"Well, we have a line *BD*, which is called the radius."

"Excellent, Juan. Now look at the columns in your handout. We've talked about the radius and diameter of the circles. What else do you see in the handout? Kim?"

"The word *circumference?*"

"And what does that mean?"

Kim appears to be thinking.

"Look again at your circle, Kim. You've identified the diameter and the radius. What is the only thing left?"

"... The distance around it. The circumference is the distance around!"

"Good thinking, Kim!"

"And how could we measure that? Could we use a ruler? Sarah?"

"We could, but it wouldn't be right because of all the curves. Instead, we could put string around the outside and measure the string afterward with a ruler."

"Excellent, you remembered how we did that with other geometric shapes. Well, today we're going to see if we can find out some things about circles. To do this, I want you to measure the circles on the handout that I've given you and put these measurements in the chart. When you're finished, we'll talk about what you've done."

With that, the class went to work measuring the circles that Ms. Morton had handed out. When she noticed that most of the class had completed the assignment, she drew the chart from the handout (shown in Table 7.1) on the board and asked the students to tell her what measurements they had gotten. As the class did this, they realized that different people got different answers, which provided an opportunity to talk about the idea of measurement error. In discussing this concept, the class decided that one way of handling the problem would be to average measurements, which they did.

Once the chart on the board was completed (see Table 7.2), Ms. Morton continued the lesson by saying, "Now let's look at our chart on the board. What patterns do you see there? Don?"

"... The values are all different."

"Yes they are," Ms. Morton smiled. "What else? John?"

"The diameters are all about twice as big as the radiuses," noted John.

Table 7.2 Completed Chart

Circle	Radius	Diameter	Circumference
A	1	2	6.3
B	1.9	4	12.5
C	2.95	6	18.9
D	4.1	8.1	24.9
E	5	10.1	32.5
F	6	11.8	38.0

"Good, John. And why do you think that is? Mary?"

Mary hesitates.

"How are the diameters and radiuses related?"

"The diameter is twice as long as the radius."

"Yes, exactly! Good, Mary. That's why the measurements are twice as long. Now let's look at the diameter and circumference columns. What do you notice here? Jamie?"

". . . When the diameter gets bigger, so does the circumference."

"That's right, Jamie," Ms. Morton smiled. "Okay—anything else? . . . Anyone?"

Not hearing a response, she continued, "Well, let's see if we can figure out how the two change. Let's have this half of the class divide the circumferences of circles A, C, and E by their diameters while the other half of the class does the same for B, D, and F."

When the class finished, Ms. Morton added a new column with their results so the chart looked like Table 7.3.

"What do you notice about the numbers in the column labeled C/D? Mary?"

"They're all just over three."

"Good, we see that the measurements aren't all exact. Why do you suppose that happened? Joan?"

"Well, we talked about measurement error, so maybe that's it."

"Good thinking, Joan. So what should we do? Leroy?"

". . . Average the numbers?" Leroy responded hesitantly.

"Good work, Leroy! Okay everyone, let's do that. Use your calculators and quickly get an average."

Table 7.3 Chart with C/D Added

Circle	Radius	Diameter	Circumference	C/D
A	1	2	6.3	3.15
B	1.9	4	12.5	3.120
C	2.95	6	18.9	3.15
D	4.1	8.1	24.9	3.07
E	5	10.1	32.5	3.14
F	6	11.8	38.0	3.22

After allowing a few moments, Ms. Morton said, "All right, what did you get? John?"

"Three point one four three."

"Fine, John. Is that what everyone got?"

She waited a few seconds while two of the students rechecked their answers, and having confirmed that 3.143 was the average, she continued.

"That is a very good average, everyone. We were very close. The actual number is three point one four. This number is called *pi*, and the symbol is this."

She then wrote the word and drew the symbol on the board.

"Now, think about a formula that we could use to find the circumference if we know the diameter. Anyone?"

"I think I know," Lacey said tentatively. "Multiply the diameter times *pi*."

"Good idea, Lacey," Ms. Morton smiled at her. "Let's everyone try that to see if it works."

With that, she drew a circle on the board using chalk and string. She measured the diameter for the class and gave them the value. While they were multiplying, she had two members of the class come up to measure the circumference for comparison. After the class discussed the results of this problem, she passed out another worksheet which contained additional circles, and the class measured these to see if they too follow the $C = \pi d$ equation.

Let's pause now to consider the example. This case study involved a teacher using a *guided discovery* approach to help students learn abstractions. In this lesson they learned both the concept *pi* and the formula $C = \pi d$. We call these lessons *guided discovery* because students are provided with information, and through the guidance of their teachers they "discover" the abstraction the teachers have identified in the objectives.

Expository lessons are more teacher-centered than discovery lessons in that the teacher is the major provider of information, relating the examples to the abstraction being taught. The abstraction is stated by the teacher *before* examples are given, and then the examples are provided to help illustrate the abstraction. To show what we mean by expository teaching, read the following anecdote which describes a teacher using this method to teach a similar lesson.

Mr. Hite wanted to teach his class the formula $C = \pi d$. He began by saying, "Today we're going to learn the formula for computing the circumference of a circle. When you're finished you'll be able to find the circumference when you're given the diameter."

He then wrote $C = \pi d$ on the board and said, "Go ahead and read this, Tim."

"C equals *pi* times D," Tim responded.

"OK, fine, Tim," he smiled. "Now what is the *C*? Jan?"

"It's the circumference."

"And what is the circumference? Derek?"

"It's . . . I'm not sure," Derek stammered.

Mr. Hite then drew on the board a circle like the one in Figure 7.1.

"Now, look at the circle. What is the circumference?" he asked as he pointed to the board and made an imaginary circle in the air.

"It's the distance around the circle," Derek said, grinning at Mr. Hite's arm movement.

"That's right, Derek," Mr. Hite grinned back.

"Now what is the d in the formula? Sarah?"

"It's the diameter."

"And where is it on our circle?" he said pointing to the board. "Cal?"

"It's the line AC," Cal responded after studying the circle.

"All right, good, Cal. Now we have one part left in the formula. What is it? Judy?"

"It's that little squiggly thing that is three point one four," she said.

"Very good, Judy. What did Tim say we called that when I wrote the formula on the board? Anyone?"

"*Pi*," three students said together.

"Okay, terrific. Now we're all set."

With that he gave each of the students a ruler, string, and a handout with three circles drawn on it.

"Look at the circles on the handout, everyone. I want you to measure the diameter and calculate the circumference. Then check your calculation by measuring the circumference with the string."

The students then went to work, computed the circumference of each circle, and checked their answers by measuring each.

These anecdotes illustrate two of the teaching strategies that are discussed in this chapter. The first involved a teacher using *guided discovery* to teach the concept of *pi* and the formula for computing the circumference of a circle. The second used an *expository* method to teach the same formula. Our discussion turns now to a comparison of the two procedures; but before continuing, complete Exercise 7.1.

EXERCISE 7.1 ⎯⎯⎯⎯⎯⎯⎯⎯⎯⎯⎯⎯⎯⎯⎯⎯⎯⎯⎯⎯⎯

Read the following teaching anecdotes and determine whether they involve expository (e) or discovery (d) teaching. Compare your answers with the ones given in the feedback section at the end of the chapter.

1. Mr. Hames was teaching a lesson on geometry. He began the lesson by passing out protractors and a sheet with a number of triangles on it. Then he said, "Today we're going to study some properties of triangles. Now, I'd like you to measure the angles of the triangles I've given you." After doing this, the class concluded that the sum of the interior angles of a triangle was equal to 180 degrees.

2. Mr. Jones, a language arts teacher, was trying to get his class to understand how rules govern the pronunciation of our language. He began by writing the words *cold, can't,* and *cut* on the board. He had

the students describe, compare, and pronounce the words. He continued by writing *cell, center, city,* and *civil* on the board and repeated the process he had used with the first list. He prompted the students to identify the letter following the *c* in each case and helped them conclude that when a *c* at the beginning of a word is followed by an *e* or *i*, the *c* is pronounced like an *s*, but when it is followed by an *a, o,* or *u*, it is pronounced like a *k*.

3. Mrs. Smith was teaching a lesson on the concept of *set*. She began the lesson by gathering her kindergarteners around on the rug and placing three clothespins in a yarn circle on the floor. Then she said, "This is a set. It's a group of objects that belong together." Then she put other objects in the yarn circle and described how they were also examples of set. At the end of the lesson, the students in the class were asked to make up their own set.

4. Miss Kirk was trying to teach her reading class to recognize inferences in written materials. She did this by going through a story and identifying a number of statements in it. Then she asked what all these had in common. After the class decided that inferences were ideas in the story that weren't actually stated, Miss Kirk gave them another story and asked them to find inferences.

A Comparison

In examining the lessons Ms. Morton and Mr. Hite did, we see that they are similar in many ways. Let's examine the similarities.

1. The objective was nearly the same for each. The scope of Ms. Morton's lesson was slightly greater in that she taught her students both the concept of *pi* and the formula $C = \pi d$, whereas Mr. Hite only taught the formula. Otherwise, the objectives were the same.
2. The planning for each was the same. Both teachers provided the students with the same materials, and the goal of having them understand the formula for circumference was identical.
3. Both the teachers interacted with their classes, which is critical for increasing student involvement and learning (Pratton & Hales, 1986). The interaction was facilitated by the questioning skills we discussed in Chapter 6. Ms. Morton prompted Kevin, Kim, and Mary when they were unable to answer, and Mr. Hite did the same when Derek had difficulty. In each case the teacher gave the student ample time to answer.
4. Both the teachers created a climate of support and promoted success through their questioning skills. As a result, the psychological safety and atmosphere conducive to motivation that we discussed in Chapter 6 were present in both lessons.
5. Both the lessons were strongly teacher-directed, and both teachers were *active* in promoting the learning activity (Good, 1983). Because of the term *discovery*, the procedure is sometimes misconceived as being one in which students are put essentially on their own to "discover" relationships among different items of information. This was not at all the case in Ms.

Morton's lesson. She had a very clear goal in mind, and her lesson was strongly directed toward the goal. Mr. Hite was equally clear in his lesson's goal and direction.

On the other hand, the following differences existed in the lessons.

1. Although the objectives and planning for the lessons were nearly the same, the sequence each teacher followed in implementing the activity was reversed. Ms. Morton began by providing the students with examples and information and guided them into deriving the formula (in addition to forming the concept of *pi*). By contrast, Mr. Hite started with the formula and then went to calculations of the examples.
2. Ms. Morton used the technique *redirection* more extensively than did Mr. Hite. She also asked a number of *divergent* questions, whereas Mr. Hite's questions were all convergent.
3. Although we can't determine length from written case studies, Ms. Morton's use of redirection and divergent questions would likely result in the lesson taking more time.
4. Mr. Hite's lesson was more focused on the topic. For example, the students in Ms. Morton's class also dealt with the concept of *radius* in their discussion, whereas those in Mr. Hite's class did not.

Based on these comparisons, we see that each of the strategies has its own advantages and disadvantages.

The expository method has two primary advantages — time and control. Because the questioning is convergent, expository lessons tend to be more time-efficient, allowing the teacher to cover more content in the amount of time allocated for the topic. Also, for inexperienced teachers who are not yet sure of their skills in leading classroom interaction, the strong lesson focus is often a source of security. They don't have to cope with channeling the divergent responses toward the content goal.

This control and efficiency can come at a price, however. Teachers using expository methods commonly slide into lecture monologues that are deadly for maintaining student attention and motivation. This need not be the case, as Mr. Hite's lesson indicates, but such techniques allow this problem to occur more readily than do guided discovery techniques. Guided discovery strongly promotes student involvement and success and, as a result, helps create the safe emotional environment needed for motivation.

Guided discovery activities, with their emphasis on observation, comparison, and explanation, are also more conducive to the development of thinking skills than are expository techniques. We discuss the topic of developing student thinking in more detail in the last section of this chapter.

Guided discovery also affords more opportunity for acquiring incidental information than do expository techniques. We saw an example of this in Ms. Morton's lesson compared to Mr. Hite's. Her students dealt with the concept of radius, whereas his did not.

On the other hand, enhanced motivation, thinking skills, and incidental learning have their price as well. As noted earlier, guided discovery lessons typically require more time because of the divergent student responses, and teachers often complain that they don't have enough time now to "get in" all the content required by their curriculum guides or published lists of objectives.

The biggest problem with guided discovery techniques, however, may be the skills they demand in teachers. Teachers using the techniques must constantly be involved in decision making and "thinking on their feet." They must decide when to begin channeling the divergent responses toward the goal, pose the right question at the right time to begin to narrow the responses, prompt when necessary—and do all this while monitoring the students' responses in order to formulate appropriate follow-up questions. Most teachers can learn to become adequate lecturers, but it takes diligence and practice to develop expertise with guided discovery. Because beginning teachers have little exposure to the technique, they are often uncomfortable initially and sometimes give up on developing their skills with the procedure before they've mastered it.

Perseverance will pay big dividends, however. Our purpose in this discussion is to help you develop your expertise with both methods, so that you will have a larger repertoire of skills, which, in turn, will allow you to add more variety to your teaching. This variety in procedures results in increased interest and achievement (Furst & Rosenshine, 1971; Good, 1983; Rosenshine & Stevens, 1986). Researchers found in analyzing the behavior of superior teachers that one important characteristic they had in common was the ability to vary their teaching methods. This allows teachers to reach students with different learning styles more effectively, and variety alone is stimulating and attention getting. For these reasons we are presenting a variety of procedures in this chapter.

This completes our introductory discussion of expository and guided discovery teaching. We turn now to a detailed description of the planning and implementing phases of each.

Expository Teaching

Planning.   There are three essential steps involved in the planning process. (This assumes that philosophical factors such as the role of the school, the teachers' function, and student needs have already been considered. They are, of course, very important, but a discussion of such philosophical issues is beyond the scope of this text.) The first step in planning is to identify a topic. This is often dictated by your textbook or curriculum guide, and any given topic can be handled at varying levels of specificity. For example, the topic in both Ms. Morton's and Mr. Hite's lessons was *circles*.

Once the topic is identified, the second step in the planning process is to determine exactly what you want the students to know, understand, or be able to do in reference to the topic. In other words, you specify a goals objective. For instance, Mr. Hite's objective could have been stated as follows:

> For fifth-grade students to understand the formula for computing circumference, so that given a ruler and four circles with the diameter drawn in, they will calculate the circumference of each without error.

The third step in the planning phase involves the selection or preparation of examples. The selection is quite simple conceptually but in practice can be difficult to accomplish. The simple part is recognizing the traits of a good example. A good example will include the important characteristics, if you are teaching a concept, or include a relationship, if you are teaching a generalization. *Include* means the learner can *see* the characteristics or the relationship in the example. The hard part involves finding examples that accomplish this task. For some unsophisticated concepts, the task is simple. For instance, the concept *quadrilateral* had the characteristics *four-sided, plane,* and *straight lines.* Examples abound.

Each of the above is composed of straight line segments, each is a plane figure, and each is four-sided. These examples are simple to prepare.

On the other hand, finding examples for a concept such as *communism* can be quite difficult. In fact, this concept is rarely illustrated with examples. Instead, it is often only defined, and how well students learn the concept depends upon the quality of the definition. As Klausmeier (1976) has stated, the problem with using only a definition is that a student may memorize the definition without understanding the concept. Feldman (1980) in a study involving sixth graders and Tennyson (1978) in a study of college students found that using a combination of examples and nonexamples together with a definition resulted in greater learning than using a definition only or examples only. Furthermore, Frayer (1970) found that students learned as much from four well-chosen examples as they did from eight examples.

In selecting these examples to teach concepts, the essential characteristics can be used as a checklist to compare the adequacy of the examples in conveying a complete and accurate concept. For example, suppose you were teaching the concept *adverb* and had determined that the key characteristics of the concept were that it was a word that modified a verb, an adjective, or another adverb. Examine the following list of positive examples to determine their adequacy:

1. The boy ran quickly across the lawn.
2. The boulder thundered loudly down the mountain.
3. She didn't know the answer to the vaguely phrased question.
4. The shark tugged relentlessly at the thin line.

As can be seen in these examples, there is no positive example showing an adverb modifying another adverb. Consequently, the concept that students will form from this lesson will be inaccurate and incomplete. By checking examples such as these against a list of essential characteristics, a teacher can avoid potential pitfalls.

An additional aid in selecting examples is to analyze the concept in terms of coordinate and subordinate concepts. (Markle & Tiemonn, 1970) The subordinate concepts can be used to generate positive examples, while the coordinate ones can provide negative examples that could be confused with the positive ones. Presenting these as negative examples helps students to understand the difference between these closely connected ideas. Negative examples generated in this manner are much more helpful to the student than other types of negative examples. For example, if a teacher were trying to teach her class the concept of *reptile*, negative examples of amphibians, mammals, and birds would be much more helpful to the learner than negative examples like car, tree, ball, or boat. These latter examples are so far removed from the concept that they contain few characteristics in common with the concept and consequently provide little valuable information about what the concept is not.

In planning for the teaching of a generalization, the teacher must also be sure that the examples used accurately illustrate the generalization. This is a slightly more complex process because the examples must illustrate the *interaction* between concepts in the generalization. For example, if you were a psychology teacher trying to teach the generalization that the amount of time between a behavior and its reinforcement is inversely related to the speed with which that behavior is learned, you would need to provide examples in which behavior was being reinforced with different time lapses and different related results. This could be done with either written anecdotes or live or videotaped examples.

In summary, the planning process, when teaching abstractions, amounts to identifying a goals objective and carefully selecting a few examples. It is a very reasonable task, but it also requires thought and insight.

In Mr. Hite's lesson, the examples were developed as the students calculated the circumference and compared their results with a string and yardstick. The use of string and rulers was important in this case because it helped make concrete a relationship that would be quite abstract based on the calculation alone. Mr. Hite demonstrated very effective planning for the lesson.

In actual classroom practice you will often have several objectives related to the same topic, some of which will be abstractions, whereas others will be facts. For example, Mr. Hite wanted his students to know the *name* of the distance around the circle and the *name* of the line through the circle's midpoint. These names are facts, so some fact-level learning was involved in his lesson in addition to understanding the formula for computing the circumference. An understanding of the form of content specified in the particular lesson's objective is important because facts and abstractions are learned differently. We've discussed the preparation of examples in planning to teach abstractions, but what do we do for fact learning?

For all practical purposes, there is little teaching strategy involved when facts are taught. The fact must be memorized, and the teacher employs certain procedures such as drill and repetition in short, frequent episodes, together with reinforcement to aid the process. Further, when the fact exists in the form of a statement, such as "The *Titanic* struck an iceberg," the terms within it must be understood. If the students didn't know that an iceberg is a massive piece of floating ice or that the *Titanic* was a ship, the statement would have no meaning.

The memorizing process can also be aided with the use of mnemonics. A familiar mnemonic is the statement "Thirty days hath September, April, June, and November." Ms. Morton designed and used a mnemonic in comparing diameter to dime and helping the students remember that the diameter goes all the way across the dime. Mr. Hite began by saying, "Today we are going to learn the formula for computing the circumference of a circle," and he then wrote $C = \pi d$ on the board.

Beyond these considerations, little *strategy* per se is involved in teaching facts or planning for their learning.

EXERCISE 7.2

Answer the following questions involving the selection of examples. Then compare your responses to the ones found in the feedback section at the end of the chapter.

1. A health instructor was trying to get her students to understand the generalization that the more strenuous the exercise, the greater the calories used. To illustrate the generalization, she selected a number of pictures of people playing sports of differing degrees of strenuousness. Analyze the quality of her examples.

_____

_____

2. An English teacher was trying to teach that a *verb* is a word that denotes action or a state of being. To illustrate the concept, he selected the following sentences:

A dog came along and chased the cat up the tree.

The man hit the car when it wouldn't start.

The ship caught the breeze and wheeled to port.

She hadn't had a decent meal in ages.

Analyze the quality of the examples.

_____

_____

_____

3. A teacher was trying to teach her class the concept *fruit*. What do the following two sequences suggest about the goals of the lesson or the ability level of the students?

Sequence A	*Sequence B*
apple	tomato
cherry	avocado
orange	mango
mango	orange
avocado	cherry
tomato	apple

_____

_____

_____

Implementing.   The implementing of expository lessons is a very logical process. The first step amounts to presenting to the students the abstraction identified in the objective. Presenting the abstraction to be learned on the board or the overhead provides a focus for the lesson and assures the students of the direction the lesson is to take. In this sense, then, the definition acts as an advance organizer, linking the new information to information in the learner's background and alerting students to the direction that the lesson will take (Ausubel, 1968; Ausubel & Robinson, 1969; Barnes & Clawson, 1975).

The next step in implementing an expository lesson depends upon the objectives of the lesson. If they involve learning factual relationships, then the primary role for the teacher is to make these facts meaningful and resistant to forgetting. Both of these can be facilitated by making sure that the facts are embedded in some meaningful organizational structure. In addition, the key terms in the fact should be examined to make sure they are clear to the students. This helps not only initial learning but also retention (Shimmerlik, 1978; Underwood & Schulz, 1960). If at all possible, this examination should be done in an interactive manner, as is illustrated in the following dialogue involving a social studies lesson.

"Okay, today we are going to talk about the Declaration of Independence. Who knows what the word *declaration* means? Kathy?"

"Oh, it means kind of like to tell something, like a declarative sentence."

"Okay, and what were we telling people? Jerry?"

"We were telling people that we wanted to be independent or free."

"And who were we primarily interested in telling this? Sue?"

"England."

"Good; what date did we do this? Mary?"

"July 4; that's why it's called Independence Day."

"And why did we want to be independent? How does this relate to what we talked about yesterday in terms of the taxes?"

A lesson like this, in which students are helped to see not only the meaning of a fact but also its significance in terms of a larger context, is quite different from one in which facts are mentioned in a lecture, to be memorized and repeated on a test.

When teaching concepts in an expository manner, the teacher must follow a number of sequential steps based upon the characteristics of the concepts. These steps are derived from suggestions by Clark (1971) and Klausmeier, Ghatala, & Frayer (1974). After defining the concept, the second step is to clarify the terms in the definition and relate the concept to a meaningful superordinate concept. This can be done by asking students to define the terms in their own words or by asking students to cite examples of the terms. The third and perhaps most critical step is to present positive examples that are linked to the definition. Negative examples should also be provided to help students understand what the concept is not. In presenting these examples, the teacher should try to get the students to relate these to the essential characteristics listed in the definition. This insures that the characteristics are meaningful to students and that they are linked to the examples in the students' minds.

After the teacher feels that the students understand the concept, he can provide additional examples for students to classify as either positive or negative. In doing this, he should encourage the students to explain the classification in terms of the characteristics listed. Having

Both negative and positive examples are important when employing an expository approach.

students classify examples and defend their answers serves several functions. It provides reinforcement for the concept being formed by the students. It encourages active participation by the students. It also provides an opportunity for both the teacher and the students to gauge how well they understand the concept. If their responses indicate that they do, then the teacher can ask the students for their own examples of the concept; if not, the teacher can provide additional examples to classify before calling for student-generated examples.

These steps are all summarized in Table 7.4 and are illustrated with an anecdote involving an elementary teacher teaching a lesson in language arts.

Table 7.4   Steps in the Expository Teaching of Concepts

Teacher:	1. Define concept and clarify terms.
	2. Link to superordinate concepts.
	3. Present positive and negative examples.
Students:	4. Classify and explain additional teacher examples as either positive or negative.
	5. Provide additional examples.

"The last few days we've been talking about different kinds of sentences. Yesterday we talked about interrogative sentences, and the day before, we talked about declarative sentences. Today we're going to talk about imperative sentences. When we're all through, you should be able to pick out the imperative sentences from a list of mixed sentences."

Then she drew the following on the board:

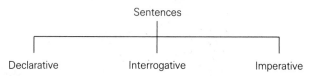

She continued, "Imperative sentences are a special kind of sentence that gives a command or an order, like these." She wrote the following on the board:

Don't do that!
Please pick up your clothes.

"Often the subject of the sentence, *you*, is understood. In the first example, the word *you* isn't in the sentence, but we understand that it means, 'Don't you do that.' You can see in both of these examples that someone is telling somebody else to do something. Also, almost always the verb in imperative sentences is in the present tense. Sometimes imperative sentences have exclamation marks in them to show that someone really wants something done. An example of this would be, 'Stop, or I'll shoot!' You would put an exclamation point at the end. Also, the verb is in the present tense, and *you* is understood."

Then she wrote the following on the board:

He didn't want to go.
Go or else I'll call the police!

"Now look at these two sentences and tell me if they are imperative sentences, Jenny."

"I think the second one is, but the first one isn't because the second one gives a command, and the first doesn't."

"Also," added Tom, "the second one is in the present tense, and the first isn't."

"Anything else? Fran?"

"Yes, you can see the subject in the first sentence. It's *he*. But in the second, the subject is understood because we can't see it."

"Excellent."

She wrote one more sentence on the board.

Don't tell me any more lies!

"How about this sentence? Is it an example of an imperative sentence? Cal?"

"Yes, because it gives a command. Also, the subject is understood, and there's an exclamation point at the end."

"Good; now who can give me some additional examples of imperative sentences?"

Note how in this example the teacher follows all of the steps listed in Table 7.4. Note, too, that the teacher made her objective clear at the beginning of the lesson and told students what they should be able to do when the lesson ended. In addition, she made the content organization clear by illustrating the relationship between this new concept and the old ones with a diagram. All of these help to make the logic of the lesson more apparent to students, which should result in better initial learning and better retention.

Because generalizations are so similar to concepts in that they are both abstractions, the steps to follow in teaching them are quite similar to those involved in teaching concepts. The only added dimension involves making sure that the concepts contained in the generalization are understood by students. This should be done at the beginning of the lesson as the generalization is being presented. The formula $C = \pi d$ is a form of generalization, and Mr. Hite clarified the terms within it when he asked Jan what the C meant, then asked Derek what the circumference was, and then continued the process as he had the students identify and describe the diameter and *pi*.

The steps involved in teaching an abstraction in the form of a generalization are shown in Table 7.5 and illustrated in the following anecdote involving an elementary science lesson.

Mrs. Swenson's class had been studying about sounds and how they are made. In this lesson, she wanted her class to understand factors that influence the pitch of a sound. She prepared for the lesson by gathering together a number of sound-making objects like a bamboo flute, a guitar, and some rubberband instruments.

She began her lesson by saying, "We've been talking about how sound comes from vibrations. Now we're going to learn how to make different kinds of sounds that are high and low. Today we're going to learn that the longer the vibrating column, the lower the pitch; the shorter the vibrating column, the higher the pitch," She wrote this on the board and continued.

"When we're through, you should be able to tell me how pitch is affected by the length of the vibrating column and show me how this works

Table 7.5 Steps in the Expository Teaching of Generalizations

Teacher:	1. State generalization.
	2. Clarify concepts within generalization.
	3. Present positive and negative examples.
Students:	4. Classify and explain additional teacher examples as either positive or negative.
	5. Provide additional examples.

with an instrument. Who knows what pitch is? (pause) No one? It's how high or low something sounds."

She then illustrated the concept of pitch with a pitch pipe, having her students listen to different sounds and identifying these as being high or low in pitch. Once she felt that the students understood this concept, she continued.

"Look at this pitch pipe closely." She showed how it had different holes in it. "These are the openings for the different vibrating columns. The noise is made here and vibrates through these columns. That's what makes different kinds of pitch."

She then took the bamboo flute and showed the class how the different holes affected the length of the vibrating column. As her next illustration of the generalization, she went to the piano and played the same key hard and softly, as well as fast and slowly, and asked the class if the pitch had changed. When they said no, she proceeded to lift up the top of the piano for the class to see. She explained how the hammer hitting the strings caused the sound and explained how strings could also form a vibrating column. Then she asked them to predict which of the strings would make high and low sounds.

As a test to determine whether the class understood the generalization, she brought out a guitar and plucked the strings several times. Then she asked the class what would happen if she held down the strings part of the way down the neck. Some of the class members could answer the question, but others couldn't, so she thought another example might be helpful. She brought out empty soda bottles and had two students in the class blow into them to make sounds. After determining that the class understood what the vibrating column was, she asked them what would happen to the pitch if they put water in the bottles.

Let's pause a second and analyze this lesson in terms of the steps suggested in Table 7.5. The teacher began the lesson by stating the generalization and determining that the students understood the concepts of *pitch* and *vibrating column*. She then illustrated the generalization with a number of positive examples and a negative one. The negative example in this case was hitting the same piano key in different ways so that the students could see that this was unrelated to pitch. (In teaching abstractions, positive examples are more useful than negative examples in helping students learn the abstraction, but negative examples still help them clarify what the abstraction doesn't include [Bruner, Goodnow, & Austin, 1956; Bourne, Ekstrand, & Dominawksi, 1971]. As a modification, some generalizations may be taught without negative examples.) The teacher followed the presentation of positive and negative examples with examples in which the students had to make predictions, which essentially involved classifying examples. The lesson ended, however, before the students had an opportunity to suggest additonal examples of their own.

This concludes our discussion of expository teaching strategies. We turn now to a discussion of guided discovery.

EXERCISE 7.3

Read the following anecdote and then answer the accompanying questions. Then compare your answers to the ones given in the feedback section at the end of the chapter.

Mr. Hanes wanted to teach his English class about figures of speech so that they would be able to understand and appreciate literature better. He began his lesson by saying, ''For the last week we've been studying about different figures of speech. Who remembers what figures of speech are? Kristin?''

''They're devices in literature to make the writing more interesting.''

Okay, and who remembers some of these that we've discussed? Larry?''

''Simile and metaphor?''

''That's correct, and, Larry, do you remember the difference between the two?''

''Similes compare two things using *like* or *as,* and metaphors compare things but don't use these terms.''

''Fine. Well today we're going to learn about a third figure of speech called hyperbole. A hyperbole is a figure of speech that uses vivid, nonliteral exaggeration.'' With that he wrote the definition on the board and drew the following diagram.

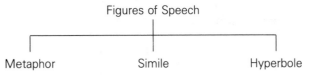

''When we're through with this lesson, you should be able to tell the difference between hyperboles and other figures of speech. Now you all know what figures of speech are, but you may not know what *nonliteral* means. Let me give you an example to help you.''

He then placed the following sentence on an overhead:

I had a ton of homework to do last night.

''This would be an example of a hyperbole because the boy didn't really have a ton of homework to do. That's what we mean by nonliteral. It isn't actually or literally true. Let me give you another example.'' He added this sentence to the overhead:

When we broke up, I cried for weeks.

''This is another example of a hyperbole because it's an exaggeration that isn't literally true. The person didn't really cry for weeks, but the hyperbole is a colorful way of communicating how broken-hearted the person was. Let's try another one.'' He wrote on the overhead,

I could talk with her forever.

''This is another hyperbole. Can someone tell me why? Sandy?''

''Because it's a nonliteral exaggeration. The person couldn't really talk with her forever; he just said that for effect.''

''Fine, now here's a sentence that isn't a hyperbole.'' He wrote,

Bill and Jim are going to see Mary.

''Can someone tell me why? Jake?''

''Oh that's easy—because the words mean exactly what they say.''

''Good. Now it's your turn. Can anyone give me an example of a hyperbole? Jack?''

"Hmmm. How about, 'I was so embarrassed I felt like dying'?"

"What do the rest of you think? Is that a hyperbole, Jan?"

"I think so because the person didn't really want to die but just said that to make an effect. And I think I've got one too. Is this a hyperbole? 'If I've told you once, I've told you a million times not to exaggerate!' "

"I think so, Jan, because the person didn't really tell the other person a million times."

1. What kind of abstraction was Mr. Hanes trying to teach?

_____

2. How did he organize his content?

_____

_____

3. Mr. Hanes made one mistake in his lesson. What was it?

_____

_____

Guided Discovery Teaching

Planning. Many teachers have the misconception that discovery lessons don't require planning and that teachers only need to turn their students loose to "discover" things about the world. While it is true that children are capable of discovering abstractions about the world on their own, this individual discovery process is often hit and miss and does not ensure that a student will learn a particular abstraction at a given time. A far more effective way of ensuring that students will learn a given abstraction is to plan explicitly for such learning. For this reason we have chosen the term *guided discovery*.

A comparison of expository and discovery teaching reveals that the planning phases for each are nearly identical. As with expository teaching, discovery strategies also begin with the preparation of an objective. Ms. Morton's objective could have been identical to Mr. Hite's. A consideraton of background is also critical. Considering adjectives again, you can see that a student could not view the sentence "He was a tall boy" and observe any relationship between *tall* and *boy* unless he had some idea of the terms *modification* or *description*. Having this background would allow the student, when prompted, to say, "*Tall* describes *boy*," or, "*Tall* modifies *boy*." The selection of examples is all the more important in guided discovery lessons because the students must rely solely on the data to form the abstraction being taught. In expository lessons, the teacher can perhaps make some allowances for the lack of adequate examples by explaining the abstraction more thoroughly (though the dangers of this have already been discussed). This option is not as available in guided discovery lessons because the students are totally dependent upon the examples provided by the teacher. If these are inadequate, the abstraction being formed will be incomplete or inaccurate.

The first question to be asked in planning for a guided discovery lesson is What illustrations can I provide to help students attain the abstraction being taught? In the case of concepts, this amounts to selecting good examples, ones that have the characteristics of the concept in them. For instance, a picture of a cow is much better than the word *cow* for teaching the concept *mammal*, because the characteristics of the concept are much more observable in the pictures. The same criteria for selecting examples for expository lessons apply to selecting examples for guided discovery lessons.

The next step in the planning process is to order the examples you will use in the lesson. Placing obvious examples of an abstraction first will lead to quicker attainment of the abstraction, whereas placing less obvious examples first will give students more practice in analyzing data and forming hypotheses. The sequence of examples can also be varied to match the difficulty level of the task with the ability of the students. A more difficult sequence might be used to challenge brighter students, while an easier one might be used to help less academically talented students learn concepts with a minimum of difficulty and frustration.

One final consideration in planning for guided discovery lessons should be mentioned. Because the students don't have a definition or the generalization written down to focus upon, their initial responses will tend to be more divergent than those in expository lessons. Therefore, the lesson may take longer than an expository lesson covering the same material. The extra time is probably well spent in terms of motivation and the possibilities for incidental learning, but time, nevertheless, is a factor the teacher should consider in planning guided discovery activities.

As a postscript to the planning phase, a comment needs to be made about facts. As we noted earlier, facts are either observed, heard, or read. Thus, there is no discovery method for acquiring them (unless you call observing facts "discovering" them), so we will focus our discussion of the guided discovery method on abstraction.

Implementing.   While the planning phase for expository and discovery lessons is virtually the same, the implementation phase is markedly different. In an expository lesson, *the abstraction is defined or described for the student, whereas in guided discovery teaching it is not.* This doesn't mean, of course, that the teacher is less concerned with the students' acquiring the abstraction. It merely means they are to acquire it themselves using the teacher's guidance. The teacher facilitates this process by providing data for the students to analyze and by asking questions that encourage the students to move beyond the information provided to "discover" the abstraction contained therein. The specific steps involved in teaching a guided discovery lesson are listed in Table 7.6 and illustrated in the following anecdote. As you read, see if you can identify the steps as they're being taught.

Miss Cane wanted to teach her students a generalization about pronouncing words. To do this, she put the following words on the board:

beat   boat
meet   main
beak

She then said, "Class, look at the words on the board and tell me what you see. Henry?"

"They all have four letters."

"Good, anything else? Pam?"

"Some are verbs, and some are nouns, and some are adjectives, like *main*."

"They could be all nouns," interjected Jerry, "because *main* could be a noun like *water main*, and *meet* could be a noun like *track meet*."

"Anything else? How about you, Jimmy?"

Jimmy paused.

"Say the word *beat*, Jimmy."

"Beat."

"And what do you notice about the sound?"

Jimmy didn't respond.

"Say it to yourself again and tell me which letters you hear."

"The *b*, the *e*, and *t*."

"Excellent, Jimmy. And was the sound of *e* long or short, Pam?"

"Long."

"And what other letter is in the word, Bill?"

Table 7.6 Steps in Guided Discovery Teaching

Teacher:	1. Present example
Students:	2. Describe example
Teacher:	3. Present additional examples
Students:	4. Describe second example and compare to first example
Teacher:	5. Present additional examples and nonexamples
Students:	6. Compare and contrast examples
Teacher:	7. Prompt students to identify characteristics or relationship
Students:	8. State definition or relationship
Teacher:	9. Ask for additional examples

"*a.*"

"What do you notice about the *a*, Stephanie?"

"You don't hear it at all."

"Good, so we say it's . . ."

(Tentatively) "Silent."

"Yes! Super, everyone. Now look at the other words and compare them to *beat*. Mike?"

"They all have two vowels."

"And what about the sound of the vowels, Judy?"

"The first one is long in each case."

"Can anyone describe the pattern we see in all these words? Missy, you have your hand up."

"If you have two vowels together, the first one is long."

"What about the second vowel?"

"Oh, yeah, you don't say it."

"That's correct; it is silent. How about the rest of you? Does what Missy says agree with the words that we have on the board? Do all of you agree? Listen again, and I'll say it, 'When two vowels go together, the first is long and the second is silent.' Is that an accurate generalization, Anne?" Anne nods. "Tell me why, using a word on the board."

"Well, boat. It has a long *o* and a silent *a*."

"Can you do the same with the last word on the list, Jason?"

"Yes, in that word the *a* is long and the *i* is silent."

"Excellent, now I'm going to give you some more words to see if they follow the rule." She wrote the following on the board:

> pain
> late
> meat
> man

"Some do, like *pain*, because the *a* is long and the *i* is silent," Janet said.

"Also, late, because the *a* is long and the *e* is silent," Jess added.

"What about *man*? Toni?"

"It doesn't fit the rule," Toni said hesitantly. "It only has one vowel in it."

"Good, Toni. The rule doesn't apply in this case. Now, give me an example that fits our pattern. Anyone . . . Go ahead, Kathy."

"How about *meat*?"

"Okay. Does Kathy's example fit, Kim?"

"Yes."

"Why do you say so?"

"We hear the sound of a long *e*, and we don't hear the *a* at all." "Excellent, Kim. Now let's look at one more. Suppose that *boat* were spelled *b-a-o-t*. If we were following this rule, how would we pronounce the word? Ken?"

"I think it would be . . . *bate*," Ken said, considering his answer.

"Bravo, Ken! Very well thought out."

Miss Cane then reminded the class again of the way *boat* is actually spelled, reviewed the rule, and closed the lesson.

Let's stop now and analyze Miss Cane's lesson. First, look again at the steps outlined in Table 7.8. Second, consider the questioning skills discussed in Chapter 6. Miss Cane displayed four examples of the generalization she was trying to teach. By doing so she actually departed slightly from the procedure as described, but sometimes alternate procedures are equally effective. All the strategies discussed in this chapter are designed to be flexible and allow for teacher judgement and preference. Miss Cane exercised her judgement in deciding to display all the examples at once.

Miss Cane displayed an excellent command of questioning skills. She began by asking the students to describe the examples: a form of divergent question. She redirected the question to several students to promote involvement and asked for comparisons among the examples. She also did a very good job of prompting when the students didn't identify the pattern in the examples immediately.

Consider also the motivation in Miss Cane's lesson. Her questioning skills were designed to motivate the learners as much as possible. Typically, in most classrooms, teachers ask questions that have one right answer, and the same bright students are the quickest to answer these questions. This leaves a significant part of the class without the opportunity to participate, and consequently, their interest often wanes. This is a natural reaction. It's not much fun to sit back all the time and watch others get all the reinforcement for giving the right answers. Guided discovery lessons with opportunities for students to make observations with little fear of being wrong induce typical nonparticipants to join in the discussion. By asking the students to make observations, all of which are correct at that time in the lesson, the teacher allows everyone in the class to participate with minimum danger of failing.

A final comment should be made about Miss Cane's teaching. Note how, at the end of the lesson, she placed the abstraction on the board for the class to see. This is important for several reasons. Most importantly, it provides a semipermanent record for the class to view. This is crucial because most classes are composed of students of different interests and abilities, and even the best-prepared lesson can leave some students behind. Placing the abstraction on the board or on an overhead allows all students to see it and provides them with the opportunity to relate it to the examples. Writing the abstraction somewhere for all the students to see also provides an alternate channel for learning by giving the teacher an opportunity to help the students phrase the abstraction well.

EXERCISE 7.4

Read the following anecdote, which describes a teacher using the guided discovery method to teach an abstraction, and then answer the questions that follow. Compare your answers to the ones given in the feedback section at the end of the chapter.

Mrs. Steere, a kindergarten teacher, was trying to teach her students the concept *set equality*. She prepared to do this by gathering together objects from around the room and by asking a number of students to come work with her in a small group on the floor. The lesson began with her saying, "Today I've got some things for us to look at and talk about. I'm going to show you some of them, and I want you to tell me what you see."

With that, she brought out two books and two blocks and put them in two separate piles beside each other. Then she said, "Who can tell me what you see?"

"There are two blocks over here."

"One of them is blue."

"The other is red."

"There's the book we read the other day, Mrs. Steere."

"Right, and what else do you see?"

"The other book is about animals."

"And it has a picture of an elephant on the cover."

"And how many books are there altogether? Jamie?"

"Two."

"Good. Now I want you to look at some more things."

She then moved the two groups of objects to the side, placing each group inside a circle of yarn, and brought out three trucks and three spoons which she placed in two distinct groups. After she did that, she asked the class to tell what they saw.

"All the trucks are red."

"And there are three spoons over there."

"One of the trucks has a wheel missing."

"And how many trucks are there?" Mrs. Steere asked. "Let's count them together — 1, 2, 3. Are there more trucks or more spoons, Shelly?"

"They're the same."

Next the teacher brought out six beanbags and six pieces of chalk and asked the class to make more observations. With prompting, the class decided that the numbers in each group were the same. She repeated this procedure with several other equal sets of objects until a student finally noticed that the numbers in the matched sets were *always* the same. With that, Mrs. Steere introduced the term *equal* to them. She wrote the symbol on the board and used toothpicks for equal signs to show the students how the matched sets were always equal. Then she mixed up the objects, formed new sets, and asked the students to tell whether the sets were equal or not. Some were, and some weren't. Then she had the students form their own equal sets from the objects in front of them.

1. Identify the following steps in the anecdote:
   a. Initial presentation of examples

   _____

   b. Presentation of additional examples

   _____

   c. Students classify examples

   _____

   _____

   d. Students provide additional examples

   _____

   _____

2. Mrs. Steere told them that the term for "the same number" was *equal*. Is this all right in a discovery lesson? Explain your reasoning.

_____

_____

_____

Guided Discovery: Developing Thinking Skills

Much is now being discussed and written about the development of student thinking (Nickerson, Perkins, & Smith, 1985; Presseisen, 1986; Baron & Sternberg, 1987; Eggen & Kauchak, 1988), and teaching thinking is being increasingly emphasized across the nation. A complete discussion of the "thinking-skills movement" is beyond the scope of this text, but we will use this section to present an overview of the movement, describe the processes involved, and illustrate how you might increase the emphasis on thinking with your own students.

The renewed interest in teaching thinking is a result of several factors. The obviously desirable goal of teaching students to think, a response to the long-standing emphasis on basic skills, and research literature indicating that recall of factual information is the dominant pattern in schools (Goodlad, 1984; Paul, 1984) have all contributed to the movement. Perhaps most important, however, are the reports of various national reform groups such as the *Carnegie Forum Task Force on Teaching as a Profession* and the *Holmes Group* stating that our society in the future will require a different product from our schools. Our students will need to function effectively in a high-tech, information-oriented society, with emphasis on flexibility, decision making, and the skills of adaptation and lifelong learning. The emphasis on thinking skills in the classroom is derived from these lofty goals.

What are thinking skills, and how can they be taught? They can be classified into three broad categories: (1) essential cognitive processes, such as observing, comparing, inferring, generalizing, hypothesizing, and reasoning inductively and deductively; (2) higher-order cognitive processes, such as problem solving, decision making, and critical and creative thinking; and (3) metacognitive processes, or literally, thinking about thinking (Presseisen, 1986).

As a classroom teacher, you can do much to encourage thinking in your students within the context of your regular classroom activities. Whenever you ask your students to look for relationships among examples or items of information, explain why a relationship exists, provide you with an additional example, explain why an existing example fits a pattern, or simply observe and describe, you're encouraging their thinking. These processes are developed with the kinds of questions you ask and the teaching strategies you use. As an illustration, let's look again at Ms. Morton's lesson on the circumference of circles and see how she prompted thinking in her students.

First, rather than give the students the value of *pi* and the formula for the circumference of a circle, her technique was to give them information that would allow them to derive both the value of *pi* and the formula on their own. Second, she provided the guidance that involved them in the essential cognitive processes. For instance, she asked questions, such as

"Look at the circles you have on the handout I've given you. What do you notice about them?"

"What patterns do you see there?"

". . . we see that the measurements aren't all exact. Why do you suppose that happened?"

"Now think about a formula we could use to find the circumference if we know the diameter."

These questions not only involved the students in the learning activity but also required them to practice the essential cognitive processes of observing, comparing, finding patterns, inferring (explaining), and generalizing (identifying a general formula)—all within the framework of inductive reasoning.

In comparing her lesson to Mr. Hite's, we see that the content was identical and the goals were very similar. The difference was in her questioning and teaching strategy. With emphasis on certain questions, she prompted thinking in her students, and you can do the same thing within the context of virtually any teaching strategy. The questions are summarized in Table 7.7.

We see that Ms. Morton incorporated several of these questions in her lesson, and because she began her lesson with data and moved to-

Table 7.7 Questions Promoting Thinking Skills

Question	Skills
1. What do you notice?	Observing
2. How are these alike or different?	Finding patterns
3. Can you give me an example?	Generalizing
4. Why? (Why is this an example? Why does this relationship exist? What told you that? and a host of others)	Inferring/Documenting inferences
5. What would happen if . . . ?	Hypothesizing

ward the general formula, her students were also involved in inductive reasoning. She could easily have asked the students for hypothetical thinking as well by asking a simple question, such as, "Now suppose that the radius were doubled. What would happen to the value of the diameter?" (or, "How would the diameter be affected?") "What would happen to the value of the circumference?" "How would *pi* be affected?" All these questions encourage hypothetical thinking on the part of the students. Ms. Morton could also have had the students engage in problem solving by giving them problems and requiring them to conclude that the solution called for finding the circumference of a circle, selecting the appropriate values, and making the calculations.

She could even have involved them in metacognitive processes by having them specify the particular processes they used in deriving the formula and the strategies they used to solve the problems.

Notice, too, that we have discussed the emphasis on thinking within the context of guided discovery. However, there is nothing that prohibits the questions from being used in an expository lesson as well.

We hope this discussion both removes some of the mystery surrounding the notion of teaching thinking skills and illustrates how teachers can readily incorporate practice in thinking in an ongoing way without any alteration in the regular curriculum. Turn now to Exercise 7.5, which is designed to reinforce your understanding of this topic.

EXERCISE 7.5

Look again at Table 7.7. Now look once more at Miss Cane's lesson and identify at least one question she asked that illustrates each of question types listed in Table 7.7. Then compare your answer to those listed in the feedback section of the chapter.

1. _____

2. _____

3. _____

4. _____

5. _____

DISCUSSION STRATEGIES

We have now completed the sections on expository and guided discovery teaching. We have found that they are planned essentially the same way but are implemented in different sequences. As a reference point for our present discussion, however, the key common characteristics are that they are both strongly teacher-directed and that they are both designed to teach specific forms of content, such as a particular concept or generalization.

Discussion strategies are quite different. They are less effective than an expository or guided discovery procedure for teaching specific content because they are typically less teacher-directed and more time-consuming. However, other important goals exist in a classroom that go beyond or are different from acquiring specific content. For example, consider the following goals:

1. To develop leadership skills
2. To summarize group opinion
3. To arrive at a consensus
4. To become an active listener
5. To appropriately handle controversy
6. To develop paraphrasing skills
7. To develop self-directed learning skills
8. To develop analysis, synthesis, and evaluative skills

There are others that could be added to the list, but you can see from those cited that an expository or discovery procedure would not be appropriate for reaching the goals. This marks the first major difference between these strategies and discussion techniques.

The second difference relates to the role of the teacher. In a discussion activity the teacher becomes less a director of learning and more a facilitator. In many ways this role is more difficult because the teacher has less control of the lesson's direction and pace. Nevertheless, the role of the teacher remains critical, for she must ensure the promotion of learning through student interaction and exchange of ideas. This can be accomplished through the teacher carefully initiating, regulating, informing, supporting, and evaluating the group activity. Let's now look at the planning and implementing phases of a discussion strategy.

Planning

While fewer actual materials are required to implement a discussion procedure than are required for an expository or discovery lesson, the thought and consideration needed are greater and will determine the success or failure of a group activity.

The bottom line in planning and implementing discussion lessons is *organization*. It is absolutely critical that the activity be carefully organized, or the activity will result in nonlearning at best or disintegrate into chaos at worst. The single biggest problem with discussion lessons is the tendency of students to drift away from the activity. Only careful organization can help prevent this problem.

There are at least five decisions that must be made when planning and organizing a discussion activity.

First, the teacher carefully considers goals. As noted previously, the goal would likely be the acquisition of a cognitive or social skill, rather than the learning of a specific concept or generalization.

Second, the teacher must decide if the activity would be best implemented in a large-group, teacher-led discussion or in small-group, student-led activities, which might be in such forms as buzz groups, a mock trial, brainstorming, case studies, role-playing, or simulation. This decision relates to the goal. If the goal is to develop leadership skills, active listening skills, or another related skill, a small-group activity would be appropriate. On the other hand, the development of analysis, synthesis, or evaluation skills should probably be teacher-directed.

Third, the teacher must consider the experience and development of the students. Young and/or inexperienced students need very explicit directions, a relatively simple task, and a short time period. As they acquire experience, they can take on more direction themselves. Discussion strategies are very developmental in this regard. A teacher hoping for success with the strategy needs a full grading period or more for the students to develop the skills for effective discussions.

Fourth, as already identified implicitly in the previous paragraph, the teacher must consider the time allotted for the activity. In general, the time given the students should be quite short. We have all had experiences where we were put into groups and we discussed the given task for a short time and then talked about everything from the weather to our clothes. This tendency to drift away from the task is one of the major problems with small groups. *A clear task that requires the students to produce something concrete in a short time period can help considerably with this problem.*

Finally, the discussion should result in a specific product such as a summary, list, series of conclusions, or something similar. The teacher in the planning stage must carefully consider the product so directions can be explicitly and thoughtfully provided.

EXERCISE 7.6

Examine the following goals and determine if they are most appropriately taught through discussion (d) or through some other technique (o) such as the expository or discovery techniques.

_____ 1. An ecology teacher wants her students to know the major causes of air pollution in a typical large city.

_____ 2. A middle school teacher would like input from his students in developing class rules for the year.

_____ 3. A language arts teacher wants her students to be able to summarize briefly the opinions of other students.

_____ 4. A literature teacher wants his students to understand the major characteristics in Steinbeck's *Tortilla Flat.*

_____ 5. A social studies teacher wants her students to determine the feasibility of nuclear power as an energy source.

Implementing

Having determined that the goal is appropriate for discussion and having considered other factors in planning, the teacher is ready to begin. As an illustration of the implementation phase in a discussion activity, read the following scenario:

Mr. Williams wanted his students to analyze and evaluate the president's constitutional right to impose a wage and price freeze without congressional approval.

He began the activity by saying, "Today we are going to analyze the president's right to make executive orders without the approval of Congress. I'm going to show you a film, and I want you to identify in the film the two positions taken and at least one item of information that supports each position. (Pause) Now tell me what you are going to do first, Tom?"

"We're going to identify the two positions on the issue."

"Exactly. Very Good. Then, what will you do next, Mary?"

"We will identify one item of information that supports each position."

"Yes, that's right, Mary. Now let's look at the film."

Mr. Williams showed the film. After he stopped the projector, he asked, "All right. What are the two positions?"

Tony volunteered, "Well, they are really simple. One position was that he had the right to impose the controls and the other was that he didn't."

"Okay," Mr. Williams said with a smile. "Now, give me an item that supports each position."

Jill raised her hand.

"Jill?"

"Inflation was running at a 12% annual rate, and some people on fixed incomes were being squeezed terribly. That supports imposing the controls."

"Tom?"

"Technically, it's unconstitutional unless a national emergency exists. While the inflation is bad, it doesn't fit the standard definition of national emergency."

"Very good, everyone. Now listen carefully. This is what we are going to do. As you walked into class today you selected a number from one to six. You also see the numbers one through six hanging on the walls of the room. When I tell you to move, I want all the people with ones to group themselves under the one, those with twos under the two and so on. Now look at your numbers. In each group, all but one of you has the number in numeral form and one has the number written out. The person with the number spelled out will be the group leader. This was done at random, and during the course of the year you'll each be a leader more than once. Leaders, it's your responsibility to appoint a recorder and lead the discussion. Recorders, you must summarize the information and report to the whole class. Each group's task is to take a position regarding the issues presented in the film, document the position in writing, and orally report your position to the whole class. Take either side of the issue. You must come to a group agreement. If one of you disagrees strongly, you may make a minority statement when reporting to the class."

Mr. Williams then reviewed the task with the class, as he had before showing the film. Finally, he said. "You have 15 minutes, starting now. Begin."

Mr. Williams then moved from group to group and announced the time at 5-minute intervals. At precisely the 15-minute point, he called the class together.

"We didn't have time to finish," Sharon complained.

"We couldn't come to a consensus," Pam said from another group.

"Those are good points," Mr. Williams said sympathetically. "Let's discuss both of those problems."

With that he explained why he only gave them 15 minutes and praised them for their diligence in the groups. He also explained that in time they would become more efficient. He then began a large-group discussion on ways of reaching a consensus. Finally, he had each group report their results and said they would analyze the results in greater detail the following day.

Turn now to Exercise 7.7. We want to particularly emphasize this exercise, and we strongly encourage you to be certain to read the feedback panel for this exercise.

EXERCISE 7.7

Consider the lesson illustrated in the scenario you just read and answer the questions that follow.

1. Mr. Williams had four goals that he wanted to develop in the lesson. Identify the four goals.

_____

_____

_____

_____

2. Mr. Williams used both large- and small-group techniques. Identify the portion of his lesson devoted to each.

_____

_____

_____

3. Describe how Mr. Williams took the experience and development of his students into account.

_____

_____

_____

4. What provisions did Mr. Williams make to ensure that the students stayed on the task to the greatest extent possible? There are at least four factors you should identify.

_____

_____

_____

_____

5. Consider our approach as authors. In presenting the description of implementing discussion activities, was our approach essentially expository, or was it more inclined toward discovery? Explain your answer, making reference to the text description.

_____

_____

_____

INQUIRY TEACHING

An Overview

In the first two sections of this chapter we discussed guided discovery, expository, and discussion techniques and expanded our discussion of guided discovery by showing how it can be used to help students practice essential cognitive processes. In this section we want to expand further our discussion of teaching strategies by describing the *inquiry* approach to instruction and how it relates to higher-order thinking through problem solving at the same time as content is being taught.

Inquiry teaching involves providing students with content-related problems which serve as the focus for the class's research activities. In working with a problem, students generate hypotheses or tentative solutions to the problem, gather data relevant to these hypotheses, and evaluate these data to arrive at a conclusion. In working with this strategy, students learn not only content associated with the problem but also procedures for solving problems in the future. The application of this teaching strategy is illustrated in the anecdote that follows:

Ms. Schmidt, a middle school teacher, was doing a unit on media and their effect on American life. During the course of the unit, her class had learned about the history of different media forms in America—the long life of the newspaper, the invention of the radio and its growth, and finally, the recent impact of television on our lives. As they investigated each of these topics, the role of advertising in each of these media was discussed. From students' comments about advertising, she realized that they didn't really understand how advertising functioned in the field of media. Therefore, she decided to let her students gather some information about this topic. She began the activity by saying, "We've mentioned advertising a number of times in our discussion of media. What are some of the things we've found out? Jack?"

"Well, advertising helps manufacturers tell people about their products."

"Also, it helps to pay for the cost of some media, like newspapers and magazines," Chad remarked. "We don't have to pay as much for them because they have advertising in them."

"And TV and radio are almost totally paid for by advertising," added Jim.

"Good, now I'd like for us to take a closer look at TV advertising and see if we can understand how it works. But first let's see how much we already know about TV commercials. Sharon?"

"Well, they're too long, and there are too many of them."

"Okay, anyone else? (pause) No one, hmmm. Well, let's see if we can ask some questions that would help us find out more about TV advertising. Pretend that there is a man here from the network to answer questions. What kinds of questions might you ask him? Let's break up into our small groups and see if we can make a list of questions."

After a period of time, the groups came back together again to share their ideas. As they did this, they found that the following two questions commonly occurred:

How often do TV commercials occur?
What kinds of products are advertised most?

When Ms. Schmidt asked the class to form hypotheses about the answers to these questions, a heated debate arose. Some people thought that commercials came on every five minutes, whereas others thought they came on every fifteen minutes. Also, the members of the class disagreed about the major products advertised on TV. Some said they were toys, others said beer and cars, and still others claimed they were food and detergent. To settle these arguments, Ms. Schmidt said, "A lot of you have different ideas about the answers to these questions. Let's write them on the board and call them hypotheses, and then let's try to gather some information to see which of these are correct."

Hypotheses

1. Commercials occur every five minutes.
2. Commercials occur every fifteen minutes.
3. The most commonly advertised products are
   a. toys
   b. beer
   c. cars
   d. food
   e. detergents

Then she added, "Well, at least we found that we don't all agree about the answers to some of these questions. Now how can we go about finding which of these hypotheses are correct? Any ideas?"

Some members of the class suggested that someone write to the stations for the answers. Others suggested that perhaps the answers could be found in magazines or books, while others suggested finding the answers by actually watching TV. After some discussion, they decided to break into teams to gather data by watching TV. In organizing for this, the class decided that each team would watch at a different time but that they all would watch the same station. They agreed to use clocks to time the commercials and to write down what they found in notebooks to share with the class. After a week, they brought their information back to class, and Ms. Schmidt helped them to organize the information into a chart, a part of which is shown in Table 7.8.

Ms. Schmidt began the discussion by saying, "Look at the first three columns of the chart and tell me what you see. Tony?"

"Well, on the same channel there are different kinds of programs during the day."

"Anything else? Terry?"

Table 7.8 TV-Viewing Chart

Time of Day	Type of Program	Product Advertised	Length of Commercials	Intervals of Commercials
early morning	cartoons	cereal toys	20 sec. 30 sec. 45 sec.	10 min. 10 min.
midday	serials talk shows	detergents food household goods	20 sec. 30 sec. 45 sec.	10 min. 8 min.
evening	sit-coms specials movies	snacks beer cars	25 sec. 35 sec. 45 sec.	15 min. 12 min.
weekend afternoon	sports	beer cars	25 sec. 35 sec. 45 sec.	15 min. 12 min.

"And there are different kinds of commercials during the day, too."

"Good, and why do you think there are different kinds of programs on at different times of the day? Josh?"

"Because different people like to watch different things."

"Anyone else? Cassie?"

"Also because people watch TV at different times. Like the only time my Dad gets to watch TV is at night and on weekends."

"And so what does the information we gathered tell us about our third hypothesis? What is the most commonly advertised product? Jim?"

"Well, it depends on when you watch. If it's during the day, the products are for kids and mothers, but at night they're for the whole family and for dads."

The class then continued to analyze the data they had collected, using the hypotheses they had formed to guide their discussion.

Let's pause for a second now and take a look at this lesson to see how it was an example of inquiry.

An inquiry lesson typically consists of four parts. In the first part, some problem is encountered by the class. Ms. Schmidt initiated this phase of the lesson by asking the class how much they knew about television commercials. In the second phase of an inquiry activity, hypotheses are formed. *Hypotheses* are tentative suggestions about how the world operates. They are, then, ideas about how the data that will be gathered might turn out. Ms. Schmidt wrote these hypotheses on the board for the whole class to see. The third part of an inquiry lesson involves data gathering. The class did this by watching TV and noting the length and kind of commercials that occurred. The final phase of an inquiry lesson involves data analysis in which the data gathered are compared to the hypotheses formulated. These steps are summarized in Table 7.9.

The inquiry strategy can be a valuable tool in a beginning teacher's repertoire for several reasons. One is that it provides the teacher with a means of teaching students problem-solving skills. By seeing how problems are solved in the classroom, they are provided with a model to follow in solving problems in other areas of their lives. In addition, the stages in the inquiry model provide students with practice in information gathering and analysis, skills with wide application in other facets of life. Inquiry is an excellent means for helping students

Table 7.9 Steps in Inquiry Lessons

Students: (with teacher guidance)	1. Identify problem
	2. Form hypotheses
	3. Gather data
	4. Analyze data and form conclusion

practice the higher-order thinking skills we discussed earlier in the chapter. A third reason for using inquiry strategies is that they provide alternate means of teaching content to students who may already be saturated with more teacher-oriented, expository techniques. Because students are actively involved in each of the phases, inquiry activities can be a motivating alternative to other approaches.

EXERCISE 7.8

Read the following anecdote, which describes a college instructor using the inquiry approach and then answer the accompanying questions. Compare your answers with the ones given in the feedback section at the end of the chapter.

Mr. Hayes's methods class had been talking about factors that influence the effectiveness of different types of media. He began this new lesson by saying, "Now I'd like to have us take a look at factors that influence the readability of different texts. Let's take a second to think about factors that might influence how easy something is to read. Any ideas? Cal?"

"How about the number of pictures?"

"Okay, that's an idea. Anyone else?"

"Also the kinds of words. Longer words are usually harder to understand than shorter ones," added Leeann.

"And the length of sentences, too. The longer the sentence, the harder it is to understand," Mike contributed.

"Another thing is the number of graphs and charts," said Christine. "These make a book hard to understand."

"Fine," answered Mr. Hayes. "Now does anyone have any suggestions of how we could find whether or not these ideas are correct?"

The class discussed the matter for a while and decided to look at textbooks at different levels in terms of the variables they had mentioned. They selected texts at the first-, fourth-, and eighth-grade levels and compared them to high school and college texts. In comparing them, they counted the average numbers of the following: syllables per word, words per sentence, illustrations per ten pages, and graphs or charts per ten pages. The results of this investigation were then compiled into the chart shown in Table 7.10.

The lesson then continued with Mr. Hayes asking, "What do the data tell us about our hypothesis linking grade level and number of syllables per word, Don?"

Table 7.10 Information on Texts

Level	Syllables	Words	Illustrations	Charts or Graphs
First-Grade	1.2	6.2	6.0	0.0
Fourth-Grade	1.3	8.4	5.1	0.0
Eighth-Grade	1.4	12.8	4.4	2.1
High School	1.6	15.0	3.1	2.4
College	1.7	17.0	2.0	2.5

"It was correct because we can see that the number of syllables per word increases with each
ade level."

"Okay, and how about the number of words per sentence? Kerry?"

The lesson continued with the class analyzing each of the columns in terms of the hypotheses
ey had formed.

where the following phases occurred in the anecdote.

)lem identification

_____

_____

_____

mulation of hypotheses

_____

_____

_____

ta gathering

_____

_____

_____

alysis of data

_____

_____

_____

Planning Inquiry Lessons

In planning for inquiry activities, the first step is identifying a problem
in a particular content area. Essentially, this involves examining the
areas of content being taught and determining if any of these can be
taught using a problem-solving approach. This isn't always possible,
but when it is, it allows the teacher to teach both content and inquiry
skills at the same time.

Often these problem situations arise spontaneously in the course
of other lessons. When this happens, the teacher has to be able to
recognize situations like this in order to capitalize on them. For
example, one of the authors witnessed an elementary science lesson in
which the class was discussing some seeds they had planted weeks ear-

lier. Some of the seeds had sprouted while others hadn't. The class was trying to figure out why. The teacher seized upon this situation to initiate an inquiry lesson focusing on what factors cause seeds to germinate. The class then proceeded to generate hypotheses about these factors and to investigate them by germinating seeds under various growing conditions.

In this case, the inquiry lesson followed naturally from a question or a problem that arose in a previous lesson. This is an especially effective way to initiate inquiry lessons for several reasons. One is that students can view the lesson as a functional response to a need rather than a perhaps nonfunctional topic imposed by the teacher. In addition, students are able to see the utility of the inquiry process in solving problems that they encounter in their environment.

Often however, inquiry lessons do not arise naturally from problems encountered in class. Or, a teacher may have a particular topic that needs to be covered. In situations like these, the teacher must be able to recognize times when inquiry activities are beneficial and structure the content appropriately. Typically, inquiry strategies are most appropriate when there is some type of causal relationship involved in the content area. For example, in the science lesson mentioned, the inquiry lesson focused on factors that caused or influenced germination. In a similar manner, the lesson on readability focused on factors that influenced or affected readability. When areas of content are addressed in this way, the first phase of the inquiry lesson, identifying a problem, is already satisfied.

The second task in planning for an inquiry lesson is to arrange for the data-gathering process. This doesn't pose any major problem if the materials needed are readily available, as was the case in the lesson on TV commercials. At other times, the teacher must plan ahead to make sure that the necessary materials will be available when needed. For example, the instructor in the methods class had to make arrangements for the availability of textbooks at different levels, and the science teacher had to bring pots, seeds, and potting soil to class to allow her students to gather data about germinating seeds. Anticipating these needs ahead of time allows the process of inquiry to proceed with a minimum of wasted time and effort. Others would argue that this efficiency imposes an artificial smoothness on the inquiry process. These same people contend that a major part of the value of inquiry lessons is to provide students with realistic experiences with problem solving. In other words, students should be given the opportunity to devise their own data-gathering procedures. Providing them with this freedom takes longer but allows them to see how inquiry works in the real world. To make the problem solving too efficient artificially distorts the picture that students get of the inquiry process. The critics who say this are more interested in the process of inquiry than in the content taught. Other more content-oriented teachers would contend that time constraints limit the amount of time that can be spent in any particular lesson, and that teachers should go ahead and help students by arranging for the data-gathering procedures. This is another educational decision that you as a professional will have to make if you decide to use inquiry strategies.

EXERCISE 7.9

Examine the following topics and determine whether they could be taught using an inquiry approach (i) or whether a discovery or expository approach (d/e) would be more appropriate. Then compare your answers with the ones given in the feedback section at the end of the chapter.

_____ 1. An elementary teacher wants students to know things that affect plant growth.

_____ 2. A language arts teacher wants students to understand the term *gerund*.

_____ 3. A health teacher wants students to know the relationship between exercising and pulse rate.

_____ 4. A home economics teacher wants students to know the effect volume buying has on the cost per unit.

_____ 5. A social studies teacher wants students to know the difference between capitalism and socialism.

Implementing Inquiry Lessons

As previously described, the first phase of an inquiry lesson involves presenting a problem. The problem provides the focus for the remainder of the lesson as well as giving direction to the next phase of implementation — making hypotheses. The problem can occur as the result of a situation encountered in a previous lesson or can be initiated by the teacher. When the latter is done, it is sometimes helpful to provide a focusing event that captures the students' attention. For example, a teacher who wanted to teach a lesson on the factors affecting the preservation of food might bring out two apples that had been cut open at the same time, one refrigerated and one not. The teacher would then ask the class to observe the condition of the two and try to explain why this occurred. The focusing event in this lesson provides a natural and tangible starting point for the inquiry lesson.

Similar events could be constructed for other types of inquiry lessons. For example, the teacher in the lesson on television advertising might have turned on a television prior to the lesson and asked the students to observe the commercials. In a similar manner, the methods instructor might have read two different passages on the same topic, one written at the fourth-grade and the other at the college level. His beginning question might be, "How and why are they the same? How are they different?" In all of the examples, the focusing event provides a concrete experience to which the students can relate. Focusing events can be motivating if they're eye-catching and helpful in getting students to see the relevance of the problem to the world around them. However the problem is introduced to the students, though, the formal statement of it should be written on the board or overhead for all to see and consider.

After the students have had time to think about the problem, the teacher should encourage them to offer ideas about solutions. Often these hypotheses are produced spontaneously; at other times it is necessary for the teacher to prompt the students to offer them. For example, the teacher wanting her students to focus on factors affecting food spoilage and preservation might ask, "What kinds of things do we do in our kitchens to keep food from spoiling?" or, "If you were going on a week-long hike, what kinds of foods would you take?" Answers to these questions would help students to identify factors that might be included in hypotheses.

Once the hypotheses have been formed, the next task for the class is to gather data to test these hypotheses. The data-gathering process can take place in several ways. It can occur as an in-class group activity or as an individual activity outside of class time. Probably the major factors to be considered here are time and equipment. If classroom time is scarce or the equipment needed is unavailable in class, then the data-gathering process can be assigned as an out-of-class activity. Having students gather data in their homes can have several advantages. One is that it reinforces the idea that inquiry is not just something that's done in the classroom. Also, having students gather data at home provides an opportunity for parents to become involved in the activity.

The final phase of the inquiry process is data analysis. The major goal of this phase of the activity is to examine the hypotheses, while analyzing the information gathered, to determine if they agree. If they don't, the hypotheses need to be revised and alternative conclusions offered. In essence, this part of the lesson involves a summing up of the activities of the lesson into some types of conclusions that students can take with them. These conclusions would form the major content outcomes of the lesson. Because of this, these conclusions should be written on the board for all the class.

As mentioned previously, organizing the data in some way facilitates the process of analysis. This can be done by placing the information in charts or by graphing it. The experience of wrestling with data and attempting to come up with an optimal organizational pattern is an educational experience in itself, in addition to its help in facilitating the data analysis. Often students will have had no previous experience with this process and will experience difficulty. The teacher who first tries to involve students in the analysis of data should not get discouraged. This is a skill that can be taught, and the best way of doing it is through the experience itself.

SUMMARY

Chapter 7 has been devoted to a discussion of four different teaching strategies. Each strategy builds on and employs the questioning skills discussed in Chapter 6. All are designed to help the teacher reach specific goals. The first two, expository and guided discovery, are designed to reach the same goals but are sequenced differently and require different skills from the teacher. Guided discovery is typically more motivating for students and is more effective for promoting student thinking skills than is expository. However, expository methods are usually more time-efficient.

Not all goals can be reached with guided discovery or expository methods, however. For goals involving organization skills, group work, human relations, and affective abilities, *discussion* strategies can be effective if they're carefully organized.

Inquiry methods are useful for developing problem-solving abilities in students within the context of the content they're learning. Inquiry problems often arise spontaneously during the course of typical learning activities, and alert teachers can seize on the opportunities to develop inquiry problems as a natural outcome of other activities. When they don't arise spontaneously, they can be planned in advance and implemented using other activities as the context.

REFERENCES

Ausubel, D. (1968). *Educational psychology: A cognitive view.* New York: Holt, Rinehart & Winston.

Ausubel, D., & Robinson, F. (1969). *School learning: An introduction to educational psychology.* New York: Holt, Rinehart & Winston.

Barnes, B., & Clawson, E. (1975). Do advance organizers facilitate learning? *Review of Educational Research, 45,* 637–59.

Baron, J., & Sternberg, R. (Eds.). (1987). *Teaching thinking skills: Theory and practice.* New York: W. H. Freeman.

Bourne, L., Ekstrand, B., & Dominawski, R. (1971). *The psychology of thinking.* Englewood Cliffs, NJ: Prentice-Hall.

Bruner, J., Goodnow, J., & Austin, G. (1956). *A study of thinking.* New York: John Wiley.

Clark, D. (1971). Teaching concepts in the classroom: A set of teaching precriptions derived from experimental research. *Journal of Educational Psychology, 62,* 253–78.

Eggen, P., & Kauchak, D. (1988). *Strategies for teachers: Teaching content and thinking skills* (2nd ed.). Englewood Cliffs, NJ: Prentice-Hall.

Feldman, K. (1980). The effects of number of positive and negative instances concept definition, and of mathematical concepts. *Review of Educational Research, 50,* 33–67.

Frayer, D. (1970). Effect of number of instances and emphasis of relevant attribute values on mastery of geometric concepts by fourth and sixth grade children. Research and Development Center for Cognitive Learning, Technical Report 116.

Good, T. (1983). Research in classroom teaching. In L. Shulman & G. Sykes (Eds.), *Handbook of teaching and policy* (pp. 42–80). New York: Longman.

Goodlad, J. (1984). *A place called school.* New York: McGraw-Hill.

Klausmeier, H. (1976). Instructional design and the teaching of concepts. In J. Levin & V. Allen (Eds.), *Cognitive learning in children.* New York: Academic Press.

Klausmeier, H., Ghatala, E., & Frayer, D. (1974). *Conceptual learning and development: A cognitive view.* New York: Academic Press.

Markle, S., & Tiemonn, P. (1970). *Really understanding concepts.* Champaign, IL: Stipes.

Nickerson, R., Perkins, D., & Smith, E. (1985). *The teaching of thinking.* Hillsdale, NJ: Erlbaum.

Paul, R. (1984). Critical thinking: Fundamental to education in a free society. *Educational Leadership, 42,* 4–14.

Pratton, J., & Hales, L. (1986). The effects of active participation on student learning. *Journal of Educational Research, 79,* 210–215.

Presseisen, B. (1986). *Thinking skills: Research and practice.* Washington, DC: National Education Association.

Rosenshine, B., & Stevens, R. (1986). Teaching functions. In M. Wittrock (Ed.), *Handbook of research on teaching* (3rd ed.) (pp. 376–391). New York: Macmillan.

Shimmerlik, S. (1978). Organization theory and memory for prose: A review of the literature. *Review of Educational Research, 48,* 103–20.

Tennyson, R. (1978). *Content structure and instructional control strategies in concept acquisition.* Paper presented at the meeting of the American Psychological Association, Toronto.

Underwood, B., & Schulz, R. (1960). *Meaningfulness and verbal learning.* Chicago: Lippincott.

EXERCISE FEEDBACK

EXERCISE 7.1

1. (d) Discovery. The lesson began with the students gathering and anlayzing data and forming the abstraction that the sum of the interior angles of a triangle is 180 degrees.
2. (d) Discovery. The sequence of the lesson was from examples to abstractions, and the class formed the abstraction themselves rather than having the teacher state it.
3. (e) Expository. The lesson began with the teacher defining the concept *set* and illustrating the concept with examples.
4. (d) Discovery. Students were provided with examples of inferences and then formed their own definition. Miss Kirk then reinforced the concept by having the class locate additional examples.

EXERCISE 7.2

1. The problem with the examples is that they don't show the interaction of the concepts in the generalization. The generalization links the concepts of strenuousness and calories. To illustrate this, the instructor would need to supplement the pictures with information about the calories burned in a given time period in each of the sports.
2. The examples used to illustrate this concept are inadequate because they only relate to one of the two kinds of verbs, action verbs. In addition, all of these verbs were in the past tense, thus giving students the impression that all verbs have to be in the past tense. These would need to be supplemented with additional examples like the following to give students a complete picture of the concept.

    The team was first on the floor.

    I am not going to be late again.

3. These two sequences of examples differ in terms of the order of difficulty or familiarity of examples. Because the initial examples used in sequence A are more familiar than the initial examples of sequence B, the goal would be attained more quickly using sequence A. Therefore, a teacher who wanted to teach this concept as quickly as possible or who wanted a more easily understood sequence for a given group of students would use sequence A.

EXERCISE 7.3

1. Mr. Hanes was attempting to teach the concept *hyperbole*. He did this in an expository manner by first defining the concept and then illustrating it with examples.
2. He organized the content by linking the new concept to the superordinate concept of *figures of speech*. This told the class how hyperboles were similar to metaphors and similes.
3. In the lesson, Mr. Hanes failed to let the students classify his examples. This wasn't a major mistake because he still had students explain his own classifications and also had students provide their own examples of the concept. However, by not having them classify his examples, he missed an additional opportunity to gather data about the students' knowledge of the concept.

EXERCISE 7.4

1. a. The teacher began the lesson by presenting the matched sets of blocks and books and asking the group to make observations.
   b. Additional examples were provided when she brought out the trucks and the spoons and then the other objects.
   c. The students classified the examples when they told the teacher whether the sets were equal or not.
   d. The students provided their own examples when they constructed equal sets of their own.
2. In discovery lessons, the responsibility for forming the abstraction is placed on the students. Mrs. Steere did this in her lesson when she had them come up with the idea that all the matched groups were the same in terms of number. This is really

the concept of *equal*. Mrs. Steere was correct in providing the symbol and name for the concept since the students had already acquired the idea. No amount of prompting would have gotten them to arrive at the symbol or concept name if they hadn't already have known it. It should be emphasized that what students discover in a discovery lesson is the *meaning* of the abstraction, not the *symbol* or *word* for it.

EXERCISE 7.5

The following questions illustrate the types specified in Table 7.7.

Observing	"Class look at the words on the board and tell me what you see."
Finding patterns	"Now look at the other words and compare them to *beat*."
	"Can anyone describe the pattern we see in all these words?"
	(Notice in response to this question that Missy said, "If you have two vowels together, the first one is long." She *generalized* in making this response.)
Generalizing	"Now give me an example that fits our pattern."
Inferring/Documenting inferences	"Why do you say so?"
Hypothesizing	"Suppose *boat* were spelled *B–a–o–t*. If we were following this rule, how would we pronounce the word?"

EXERCISE 7.6

1. This topic involves the transmission of information and would be best taught by a discovery or expository procedure. A next step for this topic could be to have students develop a plan to solve these problems.
2. Here is an example of discussion groups being used to elicit student input on classroom management rules, a topic discussed further in Chapter 9.
3. This is a goal that could be implemented in a large-group discussion activity. Large-group discussion would be preferable because it would allow the teacher to give immediate feedback to each student and other students could learn from the feedback as well. In a small-group activity the teacher would have difficulty determining to what extent the summary was accurate.
4. This goal involves acquiring knowledge and would not be an appropriate topic for a discussion.
5. This would be an excellent discussion topic.

EXERCISE 7.7

1. Mr. Williams's goals were for his students:
   a. to take and support a position with evidence
   b. to develop leadership skills

    c. to develop summarizing and speaking skills

    d. to develop techniques for arriving at a group concensus

    His first goal was stated explicitly, and the other three were more implicit.

2. Mr. Williams used a large-group activity initially when he first showed the film and asked for one item of information that supported each position. He also used a large-group procedure in discussing procedures for moving to a concensus. He planned further large-group discussion for the following day after the groups reported their respective positions. He used a small-group procedure in having the groups take and document a position. The small groups were also used in developing leadership, recording data, and summarizing information.

3. Mr. Smith understood that his students wouldn't be efficient in this activity. This was an attempt at using a discussion strategy when the students were inexperienced. He planned for their leadership development when he noted that each would have more than one chance to be a leader. Also, he discussed ways of increasing efficiency and techniques for reaching a consensus. Presumably, he would review all this prior to the next discussion lesson, and gradually the students' skill would increase with each discussion lesson.

4. Mr. Williams's organization and lesson development were excellent.

    First, he helped the students to have the necessary background by showing the film which provided them with all the information needed to carry on the discussion.

    Second, he gave very explicit directions prior to watching the film and reinforced the directions by asking students to repeat them before he turned on the projector. He also gave very precise directions for getting into the groups and in identifying the task for each group.

    Third, Mr. Williams gave the class only 15 minutes to complete the activity. It purposely was short, perhaps too short. However, considering the students' developmental level, more time probably would have become inefficient. He knew that the students were inexperienced and planned to help them develop their skills through a series of discussion activities over the course of the year.

    Finally, Mr. Williams required a product. The students had to take their position and support it in writing. These results were then reported to the whole class.

5. We used a form of discovery approach in describing implementation of discussions. We presented an example in scenario form, and the conclusions are essentially described in this feedback. This is the reason we emphasized Exercise 7.7 and particularly its feedback.

EXERCISE 7.8

1. Problem identification occurred at the beginning of the lesson when the teacher asked the class to identify factors that affected the readability of a text.

2. Hypotheses were formulated when the class listed variables that would affect readability.

3. The class gathered data when they analyzed the different texts in terms of the variables listed in the hypotheses.

4. Mr. Hayes helped the class analyze the data by asking questions that required the students to compare the data in the chart to the hypotheses they had formed.

    Several additional comments should be made about this lesson. First, note that the teacher identified the problem to be studied rather than having the class do it. This method of identifying the problem occurs when the teacher has a specific topic to be covered. Alternate ways of initiating the inquiry process will be discussed in the planning section that follows. Also, note that the teacher in this lesson organized the information that the class collected into a chart, as we have also seen earlier. Organizing data in this manner is not essential in an inquiry lesson but can be helpful when there are large amounts of data to consider. Organization makes the data easier to interpret and analyze in terms of the hypotheses formed earlier.

EXERCISE 7.9

1. (i) Inquiry. The teacher might begin the lesson by asking, ''What kinds of things influence how fast a plant grows?'' After hypotheses were formed, these could be investigated by growing plants and comparing their growth rates under different conditions.
2. (d/e) Discovery or Expository. Since a gerund is a concept, it would be more effectively taught using a discovery or an expository approach.
3. (i) Inquiry. This topic involves a cause-and-effect relationship. Such a lesson might begin with the teacher asking, ''What things affect how fast your heart beats?'' The class might then investigate this topic by surveying its members in terms of how much they exercise and then compare their respective pulse rates.
4. (i) Inquiry. The teacher could begin the lesson by asking, ''What factors affect the price of a product?'' The students could gather data relating to this question by checking the prices of different kinds and quantities of products.
5. (d/e) Discovery or Expository. Since these two terms are concepts, they would be better taught with a discovery or an expository lesson.

8 | Mastery Learning: An Implementation Strategy

Introduction

Mastery learning is rapidly being introduced in our nation's schools. School systems and individual schools throughout the nation are implementing mastery units of instruction and entire courses of study. An outstanding example of systemwide implementation is found in Johnson City, New York, and thousands of schools in Chicago, New York, Denver, New Orleans, Jacksonville, San Jose, and other cities are using mastery learning.

A growing trend is also evidenced by the numbers of workshops, institutes, and presentations at local, state and national conferences that involve mastery learning. One of the reasons for this widespread implementation is the amount of research that continues to support its effectiveness. Block's works in 1971 and 1974, reviewing literature, were highly supportive. Okey's research, published in the *Journal of Teacher Education*, involved more than 300 students in 26 classes and, in every instance, the pupils in the mastery classes outperformed the nonmastery pupils when the teacher followed the mastery plan.

Hyman and Cohen, in *Educational Leadership*, presented 10 conclusions after studying 3,000 schools' experiences with a learning-for-mastery curriculum for 15 years. They concluded that the learning-for-mastery curriculum is consistently more effective than traditional curriculums and that students in mastery learning environments master more objectives during a given period of time compared to students in nonmastery environments.

In their book *Effective Instruction*, Levin and Long reviewed mastery learning and presented current studies which support their position that mean performance level of mastery groups is significantly higher than the levels of nonmastery groups.

More recently, Whiting and Render (1987) investigated the cognitive student learning outcomes of 16 semesters of a mastery learning approach that involved 2,319 students. The data collected supported the authors' hypothesis that mastery learning does produce successful learning experiences in that this approach elevated learning to in excess of an 80% level from students who were not learning at the 25% level before their exposure to mastery learning.

These works are examples of the large amount of research which supports our position that mastery learning can be more effective than traditional methods.

An additional and equally important reason for the widespread implementation of mastery learning is that it can be easily and efficiently installed in the traditional classroom setting. Before viewing this implementation, however, let's briefly focus our attention on the basic mastery concept.

In 1963, John B. Carroll presented a conceptual model which, in its least complex form, stated that if students are given sufficient time to attain an acceptable level (regarding a specific skill or competency) and they use that time efficiently, they can succeed at the task at hand.

In 1968 Benjamin Bloom developed a practical model, based upon Carroll's work, which emphasized variations in learning time and learning materials. These variables, as pointed out by Jeter, can be easily adapted in ordinary classroom instruction and can be used at all grade levels and in all subject areas.

OBJECTIVES

After completing Chapter 8, you should be able to accomplish the following objective:

> For you as a pre/inservice teacher to increase your awareness of mastery learning so that, when given a list of statements discussing the characteristics of mastery learning, you will be able to correctly identify appropriate characteristics with 80% accuracy.

THE TRADITIONAL MODEL

When a teacher uses the traditional setting, or model, she begins with an objective and presents primary instruction to the entire group. Primary instruction is most often presented in the form of lectures, textbook readings, teacher-led discussions, mediated presentations, drills, seatwork, or possible combinations of any of these procedures. The critical point to be made is that all the students are involved in the same activity at the same time.

After the primary instruction, the teacher issues formal examinations, referred to in mastery learning as summative evaluations, in order to measure and evaluate student achievement. The teacher then moves on to the next objective regardless of the results of the examination on the first objective. As shown in Figure 8.1, this cycle of objective–primary instruction–examination–objective is repeated until the course content or curriculum has been taught.

Before we focus on how mastery learning can be incorporated into the traditional model, it is critical to note at the onset that in using the term *traditional*, we are not implying that all teachers utilize such an approach. However, it would be difficult to deny that a sizeable number of teachers do employ such a model.

Obj. #1 ⟶ Primary Instruction ⟶ Examination ⟶ Obj. #2

Figure 8.1 The Traditional Model

TRADITIONAL AND MASTERY MODELS

Mastery learning is an individualized approach that readily lends itself to implementation in a traditional environment. As with traditional teaching, the instructor using the mastery model begins with an objective but quickly inserts a step prior to the primary instruction. This step is a preassessment. The purposes of a preassessment are to determine if the students have the prerequisite skills to enable them to begin the unit of study and to establish whether or not the students have already mastered the unit's objectives. The pretest, because of the information it provides, is critical to the effectiveness of the unit of study because, according to Bloom, there is a direct relationship between student involvement in learning and prerequisite skills and knowledge.

The mastery learning teacher is now ready to begin the primary instruction which is undertaken in exactly the same way as presented in the traditional model. Lectures, readings, and other materials are offered and, again, all the students are involved in the same activity. It is therefore obvious that mastery learning begins with group-based instruction, not individualized programs. This feature makes it possible to readily incorporate mastery learning into a traditional setting, as shown in Figure 8.2.

Unlike the traditional model in which formal testing takes place at this point, the mastery model requires formative evaluations, sometimes referred to as progress checks or diagnostic tests. The purpose of these evaluations, issued immediately after the primary instruction for each objective, is to determine whether students are making progress toward the desired outcomes. Because a unit of instruction generally includes a number of objectives involving, as Bloom states, subjects broken down into short, well-defined tasks which may be sequential in nature, formative evaluations are employed throughout the unit. In this way, problem areas may be identified and remediated prior to formal or summative evaluations.

These progress checks are not graded so that the teacher may identify difficulties in a nonthreatening environment. In the event the formative evaluation shows the student is having no difficulty with the objective at hand, that student might (1) move on to the (next) objective, (2) become involved in enrichment activities, or (3) formally test out on the objective completed.

In the event the formative evaluation shows problem areas, the student is offered alternative activities, sometimes referrred to as correctives. These activities allow for self-pacing or additional time and additional learning materials, two critical components of mastery learning. These two features, time and materials, coupled with preassessments, formatives, and enrichments set mastery learning apart from traditional teaching.

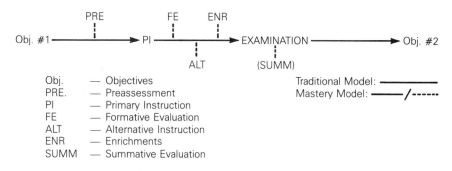

Figure 8.2   The Combined Traditional/Mastery Model

It is important to note at this point that Levin and Long list active learning time, feedback and corrective procedures, and instructional cues as three critical variables that affect classroom learning and instruction. Their entire work, *Effective Instruction,* is devoted to these variables and the authors conclude that if a teacher is successful in implementing one or more of these processes, there should be noticeable differences in students within a relatively short period of time. Such differences include increased achievement, more positive attitudes, and greater interest in and motivation for learning.

Needless to say, correctives are a cornerstone of mastery learning, while the other two variables are key considerations.

Once correctives or alternative instruction has been completed, students are checked for progress once again, a cycle which repeats itself until the student is ready to move to other objectives or formal examinations. It may be possible to provide situations in which students are formally tested at different times and begin additional objectives at different times, but this will depend upon classroom size, enrollments, materials, and other variables.

If it is necessary for all the students to begin a following objective together, enrichments and alternatives should parallel each other, with a formal examination (summative evaluation) or new instruction providing closure of a unit.

Before we turn to a discussion of the complete mastery model, let us conclude this comparison by emphasizing once again that a constantly increasing body of research coupled with widespread implementation supports our view that performance level and student achievement are higher in mastery learning environments when compared to traditional settings. This is generally so because students learn at different paces and require different materials. Mastery learning meets both of these needs.

THE COMPLETE MASTERY MODEL

Earlier, we introduced the basic mastery model and showed how it can be incorporated in a traditional setting. Now let us focus on the complete mastery model, examine its parts, and suggest techniques to implement it.

Let us begin by establishing that mastery learning basically involves three tracks: the main line track, the enrichment line track, and the alternative or corrective line track. Although we discuss the model in terms of tracks, it is a misconception that mastery does not incorporate elements of individualized instruction; to the contrary, individualization is promoted within two of the three tracks. To begin our study of the complete mastery model, let us analyze the components of the main line track.

The instruction begins with establishing an objective and then pretesting students. If the student is to be in the main line track, the preassessment will have to establish that the student has satisfied the prerequisite or entry behavior skills and the student is not familiar with the skills or objectives of the unit of instruction.

Two further observations regarding preassessments are useful at this point. The first is that it is easier to offer one preassessment which is designed to cover all the objectives in a given unit than to try to pretest individual objectives. Second, if the units of instruction are se-

Preassessments are vital in the planning of student learning experiences.

quential in nature, a summative evaluation for unit 1 would serve as a preassessment for unit 2.

Immediately after the preassessment, the student encounters the primary instruction. Again, primary instruction usually involves lectures, text readings, and various classroom activities and/or mediated presentations. Once the primary instruction has been completed, the student undergoes a formative evaluation which, in the main line track, would be completed successfully. At this point, the student would either proceed to the summative evaluation, if one is scheduled for the objective under study, or move on to the next objective. The reason a summative evaluation might not be available at this point is that it is not unusual to offer summatives for more than one objective as opposed to offering summatives for each objective.

After undertaking the summative evaluation or moving on to the next objective, the student has completed the main line track for that given objective. It is obvious at this point when following the main line track that the student does not engage in enrichment activities and is not in need of alternatives or correctives. Self-pacing is critical here if the student is to be allowed to move on. If it is not possible to send the student ahead, the student may have to move from the main line to the enrichment track.

As a final observation regarding summatives which frequently conclude main line tracks, the early mastery learning literature suggests that mastery learning units be designed to cover approximately 2 weeks of instruction and include one summative evaluation at the conclusion of the unit. Increased numbers of teachers today believe that one summative evaluation per unit of instruction puts too much pressure on the students, and they suggest administering summative evaluations at intervals throughout the unit. The number of evaluations would, of course, vary depending on the unit's length and complexity.

Now let us turn our attention to the alternative or corrective track. Once again, the instruction begins with establishing an objective, followed by pretesting students. If the preassessment provides data that suggest the student does not have needed entry behavior or prerequisite skills, the first part of the alternative track is utilized. It is here that the teacher must provide remediated instruction which will make it possible for the student to begin the unit of study.

If these entry behavior skills are required at the onset of the unit, it is obvious the student will need remediated instruction prior to the primary instruction for the first objective. However, if the entry behaviors are not needed until a later point in the unit, the student might begin the study while undertaking remediation simultaneously. Because of this factor and other constraints such as time, the teacher is urged to develop and locate remediated materials which can be used by the students on an independent basis in or out of the classroom.

If students satisfy established entry behavior levels and are not in need of information, they move to primary instruction and on to the formative evaluation. Once again, the formatives are not graded and are designed to determine whether or not the student is making progress towards the desired competency or skill.

In the event students are not successful, that is to say, the primary instruction did not meet their needs, they are sent into the alternative track which is designed to extend to the students the two critical variables of mastery learning: additional time to master the skill and additional materials to facilitate their learning.

It is at this point that the teacher must come to grips with two questions:

1. Why was the primary instruction insufficient in meeting student needs?
2. What materials or activities can be provided to solve the learning problem?

Regarding the first question, Okey and Ciesla (1975) provided a useful checklist in their tapes developed with the assistance of the U.S. Office of Education. Considerations include:

1. Were the objectives clear to the learner?
2. Did the pretest clearly establish the learner's mastery of entry behavior skills?
3. Did the primary instruction offer appropriate practice regarding the skill under study?
4. Did the primary instruction allow for a sufficient amount of practice?
5. Were feedback mechanisms employed?
6. Were possible motivational factors present or lacking?
7. Were there possible psychological or physiological factors that may have inhibited student learning or achievement?

When a teacher considers these and other factors, she must continually collect information on the nature and substance of the material under study and must continually increase a working knowledge of each and every student. In doing so, the teacher strives to reduce barriers to learning and improve efficiency, i.e., the numbers of students for whom the instruction facilitates learning of the primary instruction.

Regarding the question, What materials or activities can be provided to solve the learning problem? it is the teacher's responsibility to locate alternative resources to meet the needs of the students. This is obviously a difficult and never-ending task. It requires time, energy, and the ability to be an excellent scrounger!

However, before sending the student to alternative materials, activities, or procedures, the teacher must first be sure that the student made a legitimate effort toward learning the content of primary instruction. According to Dewey's general point of view, the teacher should generally assume the student put forth an honest effort and the primary instruction was not sufficient. However, there will be an occasional situation in which the student did not put forth his best effort, and in this case it would be acceptable to return the student to the original instruction.

When seeking alternative materials, or activities, it is worthwhile to utilize visual and audio aids as well as written instruction. If reading comprehension is a problem, modes other than books, such as films, tapes, overheads, and models, might facilitate conceptualization. In addition, there is a rather interesting and growing body of information regarding left brain and right brain function referred to in the literature as hemispheric specialization of the brain.

Briefly stated, an overwhelming majority of school activities involve linear and verbal or printed instruction which may be processed by the left hemisphere of the brain, whereas nonverbal information may be a function of the right hemisphere. In the event a student's right hemisphere might be more efficient than her left, a variety of mediated modes of instruction might promote learning, whereas the more common printed materials might provide a learning difficulty.

No matter what additional research may reveal, the major point to be made regarding alternative activities is that a variety of instructional materials should be made available to the student in the endless struggle to satisfy individual learner needs. Be sure to enlist the aid of librarians, media specialists, curriculum directors and specialists, various community sources, and colleagues when searching for resources, many of which can be obtained at no cost.

In addition to providing a variety of materials, a teacher can employ tutoring as a viable alternative. Due to time constraints, peer tutoring should be used more often than teacher tutoring. However, we caution you that peer tutoring can be highly successful or disastrous depending upon the personalities of the students involved. Teachers should do their very best to ensure that a clash of character will not occur and that the peer tutoring will be beneficial to both parties. Ehly and Larsen have made a strong case for the point that students can assist other students in the remediation of academic deficiencies. The authors fully explored these relationships in their book *Peer Tutoring for Individualized Instruction.*

It goes without saying that teacher tutoring truly individualizes a program, but, again, the teacher must pick and choose these situations because time will not allow teachers to employ themselves as alternatives too often.

Once the alternative instruction has been completed, the student undergoes additional formative evaluations and, assuming the learning problem has been solved, proceeds to either a summative evaluation or the following objective.

The third and final track is the enrichment track. As with the other two, establishing an objective begins the unit and pretesting the student follows. After it is determined that the student has the entry behaviors to begin the unit, the student may engage in enrichments through one of two channels.

The first channel is used when the preassessment shows the student already can exhibit mastery of objective 1. In this case, assuming there is consistency between the preassessment and the summative evaluation, it can be said the student has "tested out" and can choose from the following courses of action:

1. Moving on to additional objectives in the unit
2. Engaging in in-depth studies
3. Engaging in peer tutoring

If your classroom situation allows for flexibility regarding pacing, it will not be disruptive for the student to move on. However, if the management of the program is more uniform, which is particularly true if a basic curriculum is being emphasized, it is probably best to employ options 2 and 3.

A critical point to be made here is that the student should not view in-depth studies as punitive. In other words, we don't want him to feel that if he does well, the reward is additional work. On the contrary, let us once again make it clear that mastery is defined by the minimum level which certifies the student can, in fact, exhibit the desired skill or competency. This allows the teacher to support students in their pursuit of excellence, and although intrinsic rewards are critical, extrinsic rewards should be available to students involved in enrichments.

In addition to in-depth studies which are generally undertaken on an independent study or small-group basis, the student who has quickly mastered a given objective could be used in peer-tutoring situations. Peer tutoring has been discussed earlier in this chapter, and, again, the teacher is urged to proceed carefully with this approach. The major point to be made here is that it is very reinforcing for one student to be able to "teach" another student because it further supports her confidence in conceptualizing the work at hand.

The second channel in the enrichment track is found after the primary instruction and successful completion of the formative evaluation. At this point, the student is on the main line, but, as discussed earlier, if appropriate materials are available and time permits, the student could engage in some enrichment activity prior to taking a summative evaluation or proceeding to a following objective.

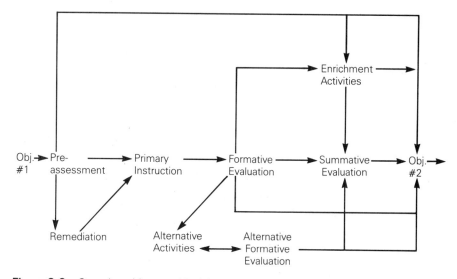

Figure 8.3   Complete Mastery Model

As a final note, parents and colleagues may question whether or not the enrichment student is being penalized while alternative instruction is being provided. Stated simply, the position here is that unlike the traditional situation, mastery learning not only promotes but actually permits and makes possible enrichments.

The traditional situation is a lockstep with all the students doing the same thing at the same time and then moving on to new tasks. There is obviously no time for enrichment or in-depth study. By contrast, advanced students in mastery environments have time to seek out ways to exhibit excellence, as shown in the complete mastery model in Figure 8.3. At the same time, there is sufficient time and material to allow increased numbers of students to succeed.

CURRICULUM DEVELOPMENT PROCEDURES

Let us assume that mastery learning will be new to your classroom. With this in mind, you need initially to employ curriculum development procedures if you are to install this innovation successfully.

The position taken here is that there is no one correct way or a magical set of procedures which guarantees that the curriculum additions will be effective. Therefore, let us offer you a variety of possible procedures described by scholars in various disciplines and offer some of our conclusions based upon their work.

An educational technologists' point of view regarding curriculum development procedures is represented by Gerlach and Ely, who offered the following:

1. Specification of objectives
2. Selection of content
3. Assessment of entering behaviors
4. Selection of strategies
5. Organization of students into groups
6. Allocation of time
7. Allocation of space
8. Selection of resources
9. Evaluation of performance
10. Analysis of feedback

It is important to note that critical features of mastery learning such as preassessments, self-pacing, and alternative materials could be considered in numbers 3, 6, and 8 respectively.

Brown, Lewis, and Harcleroad have produced a classic text in audiovisual instruction and are obviously concerned with media and materials employed during the instruction. They would instruct teachers to do the following:

1. Define (or accept) objectives and select content.
2. Select learning experiences.
3. Select formats to carry out experiences.
4. Select physical facilities.
5. Assign personnel roles.
6. Choose appropriate materials and equipment.
7. Evaluate results and recommend improvements.

With specific regard to mastery learning, we can see how numbers 2, 3, and 6 would impact upon the selection and utilization of alternative instruction.

The curriculum specialist point of view is represented by Taba and Tyler. Their steps or procedures include

1. Diagnosis of needs
2. Formulation of objectives
3. Selection of content
4. Organization of content
5. Selection of learning experiences
6. Organization of learning experiences
7. What objectives to evaluate/ways and means of evaluation

Here, diagnosis of needs might include preassessment and the problem of alternative instruction is addressed by numbers 3 through 6.

A final development procedures list is that of Gagné and Briggs, learning theory specialists. These procedures are somewhat more detailed and numerous than those previously listed and are as follows:

1. Analysis and identification of needs
2. Definition of goals and objectives
3. Identification of alternative ways to meet needs
4. Design of system components (grouping, schedules, etc.)
5. Analysis of resources required and available, and resource constraints
6. Action to remove or modify constraints
7. Selection or development of instructional materials
8. Design of student assessment procedures
9. Field testing, formative evaluation, and teacher training
10. Adjustments, revisions, and further evaluation
11. Summative evaluation (studies of effectiveness)
12. Operational installation

With specific regard, once again, to mastery learning, preassessments are implied in number 8, self-pacing might be included as a need in number 1, and alternatives are clearly taken into consideration in numbers 3, 5, and 7.

Again, we take the position that there is no one right set of procedures. However, when comparing these four curriculum development procedures, it is interesting to note that all of them employ key areas of the three-phase model:

1. What goals are to be accomplished? (Planning)
2. How, and under what circumstances, will students seek to accomplish these goals, and what resources will be needed to organize learning experiences? (Implementing)
3. How well were the goals accomplished? (Evaluation)

These are the basic questions that you must answer when you implement new units of instruction in your existing curriculum. You need to examine the procedures offered here, and others, and determine for yourself various steps that need to be undertaken when installing mastery learning. No matter what procedures you employ, considering these three questions guarantees a focus upon planning, implementing, and evaluating mastery learning units of instruction.

PREPARING MASTERY LEARNING UNITS

Now let us focus on the preparation of the actual instructional product, or mastery learning unit of instruction itself. The first point to be made is that your students are your audience and you are preparing the unit for their use. Whether or not something goes into the unit will depend upon whether or not you believe it will enhance student achievement. In addition, make absolutely sure any written material is not too difficult for your students to read.

Each unit should begin with an introduction, prospectus, or overview, which (among other things) provides the student with the general purpose of the unit of instruction. This is generally undertaken in global terms such as understanding the world of mammals or becoming increasingly familiar with energy forms. In addition, the introduction might include a description of the students for whom the unit has been prepared, a rationale or discussion regarding the importance or significance of the work to be undertaken, and a student orientation to mastery learning. This latter point, of course, is only necessary in the initial mastery learning unit.

As a final point regarding the introduction, we suggest that when implementing the initial mastery learning unit, class time should be used to orient students to the approach and thoroughly review the introduction.

The next area of the unit involves presenting specific objectives to be mastered in the unit. By clearly stating the objectives, you provide direction for the learning experience. You provide focal points and share with the student expectations of achievement.

There are a variety of styles of writing objectives that are appropriate. The critical feature and concern here is that, because a mastery environment requires the teacher to certify the student's ability to manifest a desired skill or competency, objectives must lend themselves to measurement. In that Bloom urges small units of instruction, the position here is that specific objectives limited to a single behavior per objective are most appropriate for a mastery learning environment.

The next critical area of the package is preassessment techniques. Once again, the teacher should be pretesting for entry behaviors as well as knowledge of the content to be covered. In addition to including the actual pretests, you might include feedback keys and suggestions and sources for remedial work in the event the student cannot exhibit the desired entry behaviors.

Now comes the bulk of the unit which is devoted to the activities to be undertaken. Such activities include primary instruction, alternative instruction, enrichments, formative evaluations, and summative evaluations.

The primary and alternative instructional components are frequently presented as lists of things to do. Examples might include:

1. Read Chapter 3.
2. Interact with the energy learning center.
3. Listen to the lecture on the characteristics of mammals.
4. Complete activities 3 and 4.

In addition to lists, you might choose to actually present instruction in the package itself if budget and materials are available. However, feedback from teachers using mastery learning units in the field suggests that the units or packages be as brief and to the point as possible.

Formative evaluations are usually found in the units because they are nongraded and therefore not considered to be secrets kept from students. Whether or not keys for the formatives are present will depend upon whether or not you intend personally to provide feedback.

Summative evaluations are rarely found in the units because of their formal nature. However, the summative evaluations must be consistent with the objectives, and stated objectives in the unit will provide direction for the students when it is time to prepare for these formal examinations.

Additional components may be added, of course, depending upon your needs and the needs of your students. You might utilize such things as time lines, activity/progress charts, grading mechanisms, or other variables you consider to be useful. However, at the very least, it is suggested that your mastery learning unit of instruction include

1. A general introduction
2. Specific objectives
3. Preassessments
4. Primary instruction
5. Alternative instruction
6. Formative evaluations
7. Summative evaluations (may not be in the package itself)

Finally, we suggest that you field test your mastery unit with a small but representative sample of your students. Field testing allows you to collect data and revise and refine the work before its overall implementation. This step is beneficial because it will increase your confidence in the mastery learning unit's ability to promote a successful learning environment.

PRACTICAL APPLICATIONS

The first major point to be made is that mastery learning reinforces the basic three-phase teaching model consisting of planning, implementing, and evaluating elements or phases. During the planning phase, teachers using mastery learning find they must carefully establish learning objectives or outcomes to serve as the cornerstone for the mastery sequence. In doing so, the teacher provides a focus for the remaining elements of the three-phase model.

Content, procedures and strategies, and materials are elements of the implementation phase and as such, facilitate accomplishing the objective. At this stage, the teacher is considering the most effective lecture strategies, activities, and materials to use to assist the student in "mastering" the objectives of the unit of instruction.

The third phase is evaluation, and the critical function of the teacher at this point is to certify whether or not the student has, in fact, mastered the material, shown by his manifestation of the desired learning outcomes. This responsibility requires the teacher to be very clear and specific regarding all the elements of the three-phase model, and it is because of this that teachers have found mastery learning very useful in revisiting these critical and basic teaching functions.

A second point regarding impact upon traditional components is the constant reconsideration of primary instruction. A review of Figure 8.3 (page 219) shows that, when using mastery learning, the teacher must provide alternative instruction or correctives for students for whom the primary instruction was insufficient. Therefore, it is obvious that the more successful the primary instruction, the fewer alternatives needed. Teachers using mastery learning are continually revising the primary instructions in an attempt to improve their efficiency. Theoretically, if a primary instruction met the needs of all the students, there would be no need for alternative instruction or correctives. This ideal situation will rarely if ever occur, but the important point we are making here is that the mastery learning environment becomes more manageable and streamlined as increased numbers of students succeed without the use of alternative instruction. Data appear to support the position here that teachers using mastery learning will revise primary instruction more often than teachers employing the traditional approach.

Now let us turn our attention to discussions of specific mastery learning components and the implementation experiences of practitioners.

A first and critical component is self-pacing. Many teachers find that self-pacing (allowing the students to do different things at different times with different materials) may be inhibited by such factors as a wide range of ability levels, an emphasis on testing and accountability, large numbers of students, time requirements, equipment, space, and other classroom variables. Teachers surveyed offer four suggestions that facilitate the self-pacing component.

First, as discussed previously, the teacher should engage in a never-ending effort to refine the primary instruction. The result of this effort will be that fewer students will need alternatives or correctives, and the need for self-pacing will be delimited. Numbers, time, equipment, space, and other constraints become much less of a problem as the teacher decreases the number of students in need of alternative instruction.

Another suggestion is that mastery learning units of instruction should cover small bits of information in a sequential fashion if possible. The small-bits approach generally promotes increased conceptualization and once again decreases the number of students needing additional instruction. In essence, presenting small bits keeps more of the students in the same place at the same time.

A third suggestion involves enrichments. Once again, a review of Figure 8.3 (page 219) shows that the mastery learning model basically presents a three-track approach: mainlining, or going straight through the instruction; using alternative instruction; and using enrichments. In the area of enrichments, the data suggest that teachers can minimize self-pacing difficulties by engaging enrichment students in in-depth studies as opposed to allowing them to move on to additional objectives or units of instruction. The teacher who thus engages enrichment students reduces the distance between those students engaged in enrichments and those engaged in alternatives.

Finally, it is suggested that teachers determine completion dates for units of instruction on the basis of anticipated alternative instruction. In other words, most units of instruction present concepts or learning activities that generally present problems for some students. The more experience we have with a unit of instruction and our students, the more apparent these problem areas become and the more efficient we become in reworking the primary instruction and providing effective alternatives. More often than not, as time goes by, it will require only one or two alternatives to remediate the problems, and it is suggested that the time line and points of closure be established upon the time needed to supply the primary instruction and those few alternatives.

A second critical component in mastery learning involves alternative instruction. As we have frequently mentioned, alternatives or correctives are used to remediate students for whom the primary instruction was insufficient. Feedback from practitioners provides a number of suggestions.

First and foremost, alternatives become the responsibility of the student and are frequently undertaken on an independent basis outside the classroom. These unsupervised activities often are difficult for many students, so teachers utilize a variety of methods to aid them in completing alternatives. Such techniques include special projects with clearly defined requirements, occasional research or group work, contracts, learning centers, peer tutoring, and individualized instruction which may be undertaken before, during, or after classroom instruction. The important thing to note here is that teachers should explore all the possible ways of providing alternative instruction at times other than during classroom instruction and should further seek ways to ensure student involvement in those activities.

As a final note, many teachers emphasize returning students to the primary instruction. Our position is that it should generally be assumed that the students took a legitimate shot at the primary instruction and that it did not meet their needs. We therefore believe the students should be returned to primary instruction only if it can be clearly ascertained that they did not, in fact, become academically engaged in those materials.

Another component of mastery learning involves the nongraded, formative evaluations. Because teachers have conditioned students to getting credit or grades for all evaluations, the data suggest that the term *formative evaluation* not be used. Teachers seem to be having more success, in terms of student involvement, if these evaluations are referred to as hands-on activities, check-off procedures, or other terms which do not smack of testing. Actually, the practitioners note here that if they can establish a successful relationship between the formatives and summatives for the student, the formatives can become a very strong motivational factor. In other words, if the students perceive the utility of working hard on the formatives, they are more likely to approach the progress checks seriously.

The preceding discussion leads us to one of the most controversial components of mastery learning: grading. There are many involved in mastery learning who believe to master an objective is to earn an *A* for that objective.

The positon taken here, based upon the experiences of teachers working in competency-based programs, is that mastering does not need to be conceptualized in terms of excellence. Mastery here is defined as the least amount of evidence the teacher will accept to establish that the student can, in fact, accomplish the learning task. This does not imply a lowering of standards; it simply means that this is what the students must be able to do for us to certify that they can do it.

For example, let us say first-grade students are given 20 single-digit addition problems. How many would they have to solve to prove they have mastered this skill? Possibly 80%, a common competency figure. If so, they would need to solve 16 of the 20 problems in order to establish mastery but possibly 20 to establish excellence. The point is, one can discriminate for excellence in a mastery environment.

Put in a less scholarly way, mastery means students can do it, whatever it is. At the graduate university level, the letter grade of *B* will enable students to graduate. If they can graduate, this should be interpreted as meaning they have mastered the curriculum, and those using mastery learning must adjust their grading systems to reflect the environment in which they work. At the undergraduate level, *C* means success, which leaves *B* and *A* to reflect degrees of excellence.

Finally, in terms of the logistics of implementing a mastery learning unit, practitioners have supplied a number of suggestions, which include the following:

1. Streamline and delimit paperwork, particularly in terms of formative evaluations.

2. Because of cost factors, be brief and to the point when developing units of instruction.
3. Develop effective tracking devices to monitor the activities of the students.
4. Pilot test units of instruction.
5. Do not attempt to convert your entire curriculum to mastery learning at one time.

To summarize, there can be little doubt that factors such as paperwork, expense, time, preparations, numbers, and facilities have required classroom teachers to modify mastery learning theory.

EXERCISE 8.1

Read the following statements and select the most appropriate response. Circle your answer.

1. Which of the following would be least employed in a "traditional" classroom? (a) formative evaluations (b) mediated materials (c) primary instruction (d) stated objectives (e) summative evaluations

2. Mastery learning begins with what type of instruction? (a) individualized instruction (b) group-based instruction

3. Based upon current research, what percentage in a mastery learning environment reflects success? (a) 70% (b) 80% (c) 90% (d)100%

4. Which approach describes mastery learning as conceptualized in class? (a) totally group-based approach (b) totally individualized approach (c) two-track system (d) three-track system

5. Mastery learning would place the least amount of emphasis on which of the following? (a) mediated materials (b) peer tutorials (c) rereading materials (d) small-group instruction (e) teacher tutorials

6. Mastery learning is based upon the belief that most students can learn if (a) feedback is provided (b) students are given sufficient time and appropriate materials (c) students are matched in appropriate age level (d) students are placed in appropriate learning groups (e) students are provided with materials they can read

7. Which of the following is characteristic of mastery learning? (a) diagnostic evaluations (b) learning alternatives (c) specified objectives (d) a and b but not c (e) a, b, and c

8. What are the two most critical variables of mastery learning? (a) materials and prerequisites (b) materials and tests (c) time and materials (d) time and prerequisites (e) time and tests

9. Which of the following best describes a mastery learning unit? (a) brief exercises with few diagnostic tests and few summatives (b) brief exercises with few diagnostics and many summatives (c) brief exercises with numerous diagnostics and few summatives (d) long exercises with numerous diagnostics and few summatives (e) long exercises with numerous diagnostics and numerous summatives

10. Which of the following is not true of formative and summative tests? (a) both are graded (b) both are related to instruction (c) both provide feedback regarding the instruction (d) both provide feedback regarding the learner (e) both seek to appraise change

SUMMARY

Mastery learning is a teaching technique founded upon the assumption that, given sufficient time and appropriate materials, *most* students can achieve desired outcomes. The technique differs from a more traditional approach because it emphasizes pretests, formative as well as summative evaluations, and the provision of alternatives. As presented in Chapter 8, mastery learning is a three-track system: a main track, an alternative or remedial track, and an enrichment track.

In Chapter 8 we offered in addition to a discussion of the technique itself suggestions regarding procedures to be followed when installing mastery learning in the classroom.

Finally, there can be little doubt that factors such as paperwork, expense, time, preparations, numbers, and facilities have required classroom teachers to modify mastery learning in terms of practical applications.

REFERENCES

Block, J. H. (Ed.). (1971). *Mastery learning: Theory and practice.* New York: Holt, Rinehart & Winston.

Block, J. H. (Ed.). (1974). *Schools, society, and mastery learning.* New York: Holt, Rinehart & Winston.

Brown, J. W., Lewis, R. B., & Harcleroad, F. F. (1973). *AV instruction: Technology and methods.* New York: McGraw-Hill.

Burns, R. B. (1979). Mastery learning: Does it work? *Educational Leadership, 37*(2), 110–13.

Ehly, S. W., & Larsen, S. C. (1980). *Peer tutoring for individualized instruction.* Boston: Allyn & Bacon.

Gagné, R. M., & Briggs, L. J. (1974). *Principles of instructional design.* New York: Holt, Rinehart & Winston.

Gerlach, V. S., & Ely, D. P. (1971). *Teaching and media.* Englewood Cliffs, NJ: Prentice-Hall, Inc.

Grady, M. P., & Luecke, E. A. (1978). *Education and the brain.* Bloomington, IN: Phi Delta Kappa Foundation.

Hyman, J. S., & Cohen, S. A. (1979). Learning for mastery: Ten conclusions after 15 years and 3,000 schools. *Educational Leadership, 37*(2), 104–109.

Jeter, J. (Ed.). (1980). *Approaches to individualized education.* Alexandria, VA: The Association for Supervision and Curriculum Development.

Levin, T., & Long, R. (1981). *Effective instruction.* Alexandria, VA: The Association for Supervision and Curriculum Development.

Okey, J. R. (1977). Consequences of training teachers to use a mastery learning strategy. *Journal of Teacher Education, 28*(5), 57–62.

Okey, J. R., & Ciesla, J. L. (1975). *Mastery teaching.* Bloomington, IN: National Center for the Development of Training Materials in Teacher Education.

Taba, H. (1962). *Curriculum development: Theory and practice.* New York: Harcourt, Brace & World.

Whiting, B., & Render, G. F. (1987). Cognitive and affective outcomes of mastery learning. *Clearing House, 60*(6), 276–280.

EXERCISE FEEDBACK

EXERCISE 8.1

1. (a) Formative evaluations. Progress checking without assigning grades is the least common practice listed.
2. (b) Group-based instruction
3. (b) 80%
4. (d) Three-track system
5. (c) Rereading materials. The assumption here is that the student tried to understand the written material.
6. (b) Given sufficient time and appropriate materials. Again, these are the two key characteristics of mastery learning.
7. (e) a, b, and c
8. (c) Time and materials
9. (c) Brief exercises with numerous diagnostics and few summatives. It is important to progress check every objective.
10. (a) Both are graded. Summative tests are graded by assigning a number or letter grade; formative tests are not graded.

9 Classroom Management: Antecedents

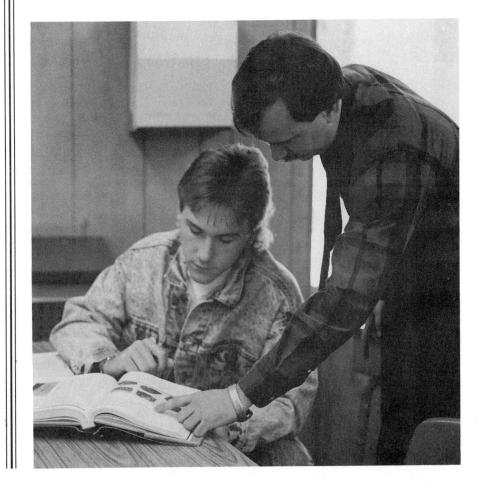

INTRODUCTION

Understanding the content you want to teach and being able to form objectives and construct unit and lesson plans are all essential teaching skills. Being able to implement these plans through a particular teaching strategy is also a central skill in teaching. But there is one additional skill that is so important that it sometimes overshadows the rest—managing a classroom so learning can take place.

A well-managed classroom can be thought of as a prerequisite to learning. Thoughtful planning and organization in terms of classroom management lay the foundation for success. Conversely, poorly managed classrooms are chaotic places where teaching and learning are hampered.

In this chapter we discuss the general idea of classroom management and key concepts in this area. In Chapter 10 we build on this foundation, describing specific approaches to management problems once they occur.

OBJECTIVES

After completing Chapter 9, you should be able to accomplish the following objectives:

1. For you as a pre/inservice teacher to understand classroom organizational patterns so that, given descriptions, you will identify the pattern as competitive, cooperative, or individualistic.
2. For you as a pre/inservice teacher to understand factors involved in classroom incidents so that, given classroom scenarios, you will identify each incident as related to teacher characteristics, classroom organization, or classroom environment.

CLASSROOM MANAGEMENT: OVERVIEW

Concerns

The problem of classroom management has long been recognized as complex, and the setting up and running of a class of 30 students is one of the most time-consuming and energy-draining activities engaged in by teachers. Poll after poll indicates that teachers' major concern is management. This concern is reinforced, then, by parents who also see discipline, or the lack thereof, as a prime problem year after year.

The reasons for this concern can be traced back to changes in schools as well as changes in society at large. Anyone who has walked through a school recently will notice factors that make management problems more complex. Unquestioned acceptance of schools and teachers as authorities has been replaced by attitudes of questioning, doubt, and hesitancy. Earlier faith in the schools as instruments of socialization and acculturation has been replaced by doubts about the role of the school in society at large. Attitudes towards child raising in general have changed, and these attitudes have found their way into the schools. No longer are students expected to sit quietly for hours through dull presentations. Instead, part of the teacher's prime responsibility is that of motivating, with direct student involvement often used as a barometer of success. No longer can teachers walk into the classroom and expect the individual attention of students who are products of today's television society. Teachers must now contend with a new generation of students who have grown up watching "Sesame Street" and action-packed programs and commercials. All of these conditions make the management of a classroom a more complex and demanding task.

From the outset, we wish to make clear our preference for the term *management* over the other often-used term *discipline*. By *management*, we mean the complex set of plans and actions that the teacher uses to ensure that the learning in the classroom is effective and efficient. Our concept of management is broader than that of discipline, which often connotes a central goal of keeping students quiet and in their seats. There is nothing wrong with having students quiet and in their seats, but that shouldn't be the teacher's central goal. Effective classroom managers place discipline in its proper perspective in the total instructional scene.

Management also involves teaching students how to manage their own behavior in classroom settings by establishing learning situations that will allow them to do this. It is in this sense that management is broader than discipline and encompasses the teacher's overall educational goals. Through the implementation of management plans, the teacher not only hopes to increase student learning but also helps students develop ways to understand and direct their own behavior.

Management and Instruction

When defined in this way, the concept of management is often hard to differentiate from the concept of instruction, and the two are closely related in theory and practice. Good classroom managers are often good instructors. They structure the classroom environment so as to maximize the student's instructional opportunities, thus minimizing the opportunity for management problems.

This interrelationship of effective management techniques and student learning has been documented by research in the classroom. Practices such as maintaining focus on the total group rather than on individual students and keeping lessons moving along at the appropriate pace were found to be associated with better student learning (Doyle, 1986). Indirect evidence for this position comes from a mounting body of research that links academically engaged time to student learning (Berliner, 1987). *Academically engaged time* refers to the amount of time students actually spend working on task-related projects. The more time spent, the more learned. This relationship of academically engaged time and learning, in addition to being empirically valid, is also intuitively sound. It makes sense that placing students in opportunities where they can learn and giving them time to do so will make a difference in how much they learn. Effective classroom management procedures ensure that this can happen.

Classroom Climate

Classroom climate is also related to student achievement in classrooms (Johnson & Johnson, 1975). Organizational patterns that result in students feeling capable, included, and secure seem to produce students who achieve better. A classroom that (1) maintains a balance between teacher directiveness and student choice, (2) provides specific direction and clarity, (3) maintains a large amount of freedom for students to think and weigh alternative solutions, and (4) provides training in interpersonal skills appears likely to be a classroom in which students will achieve and value learning, therefore minimizing the likelihood of disruptive behavior.

The ideal classroom just described does not result from one magic managerial scheme, nor can we point to one set of teacher behaviors that is sure to produce such a climate for learning. Many organizational patterns may or may not produce such a classroom. The teacher who directs or facilitates the action within a classroom appears to be the crucial element; however, considering the large number of tasks that teachers already need to contend with, you might ask, "Why complicate an already full teaching schedule with the additional task of management?" In addition to the cognitive considerations just discussed, there are affective reasons. Students don't like to learn in chaotic environments, and any teacher who has had to teach in problem classrooms will attest to the strain involved. Poorly managed classrooms are unpleasant places to teach as well as to learn. A certain degree of calm, quiet, and certainty from day to day is necessary for the teacher's mental health as well as the students'. Let's look now at some general considerations involving classroom management. In doing so, we will look at teacher characteristics, classroom organizational patterns, and the general learning environment.

EFFECTIVE CLASSROOM MANAGEMENT

Teacher Characteristics

Some attempts at helping teachers become more effective classroom managers have focused upon general characteristics of teachers. For example, Brophy and Putnam (1979) characterized an effective teacher as possessing a cheerful disposition, friendliness, emotional security, good mental health, and a high degree of personal adjustment. More specifically, effective teachers were described as persons who were able to remain calm in crises, listen actively without becoming defensive or authoritarian, avoid win-lose conflicts, and maintain a problem-solving orientation rather than resorting to withdrawal, blaming, hysteria, or other emotional overreactions.

Additionally, Brophy (1977) pointed out that some traits and behaviors associated with effective child-raising techniques were also associated with effective management. These included accepting and respecting each child as an individual; imposing firm but flexible limits and changing these as the child's development and the situation permit and require; emphasizing positive rather than negative expectations; explaining the rationale behind rules; being consistent in stating and enforcing demands, both within and among individuals; and being consistent in modeling ideal attributes.

Moskowitz and Hayman (1976) studied first-year teachers in an inner-city junior high and empirically validated many of Brophy's suggestions. They found that the best teachers used more behaviors that conveyed personal acceptance to students, gave more beneficial suggestions and verbal reinforcement, kept close tabs on behavior problems and corrected them before they got out of hand, made the classroom atmosphere positive and exciting, and joked more. These effective characteristics were contrasted with less effective practices which included criticizing, being negative, and allowing situations to get out of hand before correcting them.

The picture that emerges from these studies is that effective classroom managers are positive and task-oriented. They communicate positive expectations through their actions and deeds. They treat students fairly and place learning as the number-one item on the classroom agenda. Let's see how they translate these positive expectations into teacher actions.

Teacher Strategies

Kounin (1970) analyzed the classroom practices of effective and ineffective classroom managers and attempted to isolate variables that differentiated the two. One of the most important teacher behaviors in this regard was "withitness." *Withitness* refers to the teacher's ability to remain continuously aware of what's going on in all parts of the classroom and to communicate this awareness to the students. Related to "withitness" is the variable of *overlapping*, which refers to the ability to do more than one thing at a time. Both of these variables involve the ability to deal with individual problems while maintaining a group focus. One of the most persistent problems that beginning teachers have is the tendency to attend to one student while the rest of the class degenerates into chaos. You should keep contact with individual students brief during group instructional time so bottlenecks are not created, making every effort to maintain the pace of ongoing instructional activities.

Another characteristic of effective classroom managers is the ability to generate interest and challenge in daily lessons. Although this is difficult to discuss in general terms because it encompasses so much of good teaching, we can say that the instructional strategies selected for inclusion in Chapter 6 were specifically chosen for their ability to focus clearly on important ideas and to actively involve students in the learning process. Van Til (1974), citing a study of Baltimore teachers, found that good classroom managers use audiovisual and other resources to make lessons interesting by presenting subject matter in a vital and enthusiastic manner. He concluded that easier management "will prevail when learning experiences relate closely to the present interests and needs of children who see the use of what they are learning" (p. 35).

Related to these ideas, Kounin found that students were attentive and involved when lessons followed a logical structure and moved along at a good pace, but problems occurred when the lesson's momentum was lost. Common reasons for loss of momentum included teachers wandering off the topic, repeating or reviewing material that was already understood, pausing to gather thoughts or prepare materials, and interrupting to deal with behavior problems or other concerns. Underscored in all of these problems is the need for you to understand your instructional goals clearly and to select and implement instructional strategies that will permit students to reach them. Nothing is harder to manage than a class that doesn't know why it is there or what is happening.

The same ideas apply to the assignments students are given for in-class work. Kounin found that student involvement in such activities was dependent upon the challenge and variety that the work presented. Students quickly became satiated with tasks that required no thinking or challenge, especially if they were repetitive or lacking in value. In addition, Kounin and Gump (1974) found that activities that required interaction among students posed more potential management problems than activities in which students could work effectively by themselves. Being aware of this, you can plan student activities that

Interacting with students as individuals promotes a well-managed classroom.

match the students' management capabilities, reserving more interactive assignments for calmer days or periods. We will discuss this further in the sections on classroom organization.

In addition to ensuring that lessons and seatwork have an internal logic and structure that is communicated to the students, you can make your lessons more dynamic and alive by the interaction patterns that you choose. In some ways, teaching lessons can be thought of as conversations or dialogues between the teacher and the students. Nothing is more boring than a one-sided conversation. It's helpful to break up teaching monologues with questions that not only evoke the ideas and comments of students but also provide essential feedback about whether important ideas are being communicated. Suggestions for doing this are presented in Chapters 4, 6, and 7.

In calling on students, Kounin suggested creating suspense by posing a general question, looking around the room, and then calling on a student. He termed this "group alerting and accountability." He also suggested that students should be called on randomly rather than in a fixed order, with the teacher making a special effort to get around to everyone in the class frequently. All of these suggestions not only get the students actively involved in the lesson but also communicate "withitness" to the students.

Another practice that Kounin found to be characteristic of good teachers was the ability to make smooth transitions. Making smooth transitions involves communicating to students that one activity is ending and another is beginning, including what actions by the students are necessary to make that change. Often teachers have a clear idea of where they are going in changing from one topic to the next but don't realize the logistical problems involved in moving 30 students in that direction. A great deal of the confusion involved in making these transitions could be avoided by (1) waiting until the whole room is quiet and attentive before making the transition, (2) telling students what changes are being made, (3) writing pertinent directions on the board for quick reference if confusion occurs, and (4) monitoring the transition with a "withit" frame of reference.

Another dimension of effective classroom management is a sensitivity to the capability of students to handle different activities at different times. Anyone who has observed in classrooms for any length of time will notice that all periods and all days are not the same in terms of the amount of human energy or electricity in the air. Grambs and Carr (1979) identified the following times as being potentially high-energy times in secondary schools, but many of these apply to all levels:

The last period on Friday

The last period of the day

The last 5 minutes before lunch

The day before a big day or event

The first part of a period after a rally, school assembly, or fire drill

The time before, during, and after the distributing of report cards

The day (or days) before or after a big holiday

The appearance of a substitute teacher

The first few minutes of a period

To this list we'll add

The day before Halloween in an elementary school

How a teacher handles times such as these depends upon each teacher's individual philosophy, but some general options include being aware of, but ignoring, these special times and proceeding with normal business; selecting special high-motivation learning activities; or discussing these times with the students to help them understand their own behavior.

In addition to these special times, different types of students place various management demands on teachers. While it is hard to make generalizations about this interaction, we can say that any type of class will have management problems if students aren't learning or if there is a poor match between their instructional needs and the teaching strategies being employed. For example, Webb and Cormier (1972), in working with disruptive junior high school students, specially designed a highly structured math program for these students. Included in the program were specific objectives, matching criterion tests, and remedial activities designed to help the students correct problems identified by the tests. In addition, the students were provided with free-time reward periods when their assignments were completed. The researchers found that these structured instructional procedures not only increased the task-relevant behavior while reducing disruptive behavior in the math class, but also allowed this improvement to be maintained later in regular classes. This example is not an argument for highly structured classrooms, but it is an illustration of how instructional procedures interact with different types of students. You should keep the total instructional environment, including the students, in mind when you think of classroom management.

Additional suggestions for teachers' general orientation to students regarding the task of classroom management come from the classic study of group dynamics by Lewin, Lippitt, and White (1939). In this experiment, adult leaders working with 10-year-olds adopted one of these three leadership styles: authoritarian, democratic, or laissez-faire. The authoritarian leaders gave orders without much explanation, telling everyone what to do and with whom. The democratic leaders solicited opinions about learning tasks, tried to achieve group consensus about what to do and how to do it, and allowed some choice in working arrangements. The laissez-faire leaders didn't lead at all, instead giving vague directions and answers to procedural questions. The results, encompassing both affective and cognitive measures, showed that the students in the democratic group developed positive attitudes toward their fellow students and the leader and enjoyed the experience more than those in the other groups. These affective gains were achieved with only a slight decrease in group efficiency. The authoritarian group was most efficient in meeting the goals, but the members of the group showed tension and generally negative attitudes toward the group and the leader. The laissez-faire group measured generally poorer both cognitively and affectively. Again we can see an intuitively logical prediction that has been verified by experimental evidence—students learn best when placed in a positive environment where they have some choice about what and how they'll learn.

Baumrind (1971), in expanding upon the work of Lewin and his associates, clarified the difference between the terms *authoritarian* and *authoritative.* Teachers can't legally or morally abdicate their responsibility of providing for learning in the classroom through using either purely democratic or laissez-faire techniques. Instead, they must use authoritative leadership techniques that stress the fact that the teacher is an authority on learning, thereby accepting responsibility for what goes on in the classroom and retaining the ultimate decision-making power. However, teachers need not be authoritarian; they can solicit input from students, seek consensus on solutions to management problems, and generally take care to see that everyone in the class is clear about decisions and their rationale.

This concludes our discussion of teacher characteristics and general management strategies. How these are translated into action in terms of the social and physical environment of the classroom is an important determinant of management success. This is the topic of the next two sections.

Organizational Patterns

Social Environment Organization.   The way a teacher organizes a classroom has significant implications for management. For example, a classroom filled with groups of students working on projects is certainly apt to be noisier than one that has children involved in individual seatwork. These are forms of social organization, the topic of this section. Classroom social organization can be characterized in one of three ways—competitive, cooperative, or individualistic.

The *competitive* pattern of organization stresses individual excellence and achievement. It uses a system of evaluation that compares each student with the others. There is always someone on top and someone on the bottom, with other students ranked between. Students are urged to do better than their neighbors, to keep reaching higher for a better position on the academic ladder. Classrooms that are organized competitively typically have students working alone or in small groups. Students work on separate tasks while striving for an acceptable standard within that classroom situation. The teacher is the initiator and director of the learning tasks. The pace, set by the teacher, is usually based upon the average or slightly above average ability level in the class. This pattern of organization is by far the most prominent in schools today.

The *cooperative* pattern stresses students working together upon problems. All members of the group are important, with all students capable of making unique contributions, no matter what their ability levels. Students are encouraged to contribute, to set group goals and tasks, to divide and assign work equitably, to listen to all viewpoints, and to weigh alternative solutions. The product of such an enterprise is viewed as a group accomplishment with the input of several individuals. Creativity, initiative, application of previous knowledge to the present situation, organization, and evaluation are all tasks expected of students participating in this pattern. The teacher in this organizational pattern is a facilitator who asks for, listens to, and uses student ideas in planning instructional activities.

The *individualistic* pattern involves students working at their own levels and their own paces to achieve cognitive tasks. They must be able to follow directions, accept repetitive practice, and interpret self-evaluations. The teacher is the director, diagnosing and placing students at their correct levels, evaluating and encouraging progress, and serving as a source of information. Students usually work alone on a task that may be quite different from that of their neighbors. The objective of this type of organizational pattern is mastery of cognitive material, with steady progress upward.

Often in real classrooms, a combination of several organization patterns may be observed. Teachers may use different patterns at different times of the day and for different instructional purposes. As noted earlier, the organizational pattern significantly influences the management considerations a teacher must make. A cooperative climate may lead to the appearance of some disorder but, at the same time, helps improve the students' socialization skills, creativity, and decision-making capabilities (Slavin, 1986). An individualistic approach, by contrast, may prove most effective in terms of cognitive growth and would most likely result in fewer management problems. As with most considerations in teaching, the decision depends on your style and goals.

EXERCISE 9.1 _____

Read each statement below and decide if it is a feature of a competitive (CM), a cooperative (CP), or an individualistic (I) classroom. Then compare your responses with the ones given in the feedback section at the end of the chapter.

_____ 1. Students are valued for their unique contributions.

_____ 2. Achievement is expressed in terms of the highest grade assigned to the highest-performing student and the lowest grade assigned to the lowest-performing student.

_____ 3. Students must organize and evaluate their own instructional activities.

_____ 4. The teacher sets the pace for learning with certain set standards to be achieved.

_____ 5. The teacher serves a supporting, encouraging function.

_____ 6. The teacher helps each student find work at his or her own pace and speed.

Physical Environment Organization. A third factor affecting management is the physical environment in the classroom. This often overlooked dimension of teaching not only affects how easily students are managed but also how well they achieve. An attractive, well-lighted, comfortable, and colorful classroom is certainly more conducive to a feeling of well-being than a dim, drab, and colorless one. Other factors such as materials and the arrangement of seating can significantly affect learning and its management.

For example, learning materials that are attractive, accessible, and easily used influence students' overall feelings toward the classroom and their own capacity for learning. The visual impression received from features such as color, size of print, and spacing on the page can have an impact. Students respond positively to attractive learning materials, and you should consider this when choosing among the vast array of already prepared materials or when preparing your own. A positive reaction to learning materials certainly decreases the probability of management problems.

In designing the physical layout of the classroom, certain considerations should be kept in mind:

Visibility
Can students see the board and other visual displays?

Does the teacher have a clear view of all instructional areas to allow monitoring?

Accessibility
Do high-traffic areas (e.g., pencil sharpener, door) allow for efficient movement in the classroom?

Are these high-traffic areas designed so they minimize disruption in the classroom?

Distractibility
Are potentially noisy areas separated from other areas?

Do doors or windows invite students to drift off?

With these general considerations in mind, let's turn to some alternate ways to arrange desks.

The traditional setting with rows of desks and teacher's desk at front, shown in Figure 9.1, focuses all attention upon the teacher and discourages communication among students. This might be ideal when a teacher is presenting a lesson to the entire class, but can make peer teaching or group work difficult. Students at the rear of the room tend to be physically separated from the teacher and are most likely to be the ones causing problems.

Some classrooms use tables for seating, with the teacher's desk located somewhere on the periphery, as in Figure 9.2. This seating

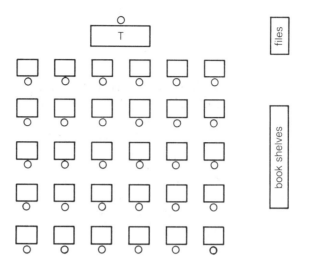

Figure 9.1 A Traditional Classroom

arrangement can be used by all organizational structures—competitive, cooperative, and individualistic.

An arrangement whereby students are provided their own workspace with as little distraction as possible is often used in an individualized instructional situation is as shown in Figure 9.3. Access to materials and teacher is maintained, with the side-by-side seating not being so distracting as across-table seating.

In considering seating arrangement, factors such as inclusion are important. One of a child's basic needs is to be included, and a physical arrangement that promotes inclusion is conducive to a feeling of well-

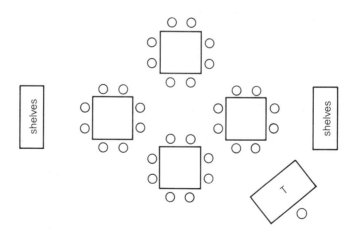

Figure 9.2 An Alternate Seating Arrangement

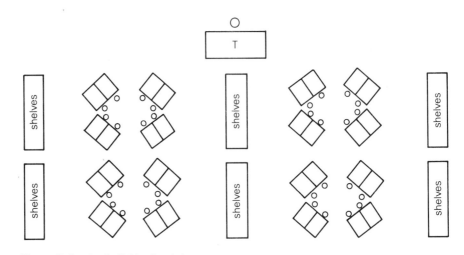

Figure 9.3 An Individualized Arrangement

being while deterring management problems. Again, when considering the physical arrangement of your classroom, consider management and academic goals. What type of learning is required? Will students need to interact with one another? Will contact be primarily between the teacher and the individual students? Is communication among students desired? Are spaces for individual work, as well as group activity, important?

Having reviewed some general considerations of factors affecting management, we can see that many management problems can probably be eliminated before they arise. The notion of preventing rather than coping with problems is called *preventive management* and is the topic of our next section.

PREVENTIVE CLASSROOM MANAGEMENT

Planning

Nowhere in teaching is planning more important than in theories of management. Effective classroom management practices don't just magically occur; they must be thought about and planned. While some teachers are "naturals" in this area, the majority of you need to prepare for and work at effective classroom management. Even "naturals" can make your practices more effective by understanding how and why your techniques work and by making conscious efforts to improve upon them. With these thoughts in mind, let's discuss the concept of preventive classroom management.

Preventive classroom management involves anticipating problems before they occur, consciously planning how to avoid their occurrence, and developing systematic procedures to use when they do. The idea here is that most classroom management problems can be anticipated and prevented by knowing their causes as well as mechanisms for their prevention. Implicit in this idea is the notion that the skills crucial to managing a classroom involve organizing, creating, and maintaining a learning environment that minimizes the need to deal with problems in the first place.

This idea is not new, having been hinted at in such sayings as, "Keep your students so busy that they won't have time to get into trouble," and, "Idle minds are the workshop of the devil." Like many folk sayings, these expressions have enough validity to ensure their existence over time. Kounin (1970) verified this notion in his study of classrooms in which he found that the important differences between successful and unsuccessful classroom managers were not in their reactions once problems arose, but rather in their planning and preparation for effective instruction and group management to prevent inattention and disruption.

Accordingly, while a major portion of our initial discussion of management techniques focuses on ways to prevent problems before they occur, realistically we realize that, even with the best of planning, some problems will still surface. Ways of dealing with management problems once they occur are discussed in Chapter 10.

Establishing Classroom Rules

Probably the most fundamental technique in preventing classroom management problems is the establishment and teaching of classroom rules. Classroom rules define general expectations or standards of behavior that apply to a large number of situations (Evertson, 1987). For example, "Raise your hand when you want to talk" applies to a wide variety of settings from classroom discussions to drill-and-practice to small-group activities. The establishment of rules has been shown to be a significant factor in reducing disruptive pupil behavior (Advanti & Beaumaster, 1973; Herman & Traymontana, 1971).

There are two parts to this technique. First, classroom rules must be thought about and established; then they must be taught to the students. As Holliday (1974) has cautioned, don't assume that students know what you mean by various rules or understand the reasons for and the implications of them. Each of these should be discussed thoroughly during one of the first sessions of class.

Rules alone will not magically produce desired behavior. It takes teacher monitoring, follow-through, and consistency, as research proves. Greenwood et al. (1974) found that appropriate behavior dramatically increased when rules were applied with feedback to the students. Sanford and Evertson (1981) found that effective teachers monitored the rules continuously throughout the year, and Moskowitz and Hayman (1976) found that successful teachers established an orderly environment at the beginning of the school term.

In establishing rules, either authoritatively or more democratically in Glasser-type classroom meetings (Glasser, 1969), you should be sensitive to general school rules and policies to know how your particular classroom rules will interface with these larger rules. For example, what are the school policies concerning food or gum in the classroom? An easy way to find out is to discuss policies with experienced teachers or administrators.

Whatever specific rules are formulated, some general ideas should be followed. One is to make as few rules as possible. This makes the rules that you do establish easier to remember and more easily accepted. When presenting rules, state them positively in terms of do this and that, rather than don't do this or that. In addition, Brophy and Putnam (1979) suggested that rules be stated in general, functional, qualitative terms rather than restrictive, absolute terms. For example, they suggested that, "When you finish you can talk and move around but do not disturb those still working," is preferable to "Remain silently in your seat when you finish." The former provides students with latitude in their choice of activities and gives them a chance to exercise their decision-making skills.

However rules are stated, it is important that students understand them. This includes not only implications for behavior but the reasons and logic behind the rules. Gudmundsen, Williams, and Lybbert (1978) proposed that rules should be taught to elementary students by holding a class meeting at the beginning of the year at which rules are not only explained but demonstrated and practiced through role-playing. If necessary, retraining could even occur. While the problem of students not understanding rules is greatest at the elementary level, students at all levels could benefit from knowing clearly what the rules are, why they were formed, and what implications they have for behavior.

Other procedures are situation specific and address student behavior in specific places, such as the teacher's desk, the cafeteria, or the playground.

As with rules, procedures need to be understood and taught. Effective teachers take extra time at the beginning of the school year to insure that all students understand what is expected of them. Classroom discussions and role-playing with younger students are effective here. Once established, rules and procedures need to be monitored throughout the school year to insure their effectiveness.

Establishing Classroom Procedures

Whereas rules are more global and fairly few in number, classroom procedures are more numerous and also more specific. They address such mundane things as

Sharpening pencils

Entering and exiting the room

Passing in papers

Procedures help organize the classroom; they provide structure to the myriad of activities that need to occur if learning is to take place in an orderly manner. Many of these procedures are driven by the tempo of the day (adapted from Evertson, 1987):

A. Entering the classroom
B. Beginning the school day
   1. Attendance
   2. Previously absent students
   3. Tardies
C. Transitions
D. Distributing and collecting materials
E. Large-group activities
F. Seatwork
   1. Asking for help
   2. Completing an assignment
G. Leaving the classroom

A Developmental Model

When formulating and implementing rules in the classroom, teachers need to consider an important point—the developmental level of the students. Developmental considerations include the ability of students to understand and follow the rules and the considerations are affected by factors such as their age, their level of emotional development, and their experience. For example, students who have never been given autonomy may have trouble adjusting to this new-found freedom if it is given without advanced preparation.

A four-stage model linking the kinds of management problems encountered to the age level or developmental stage of the student was developed by Brophy and Evertson (1976). At the first stage, encompassing kindergarten and the early elementary grades, students are learning how to be students. During this stage, teachers function primarily as instructors and trainers in regard to classroom management procedures by introducing students to life at school. In a sense, students are learning to play the game called school. The need for classroom meetings where rules are explained and demonstrated is significant.

In the second stage, encompassing the middle elementary grades, the need to stress classroom management as a primary concern is reduced, and teachers can concentrate on instructing children in the formal curriculum. During this stage, students are generally adult-oriented and are interested in following rules and pleasing teachers.

Somewhere around middle school or junior high school, students lose this adult orientation and instead start to look to their peers for pleasure as well as support. As this transition occurs, teachers begin to be resented when they act as authority figures. In addition, students sometimes find public praise from a teacher to be embarrassing, preferring instead positive interactions with teachers that occur in private. The major management problems encountered here are getting students to follow the rules and understand the logic behind them.

During the final stage, which occurs somewhere in the high school years, students become more socially and intellectually mature, and management problems for most students are reduced. In a sense, students have figured out who they are and what they should do; therefore, the kinds of management problems associated with "growing pains" are decreased.

These relationships are shown in Figure 9.4. In the diagram, the line in the upper left-hand corner of the graph represents parents and other significant adults. These people have a high influence over children during the early years, but this influence wanes as the influence of peers, shown by the line in the lower left-hand corner, becomes greater. The place where these two lines cross approximates those "troublesome years" attested to by both junior high school teachers and parents of persons in that age group.

The reasons for these developmental stages can be traced to the developmental capabilities of students as well as the kinds of problems thrust upon them at different times. Piaget (1963, 1969) and Kohlberg (1976) have written extensively about the unique reasoning styles of children at various developmental levels. First graders or sixth graders don't think about logical or ethical questions in quite the same way as do adults. In addition, students at different age levels are faced with different types of problems related to maturation and the expectations of parents, school, and society. Whatever the reasons for these management stages, we believe that these are helpful ways of thinking about and understanding types of management problems.

While teachers are primarily responsible for preventing and solving most of these problems, they are not totally without other sources of help. A brief consideration of these sources is the topic of our next section.

Using Others

There are actually several available sources for help in heading off management problems or helping to solve them when they occur. Your principal, team leader, grade-level chairperson, experienced faculty members, and perhaps most importantly, parents can all be sources of

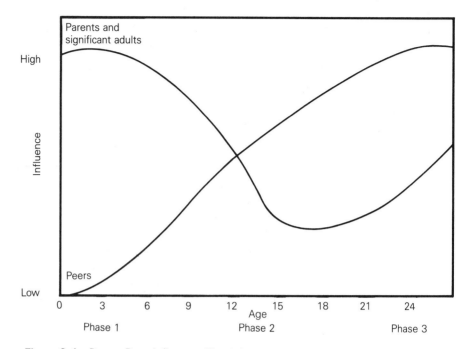

Figure 9.4   Parent-Peer Influence Chart

insight into students, allowing you to make better decisions about individuals in the management process. Simply questioning these people to discuss potential problems and gather ideas can be both a source of valuable information and a significant booster for a teacher's self-confidence. Because parents can be a teacher's most powerful ally, we will discuss the relationship with parents in a bit more detail.

One of the most promising ways of increasing student achievement and decreasing management problems in classrooms is to involve the parents of your students in teaching and learning. Research strongly supports improved learning for students when parents are actively involved in the learning process—encouraging and supporting their children at school, as well as enriching their learning environment and sharing their aspirations for learning at home (Walberg, 1984).

The relationship between parents and teachers is one that needs a great deal of nourishing. Teachers are trained educators and can, through their professional expertise, help the parents to understand just what role they play in their children's schooling. Many parents have feelings of inferiority or inadequacy when it comes to academic material, and yet their cooperation in the learning process may be vital to their children. You can build good relationships by communicating often with parents about positive topics. Strive to get to know them by inviting them into classrooms as volunteers, asking them to help with special projects, and encouraging them to send messages from home by note or telephone. Some teachers have found regular letters to parents helpful; positive interaction can be increased by short notes stressing what good things their child has accomplished during a time period.

A recent study concluded that contacts between parents and teachers can be increased if teachers send home learning activities appropriate to the child's classroom assignments (Dulaney, 1979). Other studies have shown that increased interaction between parents and teachers contributes to learning gains in students and decreases management problems.

Planning for curriculum goals and management structures should also involve planning for building positive parent-teacher relationships. Activities can be designed to include parents at home at the same time they are designed for classroom use. The parent is in a unique position to help a child apply what is learned at school and to recognize its relevance to the real world. A few minutes' attention to an activity that can carry a classroom assignment out to the home and beyond is well worth the time it takes to plan. This effort communicates to the student, through the parent, that learning is important, that school is a good place, and that the school-home relationship is a positive one. This probably can do more than any other single thing to prevent management problems.

Opportunities for parent-teacher contact can also be planned. Some teachers plan short afternoon coffee klatsches with a few parents just to get acquainted and to answer general questions. Others encourage each parent to come in for a conference at the beginning of the year. Schools often have open houses for parents. Notes or newsletters may be sent home, or telephone calls made. A few school districts encourage personal visits by teachers to their students' homes. Any means of increasing communication with the parents of students in the classroom will benefit both the teacher and the students. The important thing to remember when attempting to build relationships is to keep the interaction positive and open. Both teachers and parents have important contributions to make to a child's education. Neither one can replace the other.

When initiating increased parent-teacher interaction, it is important to keep in mind that communication does not develop in a hurry. Some parents may be reluctant or even suspicious. Some may be overeager and almost too conscientious. But any parent who is concerned about his or her child can become an instructional and management partner.

EXERCISE 9.2

Look at each of the following classroom situations and write your thoughts regarding the influence of teacher characteristics or an aspect of classroom organization. Then compare your ideas with the ones given in the feedback section at the end of the chapter.

1. Bill and Joey, in the two seats at the end of the rows, continue to talk to each other.

_____

_____

_____

2. Frank and Mike, whispering mischievously, decide to pull a prank in class. ''Let's see if we can get her mad again,'' they say.

_____

_____

_____

3. Sally says to Joan, ''Why should I try? I can never please him anyway.''

_____

_____

_____

4. The children in Ms. Stevens's class don't seem to be very friendly to each other. However, they are very quiet and well behaved.

_____

_____

_____

5. A visitor in Mr. Hanes's class went away thinking, ''What a pleasant time I had in there. I was so comfortable the entire time.''

_____

_____

_____

6. Miss Howard's class seemed to be in continual chaos, with children everywhere all the time. Her principal finally had to discuss it with her.

_____

_____

_____

7. Mr. Phillips was carrying on a discussion with a small group of students on the left side of the room. In the back, two boys were throwing paper at each other.

_____

_____

_____

8. Mr. Thomas commented to a colleague in the teacher's lounge, ''My kids are always berserk at the beginning of the period. I ask them to be quiet while I get my stuff organized, but they won't settle down.''

_____

_____

_____

SUMMARY

In this chapter we have discussed classroom organization and management from the viewpoint that such planning is part of a totally integrated instructional plan.

We have defined management as helping students learn to understand and manage their own behavior. We have also described the relationship between management and learning. A developmental model of management was presented along with the patterns of organizational structure possible in classrooms. Considerations for choosing among these structures, characteristics of effective managers, and student interaction skills, including suggested activities for their development, were discussed. We also explained these specific techniques for preventing management problems: the establishment of rules, high-energy times, the effect of the physical classroom environment, and parent-teacher relationships.

REFERENCES

Advanti, K., & Beaumaster, E. (1973). *The rise of behavior modification techniques in a class of slow learners.* Kingston, Ontario; Frontenac County Board of Education.

Anderson, L., Evertson, C., & Brophy, J. (1978). *The first-grade reading study: Technical report of experimental effects and process outcome relationships* (RDCTE No. 4070). Austin, TX: Research and Development Center for Teacher Education.

Bagley, W. (1909). *Classroom management.* New York: Macmillan.

Baumrind, D. (1971). Current patterns of parental authority. *Developmental Psychology Monograph in Developmental Psychology, 4* (Pt. 2), 1–105.

Berliner, D. (1987). Simple views of effective teaching and a simple theory of classroom instruction. In D. Berliner and B. Rosenshine (Eds.), *Talks to teachers.* New York: Random House, 93–110.

Brophy, J. (1977). *Child development and socialization.* Chicago: Science Research Associates.

Brophy, J., & Evertson, C. (1976). *Learning from teaching: A developmental perspective.* Boston: Allyn & Bacon.

Brophy, J., & Putnam, J. (1979). Classroom management in the elementary grades. In D. Duke (Ed.), *Classroom management.* Chicago: University of Chicago Press.

Collins, M., & Collins, D. (1975). *Survival kit for teachers (and parents).* Pacific Palisades, CA: Goodyear.

Doyle, W. (1986). Classroom organization and management. In M. Wittrock (Ed.), *Handbook of research on teaching* (3rd ed.). New York: Macmillan, 392–431.

Drayer, A. (1979). *Problems in middle and high school teaching.* Boston: Allyn & Bacon.

Dulaney, C. (1979). *Home learning activities as a means of increasing parent-teacher contact.* Unpublished doctoral dissertation, University of Florida.

Evertson, C. (1987). Managing classrooms: A framework for teachers. In D. Berliner & B. Rosenshine (Eds.), *Talks to teachers.* New York: Random House, 54–74.

Feldhusen, J. (1979). Problems of student behaviors in secondary schools. In D. Duke (Ed.), *Classroom management.* Chicago: University of Chicago Press.

Giannini, W. (1971). In the beginning. In M. McCloskey (Ed.), *Teaching strategies and classroom realities.* Englewood Cliffs, NJ: Prentice-Hall.

Glasser, W. (1969). *Schools without failure.* New York: Harper & Row.

Good, T., & Brophy, J. (1977). *Educational psychology: A realistic approach.* New York: Holt, Rinehart & Winston.

Grambs, J., & Carr, J. (1979). *Modern methods in secondary education* (4th ed.). New York: Holt, Rinehart & Winston.

Greenwood, C., et al. (1974). Group contingencies for group consequences in classroom management: A further analysis. *Journal of Applied Behavior Analysis,* 413–25.

Gudmundsen, A., Williams, E., & Lybbert, R. (1978). *You can control your class.* Salt Lake City, UT: Class Control Associates.

Herman, S., & Traymontana, J. (1971). Instructions and group versus individual reinforcement in modifying disruptive group behavior. *Journal of Applied Behavior Analysis, 4,* 113–19.

Hershdorfer, M. (1971). Handbook for the disorganized. In M. McCloskey (Ed.), *Teaching strategies and classroom realities.* Englewood Cliffs, NJ: Prentice-Hall.

Holliday, F. (1974). A positive approach to elementary school discipline. In *Discipline in the classroom.* Washington, DC: National Education Association.

Hoover, K. (1977). *The professional teacher's handbook* (2nd ed.). Boston: Allyn & Bacon.

Johnson, D., & Johnson, R. (1975). *Learning together and alone*. Englewood Cliffs, NJ: Prentice-Hall.

Kohlberg, L. (1976). Moral stages and moralization: The cognitive developmental approach to socialization. In T. Leckona (Ed.), *Moral development behavior: Theory research and social issues*. New York: Holt, Rinehart & Winston.

Kounin, J. (1970). *Discipline and group management in classroom*. New York: Holt, Rinehart & Winston.

Kounin, J., & Doyle, P. (1975). Degree of continuity of a lesson's signal system and the task involvement of children. *Journal of Educational Psychology, 67,* 159–164.

Kounin, J., & Gump, P. (1974). Signal systems of lesson settings and the task-related behavior of preschool children. *Journal of Educational Psychology, 66,* 554–562.

Lewin, K., Lippitt, Z., & White, R. (1939). Patterns of aggressive behavior in experimentally created social climates. *Journal of Social Psychology, 10,* 271–299.

McCloskey, M. (Ed.). (1971). *Teaching strategies and classroom realities*. Englewood Cliffs, NJ: Prentice-Hall.

McDonald, F., & Elias, P. (1976). *Executive summary report, Beginning teacher evaluation study, Phase II, 1973-74*. Princeton, NJ: Educational Testing Service.

Moskowitz, G., & Hayman, J. (1976). Success strategies of inner-city teachers: A year-long study. *Journal of Educational Research, 69,* 283–289.

Piaget, J. (1963). *The child's conception of the world*. Paterson, NJ: Littlefield, Adams.

Piaget, J. (1969). *The psychology of the child* (H. Weaver, Trans.). New York: Basic Books.

Pierce, W., & Lorber, M. (1977). *Objectives and methods of secondary teaching*. Englewood Cliffs, NJ: Prentice-Hall.

Rosenshine, B., & Berliner, D. (1978). Academic engaged time. *British Journal of Teacher Education, 4,* 3–16.

Sanford J., & Evertson, C. (1981). Classroom management in a low SES junior high: Three case studies. *Journal of Teacher Education, 38,* 34–38.

Schmuck, R.A., & Schmuck, P.A. (1979). *Group processes in the classroom* (3rd ed.). Dubuque, IA: William C. Brown.

Van Til, W. (1974). Better curriculum—Better discipline. In *Discipline in the classroom*. Washington, DC: National Education Association.

Walberg, H. (1984). Improving the productivity of America's schools. *Educational Leadership, 41*(8), 19–27.

Webb, A., & Cormier, W. (1972). Improving classroom behavior and achievement. *Journal of Experimental Education, 41,* 92–96.

EXERCISE FEEDBACK

EXERCISE 9.1

1. (cp) Cooperative
2. (cm) Competitive
3. (i) Individualistic
4. (cm) Competitive
5. (cp) Cooperative
6. (i) Individualistic

EXERCISE 9.2

In this exercise, just as with most dimensions of classroom management, many of the answers lend themselves less to specific responses than they do to teacher judgement. So, remember in reading the feedback which follows that judgements are involved, and your response may be different from ours.

1. This incident is primarily related to the classroom environment. If the seating arrangement were altered so the boys weren't at the end of rows and away from the teacher, they would be less likely to talk.
2. Here, teacher characteristics come into play. As stated in the chapter, effective teachers tend to be cheerful and calm, not resorting to hysteria or other emotional overreaction such as anger.
3. Teacher characteristics are operating in this situation. Effective teachers tend to be positive and emphasize positive expectations rather than negative.
4. This could be related to the teacher's attitude and the general classroom climate. A competitive rather than cooperative organizational pattern could also have an influence. The competitive environment would promote an orderly class but would also detract from mutual support on the part of the students.
5. This feeling was probably related in a large part to the physical environment. Bright colors, soft but adequate lighting, and attractive displays lend a feeling of comfort and well-being.
6. This incident could be related to teacher characteristics but probably is primarily related to the organizational pattern in the classroom. A cooperative setting without supervision and structure can easily disintegrate into chaos.
7. This type of activity relates to the concept of ''withitness'' as described in the chapter. Even though teachers must necessarily have some discussions with individuals or small groups, they must remain aware of the class as a whole.
8. This is the result of a teacher characteristic that is very common in the schools. The problem could easily be solved by careful preparation which would allow the teacher to begin immediately, thereby eliminating the free time at the beginning of class.

10 Classroom Management: Solutions

INTRODUCTION

In the previous chapter we discussed the general concept of classroom management and factors that affect its difficulty and complexity. We also described the idea of preventive management and suggested teaching techniques that can help prevent management problems before they occur.

However, in spite of teachers' sincere efforts to prevent these problems by such methods as establishing a positive environment, being well organized in their instructional preparation, using high-interest materials, and getting their students involved in activities, situations will occasionally occur in which these problems arise. This is inevitable; it happens to every teacher and most likely will happen to you, particularly as an intern or a beginning teacher.

In order to be an effective manager, the teacher must first have a clear definition of management problems. For our purposes *management problems* are any situations that occur in the classroom that disrupt the learning environment or cause distress to either students or the teacher. These problems can be as simple as a student sharpening his pencil during a class discussion or as serious as fighting. A list of common management problems encountered by teachers includes the following: disturbing conversations, notes being passed, refusal to comply with a request, hostility between individuals or groups, and overdependence of one student upon another. While this list isn't complete, it illustrates the scope of the problems discussed in this chapter. Notably absent are other more serious problems, such as drugs or violence, which are beyond the scope of this discussion. Teachers should not be expected to handle these problems alone in the classroom; rather they need to recognize them and refer them to the proper support personnel. The focus of this chapter's discussion, then, is on providing alternate ways of coping with the routine problems that disrupt the teaching-learning process. Here we will first discuss some general considerations in dealing with problems once they arise, then describe three specific approaches to management problems and provide some particular things you should consider in handling them.

The specific approaches are presented as possible solutions to problems that you may face in the classroom. Knowledge of and competence in using them will provide you with a repertoire of problem-solving approaches to management problems. The presentation of these techniques is based on our belief that there is no one best way to deal with all management problems. Rather, the specific strategy chosen for a particular problem should be based upon an analysis of the problem and your personality and management style. This approach, called a *models approach to management*, provides you with alternatives from which to choose in dealing with management situations in the classroom. Finally, we present a section on assertive discipline, which emphasizes both the rights of teachers as well as students.

OBJECTIVES

After completing Chapter 10, you should be able to accomplish the following objectives:

1. For you as a pre/inservice teacher to understand sources of management problems, so that when given a list of behaviors, you will identify the source as emotionally caused, teacher caused, or student caused.
2. For you as a pre/inservice teacher to understand the three theoretical approaches to discipline, so that when given a brief case study, you will identify the portions that are noninterventionist, behaviorist, or interactionist.
3. For you as a pre/inservice teacher to become aware of assertive discipline, so that without aid, you will name the three rights upon which it is based.

SOURCES OF CLASSROOM MANAGEMENT PROBLEMS

The label *management problem* is in some ways a misnomer in that what we typically describe as problems may in fact be symptoms of problems rather than the problems themselves. Kindsvatter (1978) has suggested that behaviors viewed by teachers as problems come primarily from one of these three sources: (1) teachers themselves, (2) emotional problems, or (3) casual or capricious student actions. For an example of the first case, a child's constant daydreaming or talking to her friends during a class discussion may be symptomatic of a boring activity, which is a teacher problem. The boring activity is the real problem; the student's disruption is merely a symptom of it. On the other hand, frequent fighting on the part of a student may signal an emotional problem. And last, a child walking by his friend, hitting him on the shoulder, and being hit back may be symptomatic of nothing more than children's normal tendency to clown around a little.

It is important to attempt to understand the source of misbehavior so you can take appropriate action in terms of the cause. For example, you would not treat a problem with an emotional base in the same way you would one based upon normal student behavior. Determining the cause of a problem allows you to deal with the causes rather than the symptoms. Further, if you can recognize yourself as a possible cause, you can make adjustments in your style, preparation, or the way you relate to students.

Kindsvatter has suggested that a teacher can best cope with emotional problems by communicating expectations early in the school year or immediately upon encountering the student. A clear understanding of expectation helps students understand the limits of their behavior and allows them to plan their behavior accordingly. These expectations should be phrased in a positive, supportive manner, which communicates to the student that these expectations are not punitive but are part of the regular procedures for a smooth-running classroom. In cases involving severe emotional problems, a teacher's only recourse may be to refer the student for counseling.

In dealing with teacher-caused management problems, it is often hard for you, as a teacher, to maintain a clear perspective on the situation because of your own involvement. This is to be expected, but you can do much to make your decision more objective by discussing management situations with other teachers and professionals. Both principals and teachers can provide helpful advice and different perspectives through informal consultations and visits to the classroom. A teacher encountering continual problems in this category needs in-service training in planning, organizing, and implementing various teaching strategies.

Casual or capricious actions may be the most common source of management problems in a normal school situation. You won't typically have a large portion of your class composed of emotionally disturbed students. So, the most aggravating management problems for a well-prepared and skilled teacher probably come from a base of normalcy—kids will be kids, if you will. Because of this, the main portion of our discussion focuses on problems of this type.

EXERCISE 10.1 _____

Identify the following behaviors as coming from an emotionally caused (e), teacher-caused (t), or student-caused (s) source. Then compare your answers to the ones given in the feedback section at the end of the chapter.

_____ 1. Getting out of seat without permission

_____ 2. Saying negative things to peers

_____ 3. Looking out the window during discussion

_____ 4. Writing on desks

_____ 5. Chewing gum when it is forbidden

_____ 6. Blurting out responses without raising hand

_____ 7. Throwing temper tantrum when told to wait to respond

_____ 8. Being noisy around peers but quiet around teacher

_____ 9. Continually using obscene language (although not in front of the teacher)

_____ 10. Refusing to respond to questions

SOLUTIONS TO MANAGEMENT PROBLEMS

General Considerations

The first factor in dealing with problems is perhaps as much prevention as it is treatment; the teacher and the students should have clear ideas about what kinds of behaviors are or are not acceptable in the classroom. This relates to our earlier discussion regarding the importance of establishing and communicating rules and procedures to students. In addition, you should have a clear idea of the options available when management problems occur. This plan of action, with relevant options, allows you to act decisively when problems occur and to communicate this decisiveness to your students.

In trying to decide upon a plan of action, you should clearly keep in mind your primary goal and consider how your actions will affect that goal. In general, the disruptions caused by teachers' actions should disrupt the ongoing flow of the classroom as little as possible. A major reason for this is the ripple effect (Kounin, 1970), which refers to the disturbance to surrounding students that is caused when a teacher scolds a student who is misbehaving. In instances such as this, the teacher's scolding often produces even more misbehavior because the other students' ongoing productive behavior (learning) is disrupted by the teacher. In this regard, Rosenshine and Furst (1971) found that students achieved less for the teachers who criticized the most. This effect was pronounced when the criticism was extreme. Prolonged criticism of students not only robs them of valuable instructional time but also disrupts those who are productively working and may not need teacher criticism.

In this regard, Kounin found that clarity and firmness were effective in management situations, whereas roughness was not. *Clarity* refers to the precision of the teacher's communication to her students regarding the desired behavior, whereas *firmness* refers to her ability to communicate definiteness of the expectation. For example, in terms of clarity, "Jenny, we don't talk while others are talking," is preferable to "Don't, Jenny"; it communicates not only to Jenny but the rest of the class what the problem is. In terms of firmness, compare these two requests: "Let's try to settle down and get quiet" and "Class there's too much noise. We need to settle down, NOW!" The teacher's ability to communicate intent both through words and inflection is essential to the idea of firmness. While both of these were positively related to effective management, *roughness*, which refers to noisy expression of anger, frustration, or hostility, was negatively correlated with effective classroom management.

Howard (1974) suggested that teachers should never use threats to enforce discipline. Besides the fact that management situations should be approached positively, another problem is created when students take up the threat. In addition, Howard suggests, and we agree, that teachers should avoid arguing with pupils in front of the class. You will have difficulty communicating clarity and firmness to the class if you spend considerable amounts of time arguing with individuals. This is not to say that you shouldn't spend time explaining rules and procedures, but you shouldn't spend excessive amounts of time defending them once they are established.

Management Hierarchies

With these ideas in mind, we suggest that you develop a response hierarchy which is based on the severity of your response and the amount of disruption it will cause to the class. Your actions should be based upon the student's misbehavior, and you shouldn't attempt more severe measures before trying less severe, less disruptive ones.

A response hierarchy to deal with the problem of talking in class might appear as in Figure 10.1. In using the hierarchy, you would begin by first looking at the students who were talking. If this didn't work, you could walk in the direction of the talking students and even touch them on the shoulder while continuing with the lesson. If that didn't work, you could then call on one of the students to answer a lesson-related question. Note that all of these measures can be taken without any disruption of the normal progress of class. If none of these measures works, you could then proceed to other, more severe measures such as asking the students to stop talking, separating the students, or calling in parents for a conference.

A similar hierarchy can be developed in other management areas. For example, a response hierarchy to deal with the problems of cheating might look like Figure 10.2. In this hierarchy, you might face the

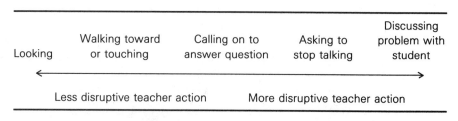

Figure 10.1 Response Hierarchy for Talking in Class

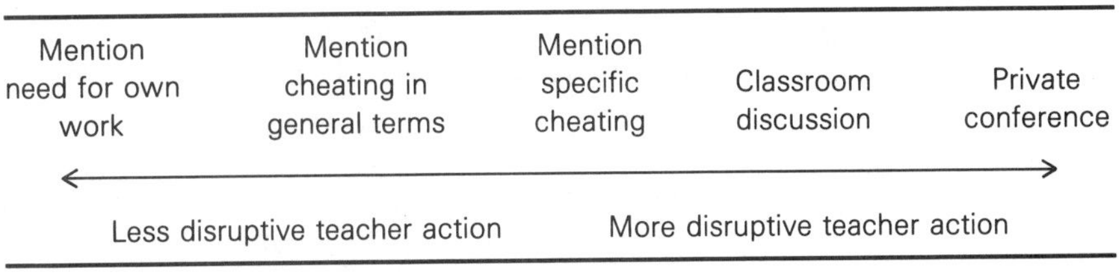

Mention need for own work	Mention cheating in general terms	Mention specific cheating	Classroom discussion	Private conference

←————————————————————————————————————→

Less disruptive teacher action   More disruptive teacher action

Figure 10.2 Response Hierarchy for Cheating

problem of suspected cheating with a casual mention of the need for students to do their own work. If this wasn't effective, the next time you gave an assignment or quiz, you could briefly mention the problem of cheating in general terms and discuss the problems connected with it. This could be followed at a later time by a specific reference to the problem of cheating in the classroom and then, a classroom discussion of the problem. Finally, you could ask the involved students to meet with you privately to discuss the problem. In each of these two examples, you choose a strategy which disrupts the progress of the class as little as possible. This approach also prevents minor problems from escalating unnecessarily into major ones and provides students with the opportunity to work out many situations in a nonthreatening atmosphere. Direct confrontation is used only when necessary.

In constructing hierarchies such as these, there are certain teacher actions that we do not recommend. These are corporal punishment, mass punishment, sarcastic remarks, forced apologies, and the imposition of school tasks for punitive purposes. We discourage the use of corporal punishment because of the implicit message that it carries—namely, that physical force is an appropriate way to resolve conflicts. Punishing the whole group for the actions of a few is not only unjust but also breeds hostility in those who feel wrongly punished. Sarcasm may temporarily solve the immediate situation, but it establishes an unhealthy means of communication between the teacher and student. Forced apologies often require students to say things in front of the class that they don't really mean. Besides being demeaning, there is an implicit dimension of dishonesty involved. Assigning school tasks for punitive purposes, such as doing 20 math problems, is ineffective because of the negative attitudes toward certain subjects that can develop as a result. Finally, none of these actions will actually solve the management problem; in fact, you will only create more problems by their use.

Approaches

In dealing with management problems in the classroom, the teacher can choose from one of three basic approaches. Glickman and Wolfgang (1979) described these as the noninterventionist, the behaviorist, and the interactionist approaches to management. Each of these approaches begins with certain assumptions about the child, and the teacher's role in the child's development. In addition, each of these approaches suggests teacher actions in response to management problems. Let's look at a brief description of each of these approaches, and then we'll see what they would look like in the classroom.

The noninterventionist approach to management, based on humanistic and psychoanalytic theories of development, believes that the child develops from an inner unfolding of potential. The teacher's role in the classroom is to facilitate that development through the development of a strong, trusting relationship and through active listening that facilitates problem solving. When management problems occur in the classroom, they result from the students' inability to understand the causes or consequences of misbehavior. Teachers help students solve classroom problems by helping them understand the nature of the problem and helping them work through solutions to that problem.

The behaviorist approach to management provides a clear contrast with the relationship/listening groups. As the name implies, this approach is based on behavioristic theories of learning, which hold that children develop as a result of external conditions, including rewards and punishments. The teacher's role in the classroom is to establish rules and procedures, communicate these clearly to students, and implement appropriate rewards and punishments for compliance or noncompliance. As students encounter consistent applications of these rules, they learn to operate within the social structure of the classroom.

Interactionist approaches are based upon social, Gestalt, and developmental psychological theories and hold that the child develops from the interaction of inner and outer forces. The teacher's role is to attempt to understand student behavior and to help students understand their own behavior and its consequences. Also called confronting/contracting (Wolfgang & Glickman, 1986), this position is intermediate to the other two in that it stresses rational decision making on the part of students but also creates a central role for the teacher in collaboratively setting rules for the classroom and confronting students with deviations from these rules.

With these overviews in mind, let's illustrate them with a typical management problem, students who forget to bring materials to class.

Ms. Bass is a seventh-grade geography teacher teaching a unit on the Middle East. Her students need to use related materials quite a bit and are expected to come to class every day with their texts, notebooks, and pencils or pens.

Ms. Bass began her Wednesday lesson by stating, "Look in your text at the pictures of the different groups found in the Middle East.

Can someone describe the difference in the people in the pictures on page 79?"

The students began describing the pictures, and then Ms. Bass said, "Ron, what can you add?"

Ron replied haltingly, "I didn't bring my book today."

Ms. Bass's reply was, "Ron, when you don't bring your materials, I have to stop the discussion, the class is disrupted, and I get frustrated." She paused for a few seconds and then went on, "Why didn't you bring your book to class?"

"Well . . .," Ron began, "I just forgot, I guess."

"Do you often forget?"

"No, I don't think so."

This discussion continued briefly, and finally Ms. Bass said, "I believe we ought to talk about this more after school, Ron. Can you stay a few minutes?"

Later, when Ron and Ms. Bass were discussing his failure to bring his book to class, she said, "I really did mean what I said earlier about being frustrated when students fail to bring their materials to class. Do you know why I feel that way?"

"I think so."

"Why is that, Ron?"

"Because we're supposed to bring our books every day," answered Ron.

"And when you don't, what does that do to the class?"

"It causes trouble because students who don't have their books can't participate."

"That's right, Ron; that's why I get frustrated. Well, do you have any idea how we can avoid this problem?"

"I'm not sure."

"Well, why don't you think about that for a while. When you think you've got something, let me know. Meanwhile, I'll be grading papers here at my desk."

In a few minutes, Ron approached Ms. Bass's desk and said, "I think I know what happens. Some nights I don't get my homework done. And then in the morning, I forget my books."

"You mean that sometimes at night you don't get a chance to do your homework, and so the next morning you're not prepared to come to school?" asked Ms. Bass.

"Yes, sometimes I try to do my homework in the morning, and there isn't time. So, then, I get rushed and forget."

The discussion continued with Ron's trying to figure out how he could avoid those disorganized mornings and Ms. Bass's helping in the process. In doing this, she attempted to be supportive by listening to his ideas and clarifying them but not trying to impose her own solutions. She felt this was important because the ultimate responsibility for the problem was with the student, and she wanted to give him practice in dealing with it.

Let's stop now and look at another teacher's approach to the same type of problem.

Mr. Gordon, fourth-grade teacher, was beginning his school year. He had gotten acquainted with his students in the first few days, had explained the grading system, and was ready to begin the instruction of his class.

He began by saying to the class, "In order for us to get the most out of school, we have to have a few basic rules. The rules are as follows:

1. No one talks while another student or I am talking.
2. No one moves around the room when we're in the middle of a discussion.
3. You always raise your hand before speaking.
4. You always write down your assignment.
5. You always bring all necessary materials to class.

"I have this jar at the front of the room, and when the class is working together to follow these rules, I'll put a marble in the jar. When the class gets 30 marbles in the jar, we'll have a class free choice at the end of the day where everyone can choose his or her favorite activity like a game, puzzle, or quiet talking. When the jar is all full, we'll plan a class party.

"If I have problems with individuals who don't follow these rules, I'll put your name on the board. That's a warning. The second time I'll put a check by your name. You'll have to stay in for recess, then. If I put two checks by your name, I'll have to call your parents to come in and talk with me. The purpose of these checks is to remind you of the rules in the classroom and to help you to follow them. So, be on your best behavior and try to follow these rules as closely as you can."

Mr. Gordon implemented his plan, and the first time Chris forgot her notebook, her name went on the board. At the end of the day, Mr. Gordon reviewed the day's happenings and discussed particular problems with individual students and general problems with the class. When necessary, the rules were adjusted or were supplemented with additional details to help particular students.

Now let's contrast these two approaches to management with a third one.

Mrs. Williams is another seventh-grade geography teacher. She began her year through such activities as getting to know the students' names and explaining the grading system.

She then began her first actual instructional day by saying to her students, "In order for us to get the most out of our classes, get along with each other, and respect each other as human beings, we must have some rules that are fair to everyone and that will help us to behave appropriately in school. I want you now to break into the following groups of four, and each group is to prepare a list of rules that we will live by during this school year. Remember, they must be fair to everyone, and they should help us all learn as much as possible about our coursework."

With that, the class broke into groups and began writing the rules. After a period of time, she asked each group to report to the whole class. In cases where one group suggested a rule that other groups did not, she asked the class if they thought it was a good rule and if it should be re-tained and incorporated into the final list. In several cases, particular rules were modified slightly until they became acceptable to everyone.

Finally, when the class was nearly finished, she noticed that no rule about bringing materials to class was mentioned. Mrs. Williams then suggested to the students that, in order to avoid disruption caused by borrowing, a rule for bringing materials be included. The class agreed, and two of the students volunteered to write the rules in large letters on a piece of poster board.

The next day Mrs. Williams referred the children to a page in their text and began a class discussion. During the discussion she noticed Kent was looking down at his desk and not responding.

She then said, "Everyone read page 96 in your text. Do that right now, and we'll continue the discussion in a few minutes."

She then went over to Kent and asked quietly, "What are you doing, Kent?"

"Nothing."

"Let's see now. You were doing nothing, but we were having a discussion. I see your book isn't in front of you. Did you forget to bring it today?"

"Yes, I did," he replied quietly.

"Do you know the rule about bringing your materials, Kent?"

"Yes."

"What is it?"

"We will always bring all our materials to class."

"Did you agree with the rule?"

"Yes."

"Okay, what do you plan to do tomorrow?"

"I will bring all my materials."

"Please write me a short letter telling me how you plan to do this. Then, at the end of the day, I'd like to discuss your plan with you."

Mrs. Williams, after completing her discussion with Kent, went on with her class discussion. Kent wrote the letter and gave it to Mrs. Williams at the end of the period. At the end of the day, they reviewed his plan and discussed its implementation in the future.

Let's now stop and analyze the three ways the problem was handled to see how they compare. Glickman and Wolfgang's ap-proaches to management are categorized on the basis of the actions of the teachers and their interactions with the students. Ms. Bass, the first teacher discussed, would be called a *noninterventionist* because her basic way of dealing with management problems was to communi-cate to students her reactions to problems in the classroom and then allow them to work out their own solutions. Mr. Gordon, on the other hand, used a *behaviorist* approach to the solution of the problem by deciding to focus on overt behavior and then structuring the classroom environment so that behaviors that led to learning were reinforced. Mrs. Williams used a third approach called *interactionist*. In dealing with the same management problem, she called upon students to help in the analysis and solution of the problem, but at the same time, assisted students in the problem-solving process. We analyze each of these approaches more thoroughly in the sections that follow.

Noninterventionist.   The noninterventionist view, also called the relationship/listening approach (Wolfgang & Glickman, 1986), has two distinctive features. The first is the assumption that children are innately good and trustworthy and the second is that they should be in control of their own actions and futures. If given the appropriate opportunities, students will learn to develop on their own and will figure out ways to deal with their own management problems. Accordingly, the teacher does not evaluate the student's actions; instead, she works to establish a nonjudgmental atmosphere of trust so that students have the opportunity and freedom to deal with their own problems. The noninterventionist teacher facilitates rather than directs or orders. Let's look now at the specific way in which Ms. Bass handled her management incident.

She began the encounter with what Gordon (1975) calls an "I" message. In reacting to Ron's not having his notebook she did the following: (1) described the behavior (the missing notebook), (2) identified the behavior's consequences (disruption to the class), and (3) stated her feelings (frustration). She was careful to avoid judgment of Ron's behavior and made no verbal evaluation of the behavior or of Ron. Her goal was to help him work through the incident by listening and clarifying.

Ms. Bass then went on to facilitate what amounts to a problem-solving approach in dealing with the incident. She first helped Ron identify the problem, being careful not to label him or his behavior as the problem or even the cause of the problem. The student then suggested alternative solutions, selected one of the alternatives, and proposed a plan for implementing the solution. The key feature in this approach is the responsibility of the student in identifying the problem and devising its solution in a cooperative atmosphere, with the teacher merely encouraging rather than guiding the process. These procedures are congruent with the basic assumptions of the approach—students are basically capable and willing to solve their own problems; they only need to be provided with a supportive environment in which they can work them out. Readers wanting to learn more about the noninterventionist view of management are referred to Rogers (1969), Moustakas (1972), or Gordon (1975).

This approach to solving management problems in the classroom is in sharp contrast to the behaviorist position, which places major responsibility for resolution of the problem on the teacher.

Behaviorist.   The assumptions behaviorists make are the antitheses of those made by noninterventionists. Rather than believing that the learners are in control of their actions and their future, behaviorists believe that the external environment is responsible for behavior. The teacher, instead of being a facilitator of student growth that comes from within the learner, creates an environment and helps the students to grow through a structured reward system. This places the teacher in a position of power and authority, responsible for molding student behavior. While behaviorists don't distrust students, the nonjudgmental atmosphere that is so critical for noninterventionists is not a consideration for behaviorists.

The behaviorist approach to dealing with management problems emphasizes the creation of environments that will prevent management problems and discourage them when they do occur. Their major tools to create problem-free environments are clear specifications of rules and specification of consequences for following or not following these rules. Reinforcement is used freely, with the function being to reward students for proper behavior and either negatively reinforce, by something such as withdrawal of privileges, or punish misbehavior.

Let's look now at how these factors came into play in Mr. Gordon's management plan. First, he had established a set of rules that governed the students' behavior. While these rules were set in the beginning of the school year, the important feature was who designed them.

The rules were then implemented and enforced in Mr. Gordon's classroom through a series of rewards and punishments. He monitored these rewards and punishments through a recording system using checks. When students followed the rules, they were given marbles which could then be used to "buy" free-time activities. Failure to follow rules resulted in the student's name being placed on the board, and subsequent checks would bring after-school detentions or phone calls to parents. If Chris forgot her notebook, she would receive a check by her name, which, if the pattern continued, could result in negative reinforcement or punishment. On the other hand, compliance with the rules would be followed by rewards.

In summary, the behaviorist position looks at the behaviors themselves rather than their causes, as important. What is crucial is creating an environment in which students are rewarded for operating within the classroom system. A teacher, operating in this position, is more concerned with establishing rules and setting a system of rewards and punishments for enforcing these rules than he is in trying to understand students and their behavior. The cognitive, or problem-solving, aspects of student behavior are for the most part ignored. Excellent sources discussing the behaviorist position include Homme (1970), Axelrod (1977), and Blackham and Silberman (1975).

This orientation is quite different from the interactionist position, which attempts to teach students to solve their own classroom problems.

Interactionist. The interactionist view of management, also called the confronting/contrasting approach (Wolfgang & Glickman, 1986), lies between the noninterventionist and the behaviorist. While the teacher assumes full authority under the behaviorist view and little authority as a noninterventionist, interactionist teachers share authority with their students. They view students as capable of making decisions but needing guidance from the teacher. This guidance function serves as the primary management role for the interactionist teacher. Mrs. Williams allowed and even encouraged participation from the students in rule making but also provided her own input into the process. She and the students jointly established rules. When Kent came unprepared, she first asked him what he was doing and then asked him if he knew the rule on bringing materials to class. She then got a written commitment from him indicating that he would bring his materials in the future.

By comparison with Mr. Gordon, Mrs. Williams didn't punish the forgetful student but, in contrast with Ms. Bass, she addressed the behavior directly. Mrs. Williams should also be prepared to take stronger steps if necessary should the materials be forgotten again. This position is called interactionist because the teacher works on the problem of management in cooperation with the student. However, in interacting with students, the teacher does not give up her responsibility to direct or manage their behavior. For further reading on the interactionist position, we recommend Dreikurs and Cassel (1972), Ernst (1972), and Glasser (1969).

Approach Summary

We'll summarize our discussion of these three positions by comparing them in terms of their different views on authority and on the source of the management problem. We will also discuss some strengths and weaknesses of each position.

The major goal of the noninterventionist position is to enhance the personal growth and freedom of the individual. While potentially bothersome to the teacher, management problems provide opportunities to function in a counselor-client relationship with students. In achieving this goal, the teacher remains as supportive and nondirective as possible.

The major goal of the behaviorist approach, by contrast, is to maintain an orderly and productive classroom. The rules established and the rewards and punishments designed to enforce these rules are not ends in themselves, but rather means towards the end, which is an efficient learning environment.

The interactionist position, while still concerned with the establishment of rules, places a major emphasis on how these rules are established and individual students' responsibility to follow these rules. In this sense the rules are not ends in themselves but rather means toward an end, the end being teaching students how to solve their own problems. In this respect the teacher acts as facilitator but is still active in the management process.

The goals of these three approaches are tied closely to the different views about the sources of the management problems. The noninterventionist approach believes that management problems come from the incomplete development of the individual but does not blame the individual for these problems. Instead, the solution is viewed as a natural part of the growth process. The behaviorist views problems as emanating from incompletely or inefficiently developed learning systems. Rather than spending time trying to figure out the reasons for the misbehavior, behaviorists spend their time trying to develop more efficient systems. The interactionist views management problems as being a normal consequence of 30 people with diverse backgrounds and interests being forced into the same classroom at the same time. The problems that arise are to be expected and should be dealt with as a normal part of the class's problem-solving activities.

The three approaches also differ markedly in their views toward teacher authority. The behaviorist view readily accepts teacher authority and uses it to establish and maintain rules in the classroom. The interactionist view maintains the idea that the teacher is ultimately in charge of the classroom, but the authority is shared with students through collaborative rule making. Students are made responsible for working out solutions to problems, but the teacher doesn't disguise the fact that these rules must be acceptable to the teacher and the school at large. The noninterventionist approach, by contrast, minimizes the authority of the teacher, instead emphasizing the relationship between teacher and students. The noninterventionist approach views the overuse of authority as an obstacle to this relationship.

As can be seen from our discussion of these approaches, none is inherently better or worse than others. What will work for one teacher won't work for another. This is the reason for our advocacy of a models approach to management. There is no best way to manage a classroom. Accordingly, we encourage you to experiment with a variety of approaches until you find which ones work for you under what situations. When armed with such a repertoire, you are then in a position to make professional decisions about your teaching.

Some workers in this area (e.g., Wolfgang & Glickman, 1986) advocate the application of these different approaches in a developmental sequence. One way of doing this would be to start with a tightly structured classroom (behaviorist approach) and then, as the classroom becomes organized, shift more control and responsibility for rule setting to students (an interactionist approach). An alternate approach begins the year at an intermediate point in the teacher-power continuum, allowing students to share in the process of rule setting. Subsequent movement from this interactionist position depends upon student behavior. If more structure is needed, the teacher can move the class more towards the behaviorist position, with a tightening of class rules and procedures. If students seem to be growing and assuming more and more of the responsibility for their own behavior, the teacher can concentrate on developing relationships with students and listening.

In reality, few, if any, teachers are strictly behaviorist, noninterventionist, or interactionist; most are a combination of all three. This is as it should be. We have presented them separately to try to make their respective positions clear and to help make your understanding as complete as possible.

EXERCISE 10.2

Examine the following statements and determine whether they reflect a behaviorist (B) position, an interactionist (I) position, or a noninterventionist (N) one.*

_____ 1. Although children can think, a structured environment is necessary to help them learn.

_____ 2. Student creativity and self-expression are the most important goals of a classroom.

_____ 3. Students need help in formulating rules and in following through with them once established.

_____ 4. Management is a means to an end; my primary job as a teacher is to teach students knowledge and skills.

_____ 5. When a student doesn't complete an assignment, the teacher's role is to understand the reasons for this.

_____ 6. Students need to understand that teachers are persons, too, with rights and feelings.

_____ 7. The best way to motivate students to learn is through grades and assignments that can be completed successfully.

_____ 8. When students persistently talk out of turn, their inner needs aren't being met.

_____ 9. When students persistently talk out of turn, they don't understand the implications of this behavior for themselves or others.

_____ 10. When students persistently talk out of turn, the classroom reward system isn't working.

*Adapted from Wolfgang & Glickman (1986).

EXERCISE 10.3

Read the following anecdote and answer the questions that follow. Then compare your answers to the ones given in the feedback section at the end of the chapter.

Mr. Rogers was a fourth-grade teacher in a typical school. He began his year by first getting to know his students and began to establish the procedures for his class.

On the first instructional day, he said, ''In order to learn the most, we must have some rules that we all want to follow carefully.'' With that, he displayed a large poster board on which were clearly printed a list of rules for the class during the year.

He then asked, ''Do all the rules seem fair? Are there others we should add?''

The class then read the rules and after a short discussion agreed that the rules were okay as he presented them. Mr. Rogers then went on with his class work.

A few days later during an explanation of a math problem, Susan was turned around talking to Shirley. Mr. Rogers ignored the talking for a moment, but it continued. As the rest of the class was working a problem, Mr. Rogers went back to Susan and asked, ''Susan, do you know why I've come to talk to you?''

Susan hesitated and then said, ''Shirley and I were talking.''

''Yes,'' Mr. Rogers continued, ''and I get upset when someone talks while I'm talking. Remember, we made a rule about talking while someone else is talking. Do you know what that rule is?''

Susan nodded.

''Now I want you to suggest some way that you can help yourself stay within the rules we agreed upon. Let me know after school.''

Mr. Rogers then continued with the lesson, and Susan stopped in at the end of the day and simply said she wouldn't talk anymore.

The next day during the same class, as Mr. Rogers was discussing another problem, Susan again turned around and began talking. Mr. Rogers went to her after he had the rest of the class involved in an activity and said evenly, ''Susan, this is the second infraction of the rules, so I'm going to have to put a check by your name. This means you won't be able to take part in our free-play activity this afternoon. Please try to obey the rules from now on.''

With that, Mr. Rogers again went back to his regular classroom activity.

1. Identify two places where Mr. Rogers illustrated characteristics of a behaviorist.

_____

_____

2. Identify two places where Mr. Rogers illustrated characteristics of an interactionist.

_____

_____

3. Identify one place where Mr. Rogers illustrated characteristics of a noninterventionist.

_____

_____

ASSERTIVE DISCIPLINE: YOU *CAN* CONTROL YOUR CLASSES

Although the importance of classroom management as a concern of all teachers, and especially beginning teachers, has remained high over the years, the popularity of different approaches has varied over time. Currently, one of the more widely discussed approaches to classroom management is *assertive discipline;* workshops in virtually every state across the country attest to its popularity.

Assertive discipline emphasizes teachers' right to an orderly classroom and outlines steps that teachers can take to insure these rights. In this section of the chapter we examine the ideas behind assertive discipline, examine its application in the classroom, and analyze some reasons for its popularity.

Assertive discipline developed out of Lee and Marlene Canter's (1976) work in the general area of assertion training. As they attempted to help their clients become more assertive, they encountered three characteristic patterns of reactions to conflict. Nonassertive people were passive and wishy-washy and were unable to express their wants or feelings. Furthermore, they were unable to back up their words with actions. Equally problematic were hostile people who could express their wants and feelings, but did so at the expense of other people; in doing this they often put down or abused others. An assertive response style, by contrast, clearly communicated wants and feelings but did so without harming other people. As they worked with teachers, they saw that many management problems involved conflict and found these different response patterns played out in the classroom.

Let's see what these might look like. Johnny has been told several times to keep his hands to himself in the classroom. The teacher turns around and sees Johnny poking at a student walking by his desk. Alternate teachers' responses are as follows:

Nonassertive: Johnny, I don't know what to do with you. Why can't you keep your hands to yourself?

Hostile: Johnny, there is something wrong with you; you just won't listen! I've told you a million times to keep your hands to yourself.

Assertive: Johnny, you've been warned before and now you've made the choice to leave the room. Pick up your books and come with me.

Assertive discipline attempts to train teachers to respond to management problems with proactive assertive behaviors rather than nonassertive or hostile actions. It is based on the premise that teachers have three rights:

1. The right to establish a classroom structure that is conducive to learning
2. The right to determine and expect appropriate behavior from students
3. The right to ask for help from parents, the principal, and other professionals to produce order in the classroom

Using these rights as a foundation, assertive discipline advocates the creation of a management system that is similar in many respects to the behaviorist approach discussed earlier. Rules and procedures are clearly laid out at the beginning of the year and reinforced with both positive rewards and negative consequences. Positive rewards include

Praise

Awards

Notes or phone calls to parents

Special privileges (e.g., games, puzzles)

Material consequences (food, prizes)

Teachers have a right to an orderly classroom.

Negative consequences include

> Time out (preferably in another classroom)
>
> Removal of a privilege (e.g., P.E. or recess)
>
> After-school detention
>
> Principal's office
>
> Home involvement

Both positive and negative consequences need to be made clear to students from the beginning and are administered with a name checklist on the board much like the one used by behaviorists.

In dealing with misbehavior, assertive discipline recommends a response hierarchy similar to ones discussed earlier. At one end of a continuum (see Figure 10.3) are nondirective statements that call students' attention to a problem; at the other end of the continuum are teacher demands that require immediate compliance.

Let's see what this continuum would like in a classroom where students are having trouble staying in their seats:

Nondirective Statement:	Class, remember what we said about staying at your desks during seatwork.
Question:	Would you get back in your seat right now?
Directive Statement:	Everyone needs to be in their seats right now.
Demand:	Janey, get in your seat and get to work or you'll choose to stay in for recess.

The way that the demand is made is important; it is neither threatening nor hostile, and puts the burden of choice for behavior on the student.

A final aspect of assertive discipline should be mentioned — the broken record. Often in dealing with student problems, teachers become sidetracked from (a) the problem at hand and (b) their requirement/request to the student. To avoid this, teachers are encouraged to use a broken-record technique, in essence, repeating their request until the message is delivered. Here's what this technique sounds like in practice.

Ms. Jackson:	Tom, you've got to stop fighting on the playground.
Tom:	But, they're always callling me names.

⌐Nondirective Statements_____Questions_____Directive Statements_____Demands⌐

Figure 10.3   Assertive Discipline Response Continuum

> *Ms. Jackson:* That's not the point. What gets you in trouble is *your* fighting. This has to stop.
>
> *Tom:* But, they pick on me first.
>
> *Ms. Jackson:* I understand. But still *your* problem is fighting. You've got to stop fighting.

If not overused (three repeats is the recommended maximum), this technique helps the teacher maintain focus in the middle of a management problem, without becoming distracted from their management objective.

In analyzing assertive discipline, let's ask these questions: What is so new about it? and Why is it so popular? A partial answer to both questions is that it emphasizes teachers' rights to a sane and orderly classroom. This is a plus for the approach; all teachers should feel they have the right to teach and enforce standards and to deal with students who infringe on this right. In addition, assertive discipline is quite structured; it describes prescriptive courses of action for most classroom problems. This is another plus, especially for beginning teachers who are sometimes unclear about their options. On the negative side assertive discipline allows for little negotiation between teacher and students and casts the teacher in an authoritarian light. In addition, there is little attempt to help students understand or control their behavior.

In terms of these strengths and weaknesses, workers in the area have recommended assertive discipline as an introductory model, most appropriate for beginning teachers (Wolfgang & Glickman, 1986). Its structure and clear delineation of alternatives simplifies the management task for teachers. The hope, then, is that teachers use this as a foundation for growth, expanding their repertoire to more complex and truly educational alternatives, as the issue becomes not so much order but growth.

SUMMARY

The purpose of this chapter has been to suggest ways of dealing with routine management problems. The discussion has been quite general because the number of specific situations that might arise is endless and the manner in which they are confronted depends upon the unique behavioral environment established by the teacher as well as the students.

Nevertheless, three specific approaches were offered that should prove useful to the classroom teacher. The approaches included the noninterventionist, interactionist, and behaviorist methods. For each approach, the role of the teacher was discussed in addition to underlying assumptions and suggestions for utilization.

It is critical to note that the successful utilization of the above approaches is dependent upon matching the appropriate method to the teacher's philosophy of education. As discussed in Chapter 10, teachers hold certain philosophical attitudes toward the nature of the learner, and these attitudes should dictate a consistent methodology for addressing management problems. In concluding the chapter, we introduced you to the concept of assertive discipline which, when employed in your classroom, can foster an atmosphere of respect and further promote student achievement and growth.

REFERENCES

Axelrod, S. (1977). *Behavior modification for the classroom teacher*. New York: McGraw-Hill.

Blackham, G., & Silberman, A. (1975). *Modification of child and adolescent behavior* (2nd ed.). Belmont, CA: Wadsworth.

Canter, L., & Canter, M. (1976). *Assertive discipline: A take-charge approach for today's educator*. Seal Beach, CA.: Canter & Associates.

Dreikurs, R., & Cassel, P. (1972). *Discipline without tears*. New York: Hawthorne.

Ernst, K. (1972). *Games students play*. Millbrae, CA: Celestial Arts Publishing.

Freed, A. (1973). *TA for kids and grown-ups too*. Los Angeles: Jalmar Press.

Glasser, W. (1969). *Schools without failure*. New York: Harper & Row.

Glickman, C., & Wolfgang, C. (1979). Dealing with student misbehavior: An eclectic review. *Journal of Teacher Education, 30* (3), 7–13.

Gordon, T. (1975). *T.E.T.: Teacher effectiveness training*. New York: Peter H. Wyden.

Homme, L. (1970). *How to use contingency contracting in your classroom*. Champaign, IL: Research Press.

Howard, A. (1974). Discipline is Caring. *Discipline in the Classroom*. Washington, DC: National Education Association.

Kindsvatter, R. (1978). A new view of the dynamics of discipline. *Phi Delta Kappan*. 322–25.

Kounin, J. (1970). *Discipline and group management in classrooms*. New York: Holt, Rinehart & Winston.

Moustakas, C. (1972). *The authentic teacher*. Cambridge, MA: Doyle.

Rinne, C. (1984). *Attention: The fundamentals of classroom control*. Columbus, OH: Merrill.

Rogers, C. (1969). *Freedom to learn: A view of what education might become*. Columbus, OH: Merrill.

Rosenshine, B., & Furst, N. (1971). Research in teacher performance criteria. In B. O. Smith (Ed.), *Research in Education*. Englewood Cliffs, NJ: Prentice-Hall.

Wolfgang, C., & Glickman, C. (1986). *Solving discipline problems* (2nd ed). Boston: Allyn & Bacon.

EXERCISE FEEDBACK

EXERCISE 10.1

As with most of the area of classroom management there are few "cut-and-dried" answers; instead, a great deal of judgement must be employed. The answers we've provided are most appropriate in a typical situation, but extremes may suggest a much different source.

1. (s) Student-caused
2. (s) Student-caused. This is probably just "kids being kids;" however, if saying negative things to peers leads to a pattern of isolation of a child or fighting, this may indicate an emotional problem.
3. (t) Teacher-caused. Looking out the window during a discussion is almost certainly a teacher-caused problem. Perhaps the teacher isn't using any materials, the discussion lacks focus, or the topic is too abstract for the student. This problem is usually easily remedied with more careful preparation on the part of the teacher.
4. (s) Student-caused. Some amount of writing on desk tops is quite normal for students. A pattern of defacing property, however, indicates emotional disturbance.
5. (s) Student-caused
6. (s) Student-caused
7. (e) Emotionally caused. Temper tantrums, particularly if they occur frequently, indicate emotional struggling within the student.
8. (e) Emotionally caused. Children, of course, are more boisterous around their peers than their teacher, but a typical outgoing child will also tend to blurt out answers and continue to be quite outgoing in class. The child who dominates or bullies his peers while withdrawing from the teacher possibly has an emotional problem. Again, the teacher must judge this at the time it occurs.
9. (e) Emotionally caused. Obscenity indicates emotional problems, although nearly every child will swear on some occasion. The pattern is the indicator.
10. (e) Emotionally caused. Refusal to respond in class to the point of withdrawing signifies an emotional disturbance.

EXERCISE 10.2

1. (B) This statement's emphasis on a structured environment indicates a behaviorist position.
2. (N) The goals of creativity and self-expression would be most emphasized by a noninterventionist who believes in the natural unfolding of the individual.
3. (I) An interactionist believes in providing enough structure so that students can operate *and* grow in a classroom.
4. (B) This view is most compatible with a behaviorist's orientation because of its functional view of management.
5. (N) Understanding students is a primary goal for noninterventionists.
6. (I) Interactionists stress the consequences of behavior, especially regarding others' rights and feelings.
7. (B) External motivation based on grades as rewards characterize a behaviorist position.

EVALUATING

11 ‖ Measurement and Evaluation

INTRODUCTION

We are now to the third and final phase of the teaching cycle. Teaching is a three-phase process that begins with planning, which includes the analysis of the content, the preparation of objectives, and the writing of lesson plans; and continues with the second phase, implementation, which is the creation and use of activities designed to help students master the objectives specified during the planning stage. This is done by employing one or more teaching strategies and selected questioning skills. We now turn our attention to describing techniques for determining whether or not students, in fact, reach the goals you as a teacher outline during the planning phase.

This book is obviously not a text in measurement and evaluation, and we will not attempt to give the complete coverage you would find in a book devoted solely to those concerns. We will, however, try to illustrate the evaluation phase of teaching and show how the entire processes of planning, implementing, and evaluating are interrelated.

Let's begin our discussion with some background related to the evaluation process. As with previous discussions regarding the planning and implementing phases, keep in mind that this material is designed to be a conceptual tool which will help you think more clearly about your own teaching.

First, note that whenever we measure student achievement, we measure the extent to which the goal is met. We do not measure the activity the teacher used to reach the goal. For example, consider the goal,

> For third graders to understand nouns.

This goal describes what we want the students to know. An activity designed to help them reach the goal, such as looking at a number of concrete objects and explaining how all of them are nouns, would follow. Finally, we would want to determine if the students had mastered the goal, in this case, whether they understand nouns.

As we found in Chapter 4, there are several different levels of understanding as shown by the following examples of evaluation statements:

> Have students recall and state in writing a minimum of five nouns.
>
> Have the students underline nouns in a list of sentences.
>
> Have students write sentences using nouns in two different ways.
>
> Have students analyze the author's meaning of certain nouns in the context of a paragraph.

Again, notice first that these measures relate specifically to the goal and not the activity designed to help the students reach the goal. Also note that the levels of the measures vary considerably, remembering that the form and the level of the measure are specified in the planning phase at the time the objective is stated. Finally, the purpose of measurements is to collect data which the teacher uses to evaluate student performance or achievement.

You will recall the term *evaluation* from the taxonomy of educational objectives for the cognitive domain in Chapter 4. Evaluation is the sixth and highest level found in the cognitive domain and is defined as making judgements based upon a criterion. Therefore, when teachers evaluate, they make judgements based upon the collected data by utilizing a variety of measurements. This chapter introduces you to the evaluation phase by distinguishing between measurement and evaluation and by explaining the preparation of measurement items.

At the conclusion of Chapter 11, you should be able to write items and design tests. These skills will give you the ability to collect and arrange information in what is usually an objective and impersonal way. The final step of the evaluation phase is to use this information to assign grades and report to both students and parents. More information than grades must be offered, and when this additional communication and feedback have been provided, the three-phase model is complete and the entire cycle begins again.

OBJECTIVES

After completing Chapter 11, you should be able to accomplish the following objectives:

1. For you as a pre/inservice teacher to understand measurement and evaluation, so that when given a series of descriptive statements, you will correctly identify them as measurement or evaluation.
2. For you as a pre/inservice teacher to understand formal and informal measurements, so that when given a series of descriptive statements, you will identify them as formal or informal measurements.
3. For you as a pre/inservice teacher to understand the background needed for students to respond to measurement items, so that when given sample items, you will describe the prerequisite skills for each.
4. For you as a pre/inservice teacher to understand differences in effectiveness of measurement items, so that when given two items, you will identify the more effective one.

5. For you as a pre/inservice teacher to be able to prepare measurements for concept learning, so that when given a concept and grade level, you will write an item to measure the students' understanding of the concept.

6. For you as a pre/inservice teacher to be able to prepare measurements for learning generalizations, so that when given a generalization, you will prepare an item to measure the students' ability to comprehend the generalization.

7. For you as a pre/inservice teacher to understand the taxonomic level of measurement items, so that when given an item, you will identify the level.

8. For you as a pre/inservice teacher to increase your awareness of tests, so that when given a list of functions, you will correctly determine the type of test for each function.

9. For you as a pre/inservice teacher to understand grading systems, so that when given a list of scores and preset levels, you will correctly assign letter grades for the participating students.

10. For you as a pre/inservice teacher to increase your understanding of grading philosophy, so that, without aid, you will list three purposes for assigning grades.

11. For you as a pre/inservice teacher to increase your knowledge of grades, so that when given a list of grade functions, you will identify all those that are compatible with the information presented in this chapter.

12. For you as a pre/inservice teacher to understand feedback systems, so that when given a list of systems for reporting grades to parents, you will discuss the most effective one and support your choice with a minimum of two points.

13. For you as a pre/inservice teacher to increase your knowledge of implementing the affective domain, so that when presented with a scenario, you will be able to identify two ways in which the teacher prevented potential conflict with parents.

MEASUREMENT

Measurement is a process that is common to all sciences, including the social sciences and education. It involves the collection of information or data; therefore, it depends on our five senses. In the process of measurement, the senses are used to collect information from the environment.

Measurement can take many forms, differing in type and precision. First, let us consider some different forms. Using a ruler on a piece of paper, lowering a weighted rope into a lake, watching an odometer on a trip, and observing the relative heights of two buildings are all methods of measuring length. Stepping on a scale, lifting two rocks, and picking up a child are all methods of measuring weight. And placing milk in a cup before use in a recipe, trying on a new dress, and appraising the size of a meal before eating it are all methods of measuring volume. What all of these measurements have in common is that perceptual processes (sight, hearing, or touch) were used to gather some type of data.

As mentioned previously, measurements differ in terms of their precision. For instance, lifting two rocks by hand is less accurate than placing them on a scale. Estimating the size of two buildings is less precise than taking ropes to the tops of the buildings, lowering them to the bottom, and then using a tape measure to calculate the lengths. In general, the accuracy of measurements is related to what is being measured and by what instrument.

How the nature of what is being measured affects the accuracy of the measurement may not readily be apparent. For example, it is much easier to measure the weight of a rock than its chemical components. Also, it is easier to measure the height and weight of children than it is to measure their intelligence. Both of these illustrations show how differences in what is being measured affect the precision of the measurement.

The availability of instruments also affects the precision of measurements. For instance, when following a very complex recipe for French pastries, a set of measuring cups and spoons is much preferred over regular ones. The measuring cups and spoons are finely calibrated to make precise measurements. In measuring a person's intelligence, the availability of instruments also affects the precision of the measurements. Some crude indicators of a person's intelligence might be the answers to such questions as "What is 11 times 11?" or "What is the capital of Maine?" or "What is a proper noun?" As rough as these measurements are, they are better than nothing at all for predicting a person's intelligence. However, a more precise indication would be his or her performance on a standardized intelligence test that had been constructed and administered by testing experts.

The topic of measurements is an especially important one for educators because of the hundreds, if not thousands, of measurements that teachers make every day. Like all measurements, these differ as to type. A teacher takes measurements when she walks around the room and observes the behavior of her students. She also measures when she asks questions or gives a quiz or a test.

Measurements differ according to whether teachers consciously plan to measure and consequently alter the environment for that purpose or whether they take the measurement as part of the ongoing flow of classroom activities. Tests and quizzes are the most obvious examples of the former, which are called *formal measurements*. However, noticing the reactions to a movie shown in class, gauging student responses in a question-and-answer session, watching students as they do seatwork, or noting significant changes in an individual's manner or dress also give teachers much information. They are called *informal measurements*, and they're valuable in providing a basis for many important decisions. For example, noticing dramatic changes in a student's manner or dress, a teacher suspecting possible drug use might decide to refer the student to a school counselor. This is a critical decision, and it cannot be made on the basis of formal measurement.

The measurements that a teacher makes do not have to be used immediately but can be stored for later use. This can be done either by writing the measurement down or by remembering it. Putting attendance figures in a book would represent the former method. Probably the most common form of measurement storage takes place in the teacher's head.

As with all measurements, the measurements a teacher makes differ in terms of their accuracy. This difference in precision is due to the two factors mentioned previously — what is being measured and by what instrument. For instance, a teacher can obtain much more precise measurements of Johnny's knowledge of multiplication tables than he can of Johnny's creative ability. The difference in accuracy here relates to what is being measured. Creativity is harder to measure because it is more nebulous. Whether a child knows the alphabet can be measured more precisely than can her reading comprehension. Again the difference in the accuracy of the measurement is related to what is being measured.

Additionally, measurement accuracy is determined by the instruments used to make the measurements. For instance, standardized reading tests, when administered and interpreted correctly can give a more accurate measurement of a child's reading level than informal methods. Also, IQ tests give more accurate measurements of intelligence than do other types of measurements such as grades in history or behavior in math class.

A primary goal of the teacher should be to increase the accuracy of measurements. The teacher should be constantly alert to factors that influence this accuracy and should try to control factors that influence it. The purpose of this chapter is to help you learn to measure student understanding as accurately as possible.

PREPARING ACCURATE MEASUREMENT ITEMS

Basic Considerations

The previous section was written to help you understand the difference between measurement and evaluation. We want you to understand evaluation so that the evaluations you make as a teacher will be rational rather than whimsical or emotional, and we want you to understand measurement so that you will be aware of the basis for your evaluations and measure as accurately as possible.

This section of the chapter is devoted to a discussion of measurement and ways of preparing items to make your measuring as accurate as possible. Keep in mind as you read that no measurement is infallible. For example, in a multiple-choice item, you are actually measuring three things. First, you are measuring the students' understanding of the material; second, you're measuring their ability to take a multiple-choice test; and third, you are measuring their reading ability. Any of these factors can affect the accuracy of the measurement. Keep this in mind as you prepare items. One way of dealing with the problem is to frequently measure each student in different ways. For example, observing a student in class and talking with him are both excellent ways of measuring. If a conversation with a student reveals that he understands the material better than his performance on a written test would suggest, that may mean the written measurement was inaccurate. The main point is that an alert teacher will not only give written measures but will supplement these with observation, discussion, and other appropriate means of information gathering.

Paper-and-pencil tests are widely used, not because they are more accurate than other forms but because they are more efficient. It's very time-consuming to discuss a topic with each student in a large class, but giving a single paper-and-pencil test can be accomplished quickly. We neither praise nor condemn paper-and-pencil tests; rather, we describe ways of making written items as accurate as possible. A good discussion of different item formats can be found in Gronlund (1988).

Let's turn now to a more specific discussion of measurement. As noted earlier, measurement is considered in the planning phase of the activity because the form of the measurement is specified in the goals objective. In considering the goal and the measurement of it, the teacher asks herself several questions and makes several decisions in answering these questions. To illustrate this, let's look at the goal statement about nouns described at the beginning of the chapter:

For third graders to understand nouns

Before even writing the goal statement, the teacher asks herself, What do I want the child to know, understand, do, or feel? The answer in this case is, I want them to understand nouns. The next and very critical question is, How will I know if they understand nouns? The answer to this specifies the remainder of the goals objective — the evaluation statement. This is not always easy. Before the teacher can answer this second question, two subordinate questions must be asked —At what level do I expect them to understand? and Will I determine their understanding through having them recognize correct statements or by having them produce statements of their own?

Recognition involves providing the students with a series of choices and having them select the correct or most appropriate one(s). Multiple-choice items involve recognition, as do true/false and matching items. In a true/false format you merely recognize the statement as either true or false, while matching involves recognizing the relationship between two words or statements. Don't be confused, however! Recognition items do not mean merely knowledge level tasks. Very high levels of thinking can be measured with recognition items. This point is illustrated later in the chapter.

By comparison, production items require that the students generate their own responses rather than recognize correct ones. Short-answer and essay questions are examples of this. We will compare recognition and production items after we've seen some examples, but first let's look at Figure 11.1, a diagrammatic representation of the decision-making process we've just described.

Teachers must answer each of these questions for themselves in order to state the complete goals objective. The evaluation statement in the objective specifies the answer to these last three questions regarding the level and the method of measuring student understanding. Again, this illustrates how powerful the goals objective is as a tool to help teachers become systematic when developing instructional units.

In a sense, this chapter should be coupled with the planning phase of teaching in that measurement *decisions* are made prior to implementing the learning activity. We are placing it here, however, because the actual measurement process occurs after the students have completed the learning activity.

Let's look now at some actual measurement items.

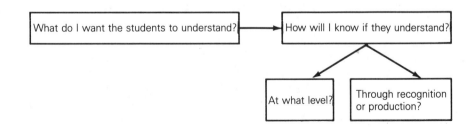

Figure 11.1   Decision-Making Model for the Planning and Evaluation Phases

Measuring the Learning of Facts

As noted in Chapter 2, facts are forms of information learned through drill, and measurement of their attainment exists only at the knowledge or low level. For example, a fact-level objective might be:

> For students to know American presidents, so that when provided with a major event in American history, they will provide the name of the person who held the presidency during that period.

An appropriate item to measure this objective could be

> The president during the Civil War was
>
> a. Alexander Hamilton
>
> b. Robert E. Lee
>
> c. Abraham Lincoln
>
> d. William Jennings Bryan

The preceding example is a recognition item. A question in the form of a production item for the same objective could be

> Who was president during the Civil War?

Measuring the Understanding of Concepts

To this point we've covered the idea of measurement, the difference between production and recognition items, and measuring the attainment of facts. We now want to move to a discussion of the process of measuring students' understanding of abstractions. However, in addition to discussing ways of measuring the learning of abstractions, we'll use examples to discuss the strengths and weaknesses of production versus recognition items. In addition, we'll discuss multiple-choice items more thoroughly than other recognition formats because that approach is the most widely used and perhaps the most efficient way of measuring. So, keep in mind both themes—measuring for abstraction, and in this section, concept learning and analysis of item formats.

First, while concepts can be measured at the knowledge level (as you will see in later paragraphs), they are most commonly measured at the comprehension level. This is accomplished quite easily and efficiently by asking students to identify unique examples of the concept. (To refresh your understanding of comprehension refer to Chapter 4.) For example, suppose you want preschool students to comprehend the concept *between*. Their comprehension could be measured with the following item.

Place an *X* on the picture where the dog is between the two boys.

Now let's turn to a discussion of measuring concepts at different levels. Note in the following discussion that some of the objectives go beyond the understanding of a concept *per se* and into the analysis of relationships. As we noted in the preceding discussion, understanding of concepts themselves is primarily a comprehension-level task.

Let's look again at the example with nouns. There are a number of evaluation statements that can facilitate the goal statement. As noted earlier, the form of the evaluation statement reflects the answers to the questions in the model (Figure 11.1). The goal and some sample evaluation statements follow:

For third-grade students to understand nouns so that
1. Without aids, they will write the definition of nouns.
2. Given a list of definitions, they will identify the one for nouns.
3. Given a list of words, they will circle all those that are nouns.
4. Given nouns, they will correctly use them in sentences.
5. Given a list of sentences, they will underline all the nouns.
6. Given a sentence, they will describe the author's intent by interpreting the meaning of the nouns in the context of the sentence.
7. Given a sentence and a list of meanings of a noun as determined by context, they will select the best interpretation.

So, you can see that decision making is not so simple! The one goal statement about a straightforward concept such as *nouns* allows for at least the seven possible evaluation statements we've listed here.

Let's look now at how the wording of the evaluation statement in the objective determines the form of the item that is designed to measure the students' attainment of the goal. Each evaluation statement and a corresponding item follow:

1. Evaluation Statement:
Without aids, they will write the definition of nouns.
Item:
On the line below write the definition of nouns.

_____

2. Evaluation Statement:
   Given a list of definitions, they will identify the one for nouns.
   Item:
   Circle the best definition of *noun.*
   a. A noun is a word that modifies verbs, adjectives, or adverbs.
   b. A noun is a word that shows action.
   c. A noun is a word that represents a person, place, or thing.
   d. A noun is a word that describes other words.

3. Evaluation Statement:
   Given a list of words, they will circle all those that are nouns.
   Item:
   Look at the words below. Circle all those that are nouns.
   a. hat   e. if   i. St. Louis
   b. is   f. and   j. Michigan
   c. door   g. to   k. pencil
   d. small   h. girl   l. under

4. Evaluation Statement:
   Given nouns, they will correctly use them in sentences.
   Item:
   Look at the following nouns and, on the line, write one sentence using each properly.

   a. sun _____

   b. table _____

   c. rock _____

5. Evaluation Statement:
   Given a list of sentences, they will underline all the nouns.
   Item:
   Read the following sentences and underline *all* the nouns in each.
   a. Jim, a large boy, rode his bike to the store.
   b. The noise in this town is murder!
   c. How fast were you going when the police officer stopped you?
   d. This is the last time I'll run through those woods.

6. Evaluation Statement:
   Given a sentence, they will describe the author's intent by interpreting the meaning of the nouns in the context of the sentence.
   Item:
   Consider the use of the noun *man* in the following sentence. Describe the meaning of the noun in each case according to the context of the sentence.

Man! That man is a *real man.*

Man! _____

man _____

man _____

7. Evaluation Statement:
   Given a sentence and a list of meanings of a noun as determined by context, they will select the best interpretation.
   Item:
   Look at the first use of the word *man* in the following sentence.

   Man! That man is a *real man.*

   Choose the best interpretation of the meaning of *Man!*
   a. It is a noun used as a subject in a sentence.
   b. It is a noun used to describe an element of masculinity or toughness.
   c. It is a noun used as a direct object in the sentence.
   d. It is a noun used as slang to express amazement or impressiveness.

Let's look now at the seven illustrations and discuss them in view of the material we've presented so far. We can say several things about them.

First, each of the seven items is a formal measurement designed to provide data to help the teacher evaluate his students' understanding of nouns. This is contrasted with informal measures such as observing the students at work or hearing a variety of responses from them.

Second, the items are written at different levels. Items 1 and 2 are knowledge level, 3 and 5 are comprehension level, 4 is application level, and 6 and 7 are probably at the analysis level. As we noted in Chapter 4, exact determinations of level are sometimes very difficult, so you shouldn't be overly concerned with uncertainty between levels such as application and analysis, or analysis and evaluation. Our primary goal is for you to be aware of and sensitive to the higher levels of the taxonomy so you can encourage your students to improve their thinking skills. Consequently, you will want to measure at the higher levels as well.

Third, some of the items are production and some are recognition. Items 1, 4, and 6 are production items; the students were asked to produce, respectively, a definition, a sentence, and an analysis. Items 2, 3, 5, and 7 are recognition items; the students had to recognize, respectively, a definition, nouns in a list, nouns in a sentence, and a correct interpretation of a noun's usage.

Let's look now at recognition and production in a bit more detail. First, production items are generally more difficult than recognition items at the same taxonomic level. For a psychological explanation of this difference, see Brown (1976) and Wickelgren (1977). Items 1 and 2 are both knowledge level, but recalling and stating the definition is more difficult than merely recognizing it. Another example of the simpler nature of recognition as compared to production is found in our vocabulary. It is generally believed that our comprehension vocabulary is several times larger than our speaking vocabulary. This means that we recognize the meaning of many more words than we are able to use in conversation.

A second observation about these two types of items is that recognition items are much easier for the teacher to evaluate. A production item results in each student giving a slightly different response, leaving you in a position of having to decide whether the produced statement represents an adequate understanding of the concept. We are not suggesting that production items shouldn't be used but are merely pointing out that they are more difficult to evaluate. For example, compare item 6 to item 7. Item 6 puts much more demand on the learner; she must interpret what is being asked, organize her thoughts, and put them down on paper. In item 7, she must merely select the choice she believes is best. Also, in item 6, students will give a variety of responses since this is a divergent question as opposed to a convergent one such as item 7. Therefore, the teacher needs to make more evaluation decisions with item 6 than with 7, where it would be much easier to be consistent in scoring.

One other factor to consider in deciding upon the item format is the amount of work involved. Production items are easier to prepare, but recognition items are easier to score. The decision of which to use depends on your concerns with the item. If you want to have students learn to express themselves in writing, you may choose to use a production item. You must keep in mind, of course, that you would be measuring writing ability in addition to the understanding of the concept. Let's look at what the student must be able to do or must know in order to respond correctly to item 6:

Be able to read

Be able to organize thoughts

Be able to write in a clear and precise way

Know how nouns are used in sentences in order to describe the way each is used in context

By comparison, let's look at what the student must be able to do or must know in order to respond correctly to item 7:

Be able to read

Know the concept *subject*

Know the concept *direct object*

Know the meaning of *slang*

Know the meaning of *amazement* and *impressiveness*

Being able to organize thoughts and express them in writing is very demanding for many students; consequently, this together with consistency, is the reason we see recognition items on standardized tests.

These factors are not mentioned to suggest that accurate measurement is extremely difficult or even impossible. On the contrary, measuring can be an enjoyable task because it gives you information about your students and your own teaching. Instead, these factors are a reminder of considerations you must make in measuring—again, all in an effort to increase rational decision making.

Let's look now at other items and consider these factors further. (You will notice that to complete this discussion we're using as an example $C = \pi d$, which is actually a generalization. We'll discuss measuring generalizations more fully in the next section.)

Think back to Mr. Hite's lesson on circles in Chapter 7 (pages 166–167). His objective was

> For prealgebra students to understand the formula for computing circumference, so that when given a ruler and four circles with the radius drawn in, they will calculate the circumference of each without error.

An item to measure Mr. Hite's objective would be:

A. Calculate the circumference of each of the following circles.

C = ___   C = ___   C = ___   C = ___

Suppose now that Mr. Hite's evaluation statement was a bit different and his objective was stated as follows:

> For prealgebra students to understand the formula for computing circumference, so that when given four diameters of circles, they will calculate the circumference of each without error.

An item to measure his objective in this case could be:

B. Calculate the circumference of each of the four circles from the following diameters:

Diameter = 2 cm. $C =$ _____
Diameter = 4.5 cm. $C =$ _____
Diameter = 13.22 cm. $C =$ _____
Diameter = 6 cm. $C =$ _____

There are still other possibilities. For instance, suppose Mr. Hite's objective was stated

> For prealgebra students to understand the formula for computing circumference, so that when given the formula and four diameters of circles, they will calculate the circumference of each without error.

An item to measure his objective in this case could be:

C. Use the equation $C = \pi d$ to calculate the circumference of each of the four circles whose diameters are given below.

Diameter = 2 cm. $C =$ _____
Diameter = 4.5 cm. $C =$ _____
Diameter = 13.22 cm. $C =$ _____
Diameter = 6 cm. $C =$ _____

We now want to compare the three items in Exercise 11.1. Because of the important discussion that follows in the feedback, it is important for you to complete this exercise.

EXERCISE 11.1 _____

Consider items A, B, and C from the previous section and answer the following questions. Then compare your answers to the ones given in the feedback section at the end of the chapter.

1. List what the student must be able to do or must know in order to respond correctly to each item.

A. (page 296)

1) _____

2) _____

3) _____

4) _____

5) _____

6) _____

7) _____

8) _____

B. (pages 296–297)

1) _____

2) _____

3) _____

4) _____

5) _____

6) _____

C. (page 297)

1) _____

2) _____

3) _____

4) _____

2. At what taxonomic level is each item written?

A. _____

B. _____

C. _____

3. Identify each item as either production or recognition.

A. _____

B. _____

C. _____

While the next section deals with the selection of possible answers, one final factor should be mentioned here about these examples. In terms of the demands on the learner, computing the circumference for $d = 13.22$ cm. is more demanding than computing it for $d = 2$ cm. Again, the choice of a difficult or easy problem depends on the judgement of the teacher and what she wants the students to be able to demonstrate. Level of difficulty is, however, a factor to be considered.

Let's look now at a common recognition item, the multiple-choice format. Our purpose here is to discuss distracters in some detail. *Distracters* are the incorrect or inappropriate choices listed in a multiple-choice item. Multiple-choice items are an efficient method of measuring all forms of knowledge. We saw in the example with nouns how recall of a definition can be measured. Let's look now at an analysis of distracters through an example of measuring comprehension of concepts.

Consider Mr. Hanes's lesson from Chapter 7 on *hyperbole* (see pages 180–181). *Hyperbole* is a concept, and, as noted earlier, an efficient method of measuring students' understanding of a concept is to have them identify examples of it. (Of course, *noun* is also a concept, and we saw that it can be measured at a variety of levels.)

Let's look at two items designed to measure students' comprehension of *hyperbole:*

1. Which of the following is a statement of hyperbole?
   a. He is like an old shoe.
   b. He was a rock of a man.
   c. The night's bright eyes shone through the inky blackness.
   d. I was so sad I could have cried a river.

2. Which of the following is a statement of hyperbole?
   a. He went to town.
   b. Three large boys rode by on their bikes.
   c. Susan looks like her mother.
   d. I was so sad I could have cried a river.

In both items the correct choice is *d,* but the distracters are much better in item 1 than those in item 2. Looking at item 1 in detail, we see that choice *a* is a simile, choice *b* is a metaphor, choice *c* is personification, and choice *d* is hyperbole. All four choices are figures of speech, and the learner must know hyperbole from other figures of speech in order to answer the item correctly. In item 2, no other figures of speech are used as distracters; therefore, the learner might not know hyperbole from other figures of speech and might still answer the item correctly. This would then be an inaccurate measurement leading the teacher to conclude that students understand hyperbole when they actually don't. The purpose in choosing good distracters is not to trick students but to measure their learning as accurately as possible.

Let's consider recognition versus production in this case. A critical factor in using the identification of examples to measure comprehension of concepts is that they are novel, having never been encountered by the students before. If they had previously encountered the example, "I was so sad I could have cried a river," as an example the teacher used to teach the concept, the measurement would merely be at the knowledge level because it had been memorized. If students are asked to produce an example, they may merely recall one rather than produce an original. In this case, a recognition item may be preferable because the teacher can be as sure as possible that the examples are unique. Again, the whole purpose is to measure as accurately as possible.

Let's look now at the recognition item distracters in the feedback for Exercise 11.1. The item was written as follows:

Look at the following circle:

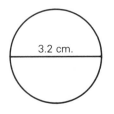

3.2 cm.

The circumference of the circle is

a.   1.6 cm.

b.   8.04 cm.

c. 10.05 cm.

d.   5.02 cm.

These numbers were not selected arbitrarily. For example:

a.   1.6 cm. = the radius (half the diameter)

b.   8.04 cm. = the area (πr^2)

c. 10.05 cm. = the correct answer (πd)

d.   5.02   = πr

If the learners are confused between area and circumference, they might choose *b*. If they don't remember that circumference relates to diameter and not radius, they might choose *d*. In either case the measurement is a more accurate reflection of the students' understanding of circumference and, therefore, more likely to help the teacher identify students' misconceptions than if the numbers were chosen arbitrarily. Again, the purpose is to measure accurately and not to trick the students.

Let's now consider another example as an exercise.

EXERCISE 11.2

Look at the following two items designed to measure a kindergarten child's concept of rectangle. Assuming the directions are given orally, choose the better item and explain your choice. Then compare your answers to those given in the feedback section at the end of the chapter.

1. Look at the three shapes on your paper and mark the one that is a rectangle.

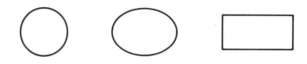

2. Look at the four shapes on your paper and mark the one that is a rectangle.

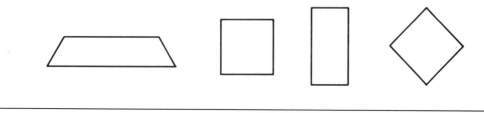

_____

_____

_____

_____

EXERCISE 11.3 _____

As a production exercise, develop a recognition item to measure a kindergarten child's concept of *mammal*. Assuming the item and the distracters would be presented in pictorial form, write a multiple-choice question with one correct answer and three distracters. Then compare your item to the one given in the feedback section at the end of the chapter.

_____

_____

_____

_____

_____

_____

_____

Measuring the Understanding of Generalizations

As with concepts, generalizations can be measured at the knowledge and the comprehension levels. However, while we noted that understanding concepts is primarily a comprehension-level task, measuring for understanding of generalizations extends readily to the application level of the taxonomy. As with concepts, levels beyond application exist for generalizations, but they are designed to measure students' ability to analyze relationships and appropriateness of generalizations and not the generalization itself.

Let's look now at the different levels. Measuring a generalization at the knowledge level primarily involves asking students to recall or identify it in a list, so we won't discuss this process here. Measuring generalizations at higher levels is quite another task. Let's look at the following objective:

> For psychology students to understand the generalization, intermittent reinforcement produces persistent behavior and slow extinction, so that when given a series of illustrations, they will identify the cases in which the generalization applies.

The item appears as follows:

> Which of the following illustrate the generalization, intermittent reinforcement produces persistent behavior and slow extinction? Circle the letter of all choices that apply.
> a. Mrs. Williams was trying to encourage Johnny's seatwork. For a week she gave him a reward every 5 minutes whenever he was working quietly at his desk.
> b. Mr. Smith assigns homework nightly but checks it only periodically.
> c. Johnny, a spirited third grader, acts up often. Generally his teacher is firm but strict. Sometimes, though, Johnny's behavior is so funny, she has to laugh.
> d. When encountering a locked door, people generally wiggle it several times and then leave or hunt for a key.
> e. Mr. Jones put 50¢ into the washing machine at the laundromat. It didn't come on, so he tried another machine.
> f. People who go to Las Vegas usually lose, but they win every once in a while.
> g. Mr. Anderson caught a fish in a particular spot in the St. Johns River. Now he fishes in that spot whenever he can and does fairly well.

In this item, the students have to identify cases where the generalization is illustrated; in other words, they are identifying examples of the generalization. In this sense, the measurement is similar to having the students identify examples of a concept, which is also a comprehension-level task.

Note the format of the item. The student, in responding, makes a decision about each choice individually. The item then essentially operates in a true/false format. The directions could just as easily have read:

> Mark as true the following cases that illustrate the generalization, intermittent reinforcement results in persistent behavior and slow extinction.

To make the item simply multiple choice, the instructor would merely have to reduce the number of choices to four or five with only one correct. We will not discuss the relative advantages and disadvantages of the true/false format and the multiple-choice format beyond a description designed to make you aware of and sensitive to the difference.

Let's look now at another example:

> People in an institution were being paid 50¢ a day for doing maintenance work around the grounds. After the work was done, the trustee, who inspected the work, would come and then pay the money to the workers. After a while, in that the work was always satisfactory and the workers always got paid, the administrators decided that they would just pay all the inmates in the morning at roll call and save the management the problem of paying people when the trustee came around.
>
> Which of the following best describes the consequence of the change in routine?
> a. There would be no change, and the operation would proceed more smoothly.
> b. The inmates would like it better because they knew they would get paid, and, consequently, they would work harder.
> c. The inmates would work less hard because they got paid whether they did the work or not.
> d. The inmates would work less hard because they would be insulted by the small amount they were being paid.

The preceding is another example from psychology. Notice the difference between the two examples. In the first, the students were asked to identify illustrations of the generalization, which is a comprehension-level task. In the second, they were asked to use the generalization, reinforcement is most effective following desired behavior, to predict consequences, which is an application-level task.

EXERCISE 11.4

Read the following item and then answer the questions at the end. Compare your answers to the ones found in the feedback section at the end of the chapter.

Which of the following cases relate to the generalization, people who smoke tend to have a higher incidence of heart disease than those who don't?

a. Mr. Smith is a robust man in his late thirties. He runs two miles a day and lives a generally healthy life. He eats two eggs and has bacon for breakfast in order to get enough protein, and loves beef because "it keeps my energy level up." His only problem is that he has a heart murmur.

b. Mr. Jones has a generally healthy living style. He has only two vices. He smokes a half a pack of cigarettes a day and has one strong drink before dinner. Otherwise he watches his diet by keeping fatty foods to a minimum and plays tennis four days a week. He is in his late thirties and is in excellent health.

c. Mr. Anderson lives a generally comfortable life-style. He smokes a few cigarettes each day but lays off the beer. He plays tennis, and everyone tells him how good he looks. However, he has two arteries par-

tially clogged that his doctor says will eventually require surgery.
d. Mr. Holt is a generally healthy man in his early thirties. His only problem is he sometimes has heart fibrillation. This is hard to imagine because he has a clean life-style. He is a vegetarian, and his weight is what it was in high school. He doesn't smoke and doesn't drink at all.

1. At what level is this item?

_____

2. Analyze the four choices in terms of the appropriateness of the distracters.

a. _____

b. _____

c. _____

d. _____

Note in each of the previous examples that measuring understanding of a generalization required a short scenario either in the stem of the item or in the distracters. When measuring generalizations, this will often be the case since a generalization is broader and more inclusive than a concept. With practice, you will learn how to write scenarios that can be used in questions used to measure your students' understanding of generalizations.

Let's look now at an example that doesn't require a scenario. Refer to Chapter 7 in which a teacher wanted her students to understand the generalization, when two vowels are together in a word, the first is long and the second is silent (pages 183–184).

An item to measure this generalization could be as follows:

(Teacher reads) Look at the list of words in front of you. I'm going to pronounce each word, and you mark the ones in which the rule, when two vowels are together in a word, the first is long and the second is silent, is illustrated.

bought	sleigh	receive
either	protein	great
read	eight	load

Notice in this item that both the words and their pronunciations were required, because the rule linked the sound of the word to its spelling. Merely showing the students the words and asking them to state in which cases the rule applied wouldn't be appropriate. In order to respond correctly, a student would have to know how the word was pronounced; that being the case, the example couldn't be unique, which would mean the item was only at the knowledge level. This example is an excellent illustration of the teacher's need to think carefully about the measurement process.

EXERCISE 11.5

Using a scenario, write a multiple-choice item to measure the following objective:

> For students to understand the generalization, climate affects culture, so that when given a description of a culture, they will identify a statement that illustrates the generalization.

Then read the item given in the feedback section at the end of the chapter.

_____

_____

_____

_____

_____

_____

_____

_____

_____

_____

Measuring Inquiry Skills

Now we will briefly consider the measurement of inquiry skills. This represents a departure from the themes of the text up to this point because measuring inquiry learning amounts to measuring an intellectual skill. The skill involved is the ability to relate data to an hypothesis or the ability to decide which of two or more hypotheses is most supported in light of the data. As an example, consider the following situation involving the relationship of data to hypotheses.

The following is a partial map of a coastline:

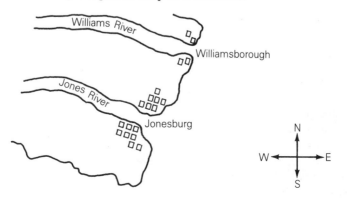

Both cities are on the coast and exist at the mouths of rivers. However, Jonesburg is a large and busy transportation center, whereas Williamsborough is small and insignificant. The following were proposed hypotheses that explained the reason for this difference:

1. While both Williamsborough and Jonesburg are on the coast and are at the mouths of rivers, Williamsborough's harbor is smaller than Jonesburg's, and the winds and tricky local currents made entrance dangerous in the early years when sailing ships were used.
2. The coastal range of mountains isolated Williamsborough but dwindled to foothills by the time they reached Jonesburg, which left it accessible to overland shipping.

The following data were gathered in reference to the hypotheses. Based on the data, decide which hypothesis is more logical and explain your choice briefly.

1. The current along the coast runs from north to south.
2. Jonesburg's harbor is larger than Williamsborough's.
3. About the same number of ships ran aground near Jonesburg as ran aground near Williamsborough in the sailing days.
4. Jonesburg and Williamsborough are over 100 miles apart.
5. The mountains around Williamsborough are more rugged than the mountains around Jonesburg.
6. The local winds around Jonesburg are more variable then they are around Williamsborough.

Keep in mind here that you're measuring the student's ability to relate data to hypotheses, which means the particular content of the item is not important. An inquiry lesson could present a topic in science while the item could involve social studies content. This is not inappropriate, because you're measuring an ability or an intellectual skill on the part of the students rather than information about an area of content. This is often a unique experience for a student and initially can be disconcerting. However, once this ability is developed, the students have acquired a powerful thinking skill.

EXERCISE 11.6

Read the following example of an inquiry situation and then respond to the data which follow. Check your responses with the ones given in the feedback section at the end of the chapter.

A study reported an investigation of longevity in various groups of people around the world. The investigators found two particular groups with a wide disparity in the average life expectancy between them. Furthermore, Group A (the long-lived group) had a much lower overall standard of living than Group B (the shorter-lived group). The average expectancies were Group A—85 years, and Group B—70 years. The investigators proposed the following explanation for this startling phenomenon:

While the standard of living for Group A is lower, they live in a manner conducive to good health. They are basically agrarian people, leading active and hard-working lives tending livestock and farms. Hence, they stay slim and avoid becoming overweight. They live in the mountains away from the psychological stresses of urban living. Their intake of potentially harmful items such as alcohol, tobacco, and high-cholesterol foods is kept at a minimum. On the other hand, Group B was sampled from an urban environment where psychological stress causing blood pressure problems is high, the air is dirty from factories, and the people lead sedentary lives.

The following are data that were found relative to the two groups. In each case, decide if the data support the explanation (s) or do not (ns).

_____ 1. Group A people averaged about 5'10" and about 190 lb., while Group B people averaged about 6'0" and approximately 180 lb.

_____ 2. The average protein intake per capita per day was
Group A: All sources — 60 g.
              Animal sources — 1 g.
Group B: All sources — 100 g.
              Animal sources — 95 g.

_____ 3. Group A people average 6 oz. per person per day of an alcohol resembling a cross between gin and vodka.

_____ 4. Group A people spent an average of 12 working hours per day walking in the mountains as sheepherders.

_____ 5. The city from which the Group B sample was drawn was noted for its "soft" industry such as insurance companies and clearinghouses for photocopying companies rather than heavy industries such as steel making.

_____ 6. The companies noted in number 5 employed many supervisors and salespeople, with each company priding itself in its success competing with rival companies.

_____ 7. The companies noted in numbers 5 and 6 also prided themselves in their comprehensive recreational programs including a variety of team and individual sports. They noted that each supervisor and salesperson averaged a minimum of 5 hours per week of vigorous physical activity.

_____ 8. Group A people enjoyed smoking a ground-up root resembling pipe tobacco in their leisure time. The investigators tried it and found it made them lightheaded when they inhaled, but the natives said it was easy to get used to.

_____ 9. In interviewing Group A people, a typical remark heard was, "It is good here where we can sit in the evening, watch the sun settle over our land, talk quietly, and watch our children grow."

_____ 10. In interviewing Group B people, typical remarks were, "I love my work. The only problem is that it's a bit of a hassle on the go all the time. It's really nice to get home and away from the grind. The traffic in this town is murder."

You've now seen what is perhaps a unique form of measurement for teachers and students, measurement of the inquiry process. Of course, the teacher could still measure the students' understanding of the content that came from the lesson in one of the conventional ways already discussed. Our purpose here is to give you a brief introduction to the idea of measuring inquiry skills. This introduction is sketchy because complete discussion of measuring for inquiry skills in beyond the scope of this text, but we hope this initial exposure will help you get started toward developing an important thinking skill in your own students.

EVALUATION

There is probably no process more central to teaching than *evaluation,* the process that involves the making of decisions. These decisions are based upon pertinent information, which you have gathered either formally or informally, and considered value judgements. The use of the term *evaluation* has at times been questioned, because of the narrow connotations of good and bad that it sometimes brings to mind. However, you should be cautioned at this point that the meaning of the term is broader in scope than merely decisions of bad and good. Evaluation will be used here to include all types of decisions.

As important as evaluation is to education and the classroom teacher, the process is not unique to education. People in all walks of life make evaluations constantly whether they realize it or not. For example, a person crossing the street makes an evaluation when looking both ways, estimating the speed of approaching vehicles, and then deciding whether to cross the street. A homemaker shopping for the family dinner makes an evaluation when checking all the meat prices before deciding on a particular cut. A person planting a vegetable garden makes evaluations as to the type of seeds to plant in the garden after checking characteristics of the plants and the growing conditions in the area.

All of these examples have two characteristics in common. One is that there was some type of decision being made; the other is that there was some type of information input before the decision was made. In all three examples, data in the form of measurements were actively gathered and utilized in the making of the decision. The measurements may have been formal or informal, but they were the basis for the evaluation.

Data gathering can occur in two ways in the evaluation process. One is by *data input,* and the other is by *data recall.* When individuals actively search the environment for information relevant to the pending decisions, they are using data input.

For example, in the case of the person crossing the street, data input would occur when the individual checked for cars and noted their approximate speeds. In the gardening example, the individual planting the garden would input data by reading the seed packages and checking the type and consistency of the soil.

Data recall occurs when the individual remembers information that is pertinent to the decision to be made. The person purchasing meat for the evening meal might recall recent dinner menus and family members' preferences regarding different types of meat. The person crossing the street might try to remember previous similar experiences in crossing that street or information such as the speed limit on that section of road or whether there were any stop lights on the street to slow down the cars.

As previously mentioned, evaluation consists of decision making based upon information gathered. One other characteristic of the evaluation process is important. This involves the influence of values on the evaluations that people make. *Values* are those beliefs that guide a person's life. Patriotism, love, honesty, and truthfulness are all values. Values influence all evaluations, whether the individual making the evaluation is aware of this or not. In the previously cited instances, personal values toward risk taking when crossing the street and the importance of money and personal health when buying meat could influence the evaluations made.

Let's look now at some examples of educational evaluations. For instance, a teacher assigns certain roles in a play according to unique characteristics of the students. In doing this, the teacher might try to match such factors as the type and the difficulty of role with specific students. These assignments would be evaluations for several reasons. First, they are decisions. Second, they are based on information that the teacher has gathered such as the personalities of the children and the demands of the different roles. Finally, these decisions are based on the teacher's belief that self-confidence, ability to speak in public, and ability to memorize are important skills to encourage in students.

Certain types of educational evaluations are readily apparent. Teachers make evaluations constantly about whether students have learned their multiplication tables, know the letters of the alphabet, or understand the experiment discussed in last Thursday's class. Often the evaluative nature of this process is emphasized by the fact that the teacher actually gives a grade, which is only one type of evaluation. This giving of grades is an evaluation because it is a decision reached by a teacher based upon data (quizzes, test papers, assignments, or participation in class) and certain values (hard work, obedience, the importance of factual knowledge, or creativity). Notice here how informal measurements and values influence teacher evaluations. A teacher valuing hard work, adherence to rules, and perseverance who notices a student reading during times allotted for homework may consciously or unconsciously react unfavorably. Here the values and the informal measurement of merely noticing the student reading interact to affect the teacher's decision. On the other hand, a teacher who values free spiritedness and a curious mind may react in precisely the opposite way when making the identical informal measurement.

Some other types of evaluations made by teachers may not be so apparent. These do not involve a grade as a judgement. A teacher allowing a student to go out to recess even though he hasn't finished his math work would be an example of an evaluation. In making that decision, she gathered information (the student's restlessness and inability to concentrate) as well as recalled information (past instances in which the student acted this way). She then used this information along with values she had toward children and education and decided that it would be best to allow him to go out and run off some of his excess energy.

If you are aware of factors that enter into the evaluation process, such as informal measurement, you can then make better evaluations. If you understand the importance of the information in the evaluation process, you can strive to make sure that the information that you use is accurate. Also, if you are aware of the values that influence your evaluations, your decisions may become more rational. Now that you have studied the process of evaluation, we hope you will be able to apply this knowledge and make better and more sensitive evaluations in your classroom.

EXERCISE 11.7

Read the scenario that follows and decide whether each numbered statement describes an informal measurement (im), a formal measurement (fm), or an evaluation (e). Then compare your answers to the ones found in the feedback section at the end of the chapter.

Miss Anthony wanted her kindergarten students to be prepared for written symbol recognition so that they could pick out the symbol when its sound was made. Therefore, she needed to determine if her kindergarten class needed more work in sound discrimination before they went into recognition of the written symbols. (1) _____ She decided to pronounce the words *bird, dog, ball, dad, man, none, nose,* and *milk* to the children individually and ask them to tell her which ones had the same first sound. (2) _____ She then checked the students to see if they could match the sounds, and she found that 8 of her 20 students matched all four of the pairs of sounds correctly, while the other 12 incorrectly matched one or more of the pairs.

She separated the children into the group of 12 and the group of 8, which she started on written letter recognition activities. (3) _____ Then, in order to have smaller groups, Miss Anthony divided the group of 12 into those whose first names started with *A* through *M* and those whose names started with *N* through *Z*, which made six students per group. (4) _____ She decided to practice first-letter sounds with both of these groups by presenting pictures of objects and pronouncing the words.

While Miss Anthony worked with the first group of six, she saw Joey poke Mary and pull her hair. (5) _____ She also noticed Joey glancing at her as he performed his little disruptions. (6) _____ She recalled that he had been making himself conspicuous in other activities as well. (7) _____ She then decided that she wouldn't call more attention to Joey by reprimanding him. (8) _____ She noticed that Mary seemed to be paying little attention to him.

After Miss Anthony completed her week-long activity with her two groups of six, she gave the children each a set of 15 pictures and told them to put all of the pictures that started with the sound of ''b'' in one pile, those that started with ''d'' in a second pile, those with ''m'' in a third, and those with ''n'' in a fourth. (9) _____ Based on the results, Miss Anthony moved the top eight into symbol recognition but held the bottom four students back for more work.

TEST APPROACHES

Norm-Referenced Tests

When students go to school, they are assigned to specific classes. This assignment may be very deliberate, based upon subject matter, ability, or age, or it may be random. The point is that students are placed in groups and are therefore measured and evaluated in a group setting. Because the students are in groups and are frequently competing against one another, *norm-referenced* tests have been very popular since World War I. In essence, this approach compares the score of one student to the scores of all the other students in the group. The population or group could be as small as a self-contained classroom or as large as a nationwide sample taking a standardized examination at one given time. When comparing scores, a student's standing within the group is clearly identified. The basic point to remember here is that norm-referenced tests are solely concerned with how one student compares with others.

Criterion-Referenced Tests

At the beginning of each chapter in this text, we clearly establish the competencies or skills you will have at the conclusion of the chapter. Our concern is not how well you do when compared to your fellow students, but whether or not you can exhibit the skills stated throughout the text; therefore, this text employs a *criterion-referenced* approach. The major concern when using criterion referencing is to establish an objective, competency, or skill with an acceptable level of performance and then determine whether or not the student can do it. Rather than compare a student to other students, with this approach the teacher compares the student to a predetermined standard. In doing so, demonstrable skills are clearly established.

The basic point to remember here is that criterion-referenced tests are solely concerned with the ability of the student to accomplish a specific skill or objective at a competent level. It is important to note that this level is clearly established prior to the test. Additional information on criterion-referenced tests can be found in Lyman (1986).

EXERCISE 11.8

Identify each of the functions listed below as characteristic of norm-referenced tests (n) or criterion-referenced tests (c). Then compare your answers with the ones given in the feedback section at the end of the chapter.

_____ 1. Determines whether or not a student is in the top 10% or bottom 10% of the group

_____ 2. Must have predetermined standards

_____ 3. Skills must be clearly demonstrated at a predetermined level.

_____ 4. Students are compared to standards.

_____ 5. Students are compared with other classmates or groups of students.

_____ 6. Students compete against each other.

_____ 7. Theoretically, all students could make an _A_.

_____ 8. The student's standing within the group is clearly identified.

_____ 9. Generally, one finds an equal distribution of letter grades.

_____ 10. More commonly used when teaching for mastery, competency, or the acquisition of skills.

DETERMINING GRADES

Test Scores and Grades

In the previous section we discussed the nature of norm-referenced and criterion-referenced test scores. For the former, the score establishes the student's relationship to a group, whereas the latter reflects performance with regard to a predetermined standard. In both cases, scores are a measurement function that provides the teacher with data regarding the success of the planned objectives and the implementation of the unit of study. Assigning grades is an evaluation function because it is the teacher's responsibility to make judgements based upon these tests scores and other data.

Methods for Determining Grades

If teachers were to use norm referencing in its pure form, they would employ what is called a _normal curve_. The normal curve is a graphic representation of a normal probability distribution. For example, the height of people tends to fit the normal distribution, as does weight. In large samples, scores on IQ tests also tend to fit a normal pattern. The normal curve is useful for very large samples being measured with standardized achievement or aptitude tests. For the typical classroom teacher, the concept of the normal distribution is valuable, but using the normal curve as a basis for assigning grades is rarely done. A more complete discussion of the normal curve can be found in Lyman (1986).

Teachers, however, often are interested in comparing students to each other. In these cases they often "eyeball" the clustering of the scores in a distribution and make judgements of the students' performance based on the clusters.

F								D		C			B	A
											X			
										X	X		X	
								X		X	X	X	X	X
		X	X					X	X	X	X	X	X	X
0	1	2	3	4	5	6	7	8	9	10 11	12 13 14	15	16 17	18 19 20

Figure 11.2   The "Eyeball Method"

When using this method, you must set up all the scores on a horizontal line and then examine them. This procedure is shown in Figure 11.2. It is possible that this will not yield A or F grades. If the highest score in Figure 11.2 had been 17, most teachers would not have assigned a grade of A for this work.

The most common method for assigning grades employs a percentage system, which is a form of criterion referencing. A sample percentage system could be:

93–100%   A

85– 92%   B

76– 84%   C

67– 75%   D

With this system a teacher determines each individual student's average percentage at the end of a grading period, such as a 9-weeks period, and this percentage determines the grade. A complete discussion of the advantages and disadvantages of this system is beyond the scope of this text. We introduce it to you here, however, because it is the most common method of assigning grades in the elementary and secondary schools in our country. A thorough discussion of the issues involved in grading can be found in Ebel and Frisbie (1986).

EXERCISE 11.9

Answer the following questions for each of the groups of scores shown below. Then compare your answers to the ones given in the feedback section at the end of the chapter.

1. Using the "eyeball method," determine the letter grades A, B, C, D, and F for the sample below.

```
                                       X
                                       X
                      X        X  X  X              X
                   X  X        X  X  X              X           X
          X        X  X        X  X  X     X  X  X     X  X
_____
 0  1  2  3  4  5  6  7  8  9  10 11 12 13 14 15 16 17 18 19 20
```

2. Using the percentage method and a pass/fail letter-grade system (with 80% being acceptable performance), how many of the following scores are passing?

```
                                       X
                                       X              X        X
                                       X              X        X
                            X  X  X  X  X  X           X  X
                               X  X  X  X  X  X  X  X  X  X
_____
 0  1  2  3  4  5  6  7  8  9  10 11 12 13 14 15 16 17 18 19 20
```

PURPOSES FOR ASSIGNING GRADES

Feedback

First and foremost, grades provide feedback for students and parents. In doing so, a grade becomes an indicator of achievement or performance in a given unit or course of study. If such feedback is to be of any use, the students and their parents should be familiar with the grading system. The most common is the letter-grade system which utilizes *A, B, C, D*, and *F* grades. These letters have more or less represented *excellent, good, average, poor*, and *failing*, respectively.

In some areas, you might encounter a pass/fail (P/F) or an honors/satisfactory/unsatisfactory system (H/S/U). Whatever the system being used, its purpose is to communicate the educational progress of the pupil. Alcorn, Kinder, and Shunert (1970) have presented an excellent review of feedback systems.

This knowledge of progress is very critical, for it allows teachers to monitor the strengths and weaknesses of a student regarding a specific objective, and knowledge of results is an important factor in student motivation (Wlodkowski, 1984). This in turn serves as a guide for further coursework. An *A* is an indicator that the student is most likely strong in that area and may be ready to move ahead, engage in enrichment exercises, or help a peer who is having difficulty with the material. A letter grade of *D* or *F* shows that the original instruction may not have met the student's need and that additional or alternative strategies or materials may be needed to advance the student to an acceptable level of performance.

Other Uses for Grades

Grades are used not only to provide feedback to parents and students but also to meet a wide range of institutional needs. They are one of a number of factors used as a basis for grouping students. If a grade truly reflects achievement, it is legitimate to use such information when assigning students to math and reading groups at the elementary level and advanced or specialized courses at the high school level.

Needless to say, grades are used by school systems to promote students from one grade level to the next and to graduate students from different levels within the system. Grades are often used to determine honor students and often serve as the basis for awards and scholarships. They may even determine whether or not a student is eligible to engage in extracurricular activities. Finally, grades are a major factor regarding college admission and eligibility to participate in athletics. For example, the National Collegiate Athletic Association, in implementing a rule called Proposition 14, has stated that any high school graduate with less than an overall *C* average is ineligible to participate in intercollegiate athletics at an NCAA member university.

Although the original purpose of grades was to provide information regarding student progress and achievement, there can be little doubt that as educational institutions have grown, grades have become a critical factor to the success in the adult world of today's students. This is true not only in the professions but also in any area that requires the student to exhibit mastery of a skill.

EXERCISE 11.10

In the spaces provided below, list three purposes for determining grades. Then check your answers with the ones given in the feedback section at the end of the chapter.

1. _____

_____

_____

_____

Feedback should be supportive and need not always be in the form of a grade.

2. _____

_____

_____

_____

3. _____

_____

_____

_____

Inappropriate Uses of Grades

As stated previously, the most critical purpose of grades is that of serving as an indicator of achievement by being the vehicle to communicate this achievement to students and their parents. However, there are many other ways in which grades are used in classrooms.

Frequently, a higher, inappropriate grade is assigned to a student whose achievement has been low but whose effort has been high. In this way, the function is that of an incentive to keep trying regardless of the degree of achievement. When this takes place, the grade becomes more important than the achievement, which is most often undesirable. The problem that arises from this situation is that a student might have solid grades yet very low scores on the standardized measurements, a situation which confuses and frustrates parents and aggravates administrators and school boards.

If the function of a grade is to transmit information regarding student achievement, one must avoid communicating inaccurate information such as would be done by assigning a grade higher than was earned. The teacher should also avoid using grades as a management axe. If a student achieves at the B level, it is illogical to report C achievement because of a lack of participation, poor attendance, or a management/discipline problem. Those situations should be handled in other ways, as discussed earlier in the text.

Affective areas must also be communicated in other ways. Grades should not be used to help students maintain a positive self-concept or help them move away from a negative one. Grades should not be given to reward the cooperative nor to punish the uncooperative student.

The best way to support students is to review and upgrade the quality of instruction continually, which will allow increased numbers of students to achieve academically, something that will be reflected in higher grades.

EXERCISE 11.11 _____

With regard to the list below, place an X in front of the statements that reflect appropriate functions of grades. Then compare your answers with the ones given in the feedback section at the end of the chapter.

_____ 1. Grades should be awarded for effort.

_____ 2. Grades should be awarded to support a positive self-concept.

_____ 3. Grades should be awarded to help students conquer a negative self-concept.

_____ 4. Grades should accurately transmit academic achievement.

_____ 5. Grades could be lowered based upon participation and attendance.

FEEDBACK SYSTEMS

Feedback to Students

Students receive feedback from teachers on a daily basis in many ways. One of the most common is that of a grade on a formal measurement such as a paper-and-pencil test. As stated earlier, the meaning of the grade must be clear and easily understood by the student so that it clearly communicates the level of achievement. Of course, teachers are always writing comments on papers and providing verbal feedback. Again, the major point to be made is that all feedback regarding communication of achievement must be comprehensible.

In addition, the teacher's grading policies and system should be simple and clear to the student. As we have emphasized throughout this book, students have a right to know their learning situations and the objectives they are expected to meet. They must know at what level they must perform in order for them to succeed. Feedback regarding performance and achievement should be continuous, and students should know their standing at all times. The "secret stuff" has gone on for too long; teachers must take the guesswork out of grades and grading schemes.

Feedback to Parents

The most common form of communicating grades to parents is the report card. The high school report card offers grades that should be reflections of academic achievement, whereas the elementary report card serves the same function in addition to providing information on satisfactory or unsatisfactory performance in other, nonacademic areas.

The parent should be familiar with as much performance information as the school can provide, most often presented in the form of grades. However, this information must be usable by clearly communicating levels of achievement. A letter grade of *B* in one class might not mean the same as a *B* of another class. As mentioned earlier, parents seeing satisfactory grades on report cards and low percentiles on standardized tests fail to understand how this can happen.

What teachers must keep in mind is that the reason for a report card or any other communication device is to increase parents' awareness of the educational progress of their children. The report card is only one way of achieving this goal.

Another method of communicating progress is a written report. Such reports should be clear, easy to read, and void of any grade reporting as such. In everyday language, teachers must communicate the general academic situation, being concerned with not only what they are trying to say but also with the way they are trying to say it.

The most effective way of communicating with parents is through a conference. Face-to-face verbal communication allows the parent to ask questions and the teacher to provide understandable information. As stated earlier, parents need to know what grades mean, and in a conference, the teacher can very clearly discuss observable achievement as well as learning difficulties. The teacher should also realize that the parent conference is a two-way street and provides the opportunity to gain increased and valuable information about the student and his or her home environment. Such information may become instrumental in helping the teacher promote further achievement.

EXERCISE 11.12 _____

Which of the following three reporting systems is the most effective: report cards, written reports, or parent conferences. Give two reasons for your choice. Then compare your answers with the ones given in the feedback section at the end of the chapter.

Most effective reporting system: _____

1. _____

_____

2. _____

_____

Parents and the Affective Domain

During the 1970s, mastering the basics became the publicly proclaimed goal of American education. Although the zealousness of individuals committed to this effort has abated somewhat, basic skills continue to dominate modern curriculums. Nevertheless, the majority of today's professional educators enthusiastically support the concept of educating the "whole child."

A significant component of this concept involves the affective domain. As you know from your reading of Chapters 2 and 4, it is in this area that teachers provide educational opportunities for students to express and share values, attitudes, feelings, opinions, and a variety of viewpoints. It is in this area that students become more aware of their surroundings, exhibit the willingness to listen to varying positions, and choose to become actively involved in the educational environment.

Needless to say, affective units of instruction have become somewhat controversial in the public sector and are particularly so when labeled with such concepts as the humanistic curriculum and values clarification.

Based upon the assumptions that (1) affective units are essential to the "whole child" concept and (2) affective units can stimulate parental involvement, teachers need to consider coping behaviors regarding parental attitudes toward the affective domain.

In line with most management-type situations, teachers should first consider preventive strategies, methods, and approaches. They should anticipate conflicts with parents and be as prepared, in advance, as possible. Points for consideration here include

Using state- and district-adopted materials

Providing parents with opportunities for suggesting topics

Checking in advance with potentially sensitive parents

Utilizing guidance counselors

Guiding the discussions

Establishing a rationale for the activity

Securing the backing of chairpersons or team leaders

Securing administrative approval

Avoiding discussions regarding specific classroom individuals

Focusing on situations

Utilizing indirect teaching approaches such as questioning and paraphrasing

Stressing the ground rule that all opinions are acceptable with regard to the discussion

Stressing that overt participation is not required

Increasing knowledge of students' backgrounds

Introducing many points of view

Having thorough lesson plans

Serving in the role of a facilitator

Delimiting influence

Providing parents with outlines and descriptions of exercises

Assuming that preventives may, on occasion, fall short, teachers must anticipate face-to-face meetings with parents (regarding a component of the affective domain with which the parent is displeased) and should consider ways of minimizing conflicts. Suggestions here include

Being courteous and explaining your rationale

Listening to the parent's point of view

Discussing the situation frankly and supporting positions with policies

Bringing in outside support in the form of colleagues, counselors, and administrators

Discussing alternatives

Focusing on the child

Having a third party present

Being prepared to professionally defend your curriculum

Inviting parents to observe the class

Being friendly and concerned

Establishing the value of the exercise

Being positive about the impact of the exercise

Being prepared to cite possible solutions

Understanding and respecting the parent

Using records to support the curriculum

Having sample techniques available

Documenting meetings with parents

Finally, a published set of administrative guidelines, which could be made available to parents as well as faculties, can do much to enhance effective communication, provide focal points for discussion, and, to some degree, educate the public about the process and value of affective units. Such guidelines might include defining exercises as a nonthreatening communications process for helping students understand positive or negative consequences of holding interests, attitudes, and beliefs; directing exercises toward the teaching of decision-making skills based upon democratic principles; requiring lesson plans for the purpose of administrative approval; and being sure activities are conducted by certified, professional employees who are trained and qualified to use affective processes.

In the long run, the key to the successful implementation of affective experiences in the classroom will be found in the professional educator's ability to assist parents in understanding the meaning of the affective domain and the value of having their children's total growth stimulated by such a learning environment.

EXERCISE 11.13

Read the following scenario and identify two ways in which the teacher attempted to prevent potential conflict with parents regarding a unit involving the affective domain.

Mr. Larsen decided to design a unit of instruction on the nuclear disarmament issue. As always, he prepared his objectives and then began to select appropriate content, strategies, and materials that would facilitate the unit. He located some excellent materials suggested by the National Council for the Social Studies (NCSS). He also found a simulation that required the students to discuss their individual opinions regarding the nuclear disarmament issue. His principal assured him that it was an appropriate exercise within the unit. He also located a rather controversial film on atomic warfare and decided it was too powerful to pass up. He further decided that all his students would watch the film and write a brief paper on their reactions to it. Finally, he decided to tie all the instructional activities to a series of penetrating problems and questions offered at the conclusion of the chapter on World War II in the students' state-adopted textbook. As was his custom, Mr. Larsen then set about the task of developing compatible measurements that would allow him to evaluate student progress.

SUMMARY

In this chapter we've presented much of the third phase of the three-phase model of teaching. We discussed the differences between measurement and evaluation and then focused on measurement accuracy.

The idea of measurement accuracy was developed around sample items designed to measure the production or recognition of facts, concepts, and generalizations. A detailed discussion of multiple-choice items was woven into the description. We then closed this section with a brief introduction to the idea of measuring for inquiry skills.

A complete discussion of all the forms of measurement items, including various observational items, is beyond the scope of this text, and the reader wishing more information in this area should consult a text devoted primarily to measurement and evaluation.

The determining and communicating of grades, as discussed in this chapter, mark the last step of the three-phase model. When determining grades, teachers must first decide whether they are going to compare students to students or students to preset standards. Once this decision is made, the next step is to select an appropriate grading system that allows the teacher to assign letter grades objectively. It is important to note that a certain amount of subjectivity is always present, no matter how objective the grading system.

Once letter grades have been assigned, the next step is to clearly and understandably communicate them to students as well as parents. The critical point here is that the letter grade must accurately represent student performance. Once this step is accomplished, the utilization of the three-phase model is complete.

As a final point, it should be understood that using this model involves a never-ending process. Although the process of assigning and communicating grades completes the evaluation phase, the teacher must now examine student achievement in order to plan, implement, and evaluate subsequent instruction. Therefore, the utilization of the three-phase model is a circular situation in which the teacher is engaged in an endless instructional series. Only through such a process can teachers hope to improve instruction on a continual basis and thereby promote student achievement and a success-oriented environment.

As stated at the onset, it is our firm conviction that your use of the three-phase model as described throughout this work will increase your effectiveness in the classroom.

However, we hasten to add that the conclusion of the three-phase model does not conclude the teaching act. On the contrary, it is merely a beginning in that your original planning, implementing, and evaluating—effective as these may have been—enable you to revisit the unit or lesson and revise your work by replanning, reimplementing, and reevaluating.

We hope the three-phase model will be invaluable to you in your efforts to maximize achievement in the three areas (knowledge and information, attitudes and values, and manipulative skills) of student learning. The utilization of this never-ending cycle truly marks the professional educator who continually strives to provide learning experiences and a classroom environment that facilitates the growth of each and every child.

References

Brown, J. (Ed.). (1976). *Recall and recognition.* New York: Wiley.

Ebel, R., & Frisbie, D. (1986). *Essentials of educational measurement* (4th ed.). Englewood Cliffs, NJ: Prentice-Hall.

Gronlund, N. (1988). *How to construct achievement tests* (4th ed.). Englewood Cliffs, NJ: Prentice-Hall.

Lyman, H. (1986). *Test scores and what they mean* (4th ed.). Englewood Cliffs, NJ: Prentice-Hall.

Wickelgren, W. (1977). *Learning and memory.* Englewood Cliffs, NJ: Prentice-Hall.

Wlodkowski, R. (1984). *Motivation and teaching: A practical guide* (2nd ed.). Washington, DC: National Education Association.

Exercise Feedback

EXERCISE 11.1

In each of the items the students must, of course, be able to read. In addition they must be able to do or know the following:

1. A.
   1) Be able to measure.
   2) Know that $C = \pi d$ applies to this problem.
   3) Know the formula $C = \pi d$.
   4) Remember the value of π.
   5) Know the relationship between radius and diameter.
   6) Be able to put the numbers in the equation.
   7) Be able to multiply decimals.

   B.
   1) Know that $C = \pi d$ applies to this problem.
   2) Know the formula $C = \pi d$.
   3) Remember the value of π.
   4) Be able to put the numbers in the equation.
   5) Be able to multiply decimals.

   C.
   1) Know the value of π.
   2) Be able to put the numbers in the equation.
   3) Be able to multiply decimals.

   From these lists we see item A is the most demanding. It requires more prerequisite knowledge than either of the others. It is also the most realistic in that concrete examples of circles are in the item rather than making the students think about circles in the abstract.

2. A. Application
    B. Application
    C. Comprehension

Both items A and B are at the application level in that they both require the students to select the formula and calculate the circumference. Item A requires abilities such as measuring and knowing the relationship between radius and diameter that the teacher may not want to require. In order to capture realism, the teacher could rewrite item B as follows:

Calculate the circumfrerence of each of the following circles.

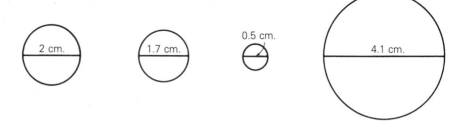

Item C is written on the comprehension level because the equation was given, and the students only had to put the numbers in it and compute the result.

3. A. Production
    B. Production
    C. Production

Because the responses are convergent in each case, production items are a better choice than recognition. However, a recognition item could have been written (although, of course, a different evaluation statement would have to appear with the goal statement in Mr. Hite's objective). A recognition item can be written as follows:

Look at the following circle:

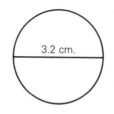

The circumference of the circle is
a.   1.6 cm.
b.   8.04 cm.
c.   10.05 cm.
d.   5.02 cm.

EXERCISE 11.2

Item 2 is definitely better than item 1. In item 1 the correct choice is obvious since it is the only four-sided figure. In item 2, the children must discriminate among four different four-sided figures. Also, they must know the difference between a rectangle and a square and between a rectangle and a trapezoid. A teacher could be quite certain the children had a concept of rectangle if they marked item 2 correctly, while he or she might be mistaken with a correct response to item 1.

EXERCISE 11.3

The following would be an appropriate item to measure a small child's comprehension of the concept *mammal*. Of course, your item is probably somewhat different, but it should have good distracters.

> Circle the animal that is a mammal. (Assume this would be read to the students and that the four choices would be in pictorial form.)
> a. Frog
> b. Cow
> c. Alligator
> d. Eagle

The correct answer, of course, is *cow*. The distracters are good ones, though, because a frog is an amphibian, an alligator is a reptile, and an eagle is a bird. Each represents a concept coordinate to the concept *mammal* and measures the child's ability to discriminate among coordinate concepts. (For a review of cordinate concepts refer to Chapter 2.)

EXERCISE 11.4

1. Comprehension. The students are asked to identify an illustration of the generalization.
2. In order to respond correctly, students must relate smoking and heart disease.
   a. Heart disease but no smoking
   b. Smoking but no heart disease
   c. Correct — heart disease and smoking
   d. Heart disease but no smoking
   If the distracters were written without any reference to either smoking or heart disease, the students could respond correctly without understanding the generalization. This would make the item invalid and could give the teacher some misinformation about student understanding.

EXERCISE 11.5

The following is an item that could be used. In this case, as with many others in this chapter, there are a number of appropriate possibilities.

> The Tahitians have a peaceful, fun-loving culture. Life in Tahiti hasn't changed much in the last 100 years. Many Tahitians still fish for a living. Because it is warm, many wear a sarong the year round, just as their ancestors have for centuries.

The sentence that illustrates the generalization, climate affects culture is
a. Tahitians have a peaceful, fun-loving culture.
b. Life in Tahiti hasn't changed much in the last hundred years.
c. Many Tahitians still fish for a living.
d. Because it is warm, many wear a sarong the year round, just as their ancestors have for centuries.

EXERCISE 11.6

1. (ns) Does not support. The explanation says Group A people are slim, but, according to the data, their weight-to-height ratio is higher.
2. (s) Supports
3. (ns) Does not support. The explanation says Group A people drink little, but the data say they drink an average of four drinks per person per day.
4. (s) Supports
5. (ns) Does not support. The explanation says Group B people breathe dirty air, but the data say the city in which they live is noted for ''soft'' industry, which is nonpolluting.
6. (s) Supports
7. (ns) Does not support. The explanation says Group B people are sedentary, but the data say they exercise.
8. (ns) Does not support. The explanation says Group A people avoid harmful items like tobacco, but the data say they smoke.
9. (s) Supports
10. (s) Supports

EXERCISE 11.7

1. (e) Evaluation. A decision was made based on some previous measurement.
2. (fm) Formal measurement. Miss Anthony consciously planned to gather some information about her students and did so by checking to see if they could match similar first sounds.
3. (e) Evaluation
4. (e) Evaluation
5. (im) Informal measurement. The teacher, in an unplanned way, gathered some information.
6. (im) Informal measurement
7. (e) Evaluation
8. (im) Informal measurement
9. (e) Evaluation

EXERCISE 11.8

1. (n) Norm-referenced. With criterion-referenced tests, bottom and top percentages are not identified.
2. (c) Criterion-referenced
3. (c) Criterion-referenced
4. (c) Criterion-referenced
5. (n) Norm-referenced
6. (n) Norm-referenced. The highest scores receive a letter grade of A and the lowest a letter grade of F.

7. (c) Criterion-referenced. If the highest score, based upon 100%, was 99% and the lowest was 95%, all might be awarded the letter grade of *A*.
8. (n) Norm-referenced
9. (n) Norm-referenced. The usual grade distribution is mostly the letter grade of *C* with some *Bs* and *Ds* and a few *As* and *Fs*.
10. (c) Criterion-referenced. These approaches require the establishment of predetermined standards.

EXERCISE 11.9

1. *A* — scores 18-19
   B — scores 14-16
   C — scores 10-12
   D — scores 7-8
   F — score 3
2. 13. A passing score would be 80% of 20 or $0.80 \times 20 = 16$. Therefore, any score of 16 or over, of which there are 13, would be awarded a passing letter grade.

EXERCISE 11.10

Any of the following would be acceptable responses:
1. Inform students of educational progress.
2. Inform parents of educational progress.
3. Guide further coursework.
4. Provide a basis for grouping.
5. Provide a basis for promoting.
6. Provide a basis for graduating.
7. Provide a basis for college admission.
8. Provide a criterion for honors.
9. Provide a criterion for extracurricular participation.
10. Provide a motivational factor.
11. Identify student strengths and weaknesses.
12. Provide a basis for employment.

EXERCISE 11.11

1. No X
2. No X
3. No X
4. X
5. No X. If the grade accurately reflects student achievement, there can be no legitimate reason for lowering the grade. However, teachers often build participation and attendance into their grading scheme.

EXERCISE 11.12

The most effective reporting system is the parent conference. Any two of the following are acceptable reasons:
1. Allows parent questions and teacher answers
2. Allows parents to learn exactly what a grade means
3. Allows the teacher to explain both progress and problems

4. Allows the teacher to learn more about the student and his or her home environment.

EXERCISE 11.13

1. Mr. Larsen secured the approval of his principal.
2. Mr. Larsen used a state-adopted textbook.

> NOTE: Mr. Larsen may have been encouraging some difficulty in the following ways:
> 1. He used materials that had not been approved.
> 2. He required all students to participate in an overt way.

TRENDS

12 ‖ Recent Directions in Education

INTRODUCTION

In this, the final chapter of the text, we focus on recent trends in education that have impact on the classroom teacher. The first of these, the accountability movement, has come from a demand by the public and legislators for teachers and teacher educators to document the quality of their work. The accountability movement, which began in the early 1970s, has resulted in two recent phenomena: minimum competency testing and increased interest in testing teachers.

Minimum competency testing is based on the idea that schools need to document student ability and hold students accountable for their educational progress. The major way that this is done is through the use of tests administered periodically throughout students' educational careers. In many states where minimum competency testing occurs, progression to the next grade, as well as the awarding of a graduation diploma, may be contingent upon passing a test.

This increased interest in the quality of public schools has resulted in two major trends: the redesign of teacher education programs and increased requirements for teacher testing. A number of national reports (e.g., *A Nation at Risk*, 1983; *A Nation Prepared*, 1986) identified the teacher as a central component in improving our schools. Teacher education programs have responded with increased emphasis on basic communication skills such as speaking and writing, greater attention to subject matter mastery, and knowledge of research on teaching. State legislators have responded with requirements for either state-constructed or nationally standardized tests for prospective teachers. In many states, these tests are significantly altering certification requirements, which used to be simply the completion of an approved teacher education program.

Another major trend has been a growing recognition of the diversity of clients of today's schools. Multicultural education has made us aware of the powerful influence that culture has on schools and schooling. Research from psychology affirms the significance of individual differences in learning styles and preferences. Mainstreaming, the incorporation of handicapped learners into the regular classroom, has made classroom life not only more complex but more enriching. The rationale behind mainstreaming is that a large number of handicapped children would benefit from the regular classroom, and research seems to support this hypothesis (Madden & Slavin, 1983).

The most recent development in education and the last to be discussed in this chapter is the arrival of computers in the schools. The computer revolution has had an impact on the schools in a number of ways, including simplifying administrative record keeping and scheduling and providing computer-assisted instruction. But, the biggest thrust of computers in the schools has been in the area of computer literacy. The basic idea here is that the schools should take a positive role in helping all students understand the role that computers are having in shaping our technological society. How to do this is the topic of the final section of this chapter.

As a concluding note, let us mention that the five exercises included in Chapter 12 involve contemporary issues and have a wide variety of possible responses. Therefore, feedback panels have not been provided, and we urge you to discuss these issues in class with your fellow students and instructor.

OBJECTIVES

After completing Chapter 12, you should be able to accomplish the following objectives:

1. For you as a pre/inservice teacher to understand the concept of teacher alignment, so that when provided with a short-answer test, you will be able to describe the idea in your own words and explain the political forces that shaped it.
2. For you as a pre/inservice teacher to understand minimum competency testing, so that on a short-answer test, you will be able to explain the concept itself, and discuss the pros and cons of this practice. Your answer should be in your own words and reflect the major points in the text.
3. For you as a pre/inservice teacher to understand the effect of the teacher-testing movement, so that on a short-answer test, you will be able to describe the origins of the movement and its consequences for teacher certification.
4. For you as a pre/inservice teacher to understand mainstreaming, so that on a short-answer test, you will be able to explain mainstreaming and its relationship to P.L. 94–142.
5. For you as a pre/inservice teacher to increase your awareness of classroom diversity, so that, without aid, you will be able to list five goals of multicultural education.
6. For you as a pre/inservice teacher to become more familiar with classroom interaction, so that, without aid, you will be able to define the term *cooperative learning*.
7. For you as a pre/inservice teacher to increase your knowledge of hemispheric brain research, so that, without aid, you can describe two functions of the left hemisphere and two functions of the right hemisphere of the brain.
8. For you as a pre/inservice teacher to understand the concept of computer literacy, so that on a short-answer test, you will be able to give a definition of computer literacy that includes the following components: hardware, software, and computer control.

ACCOUNTABILITY

Probably the most pervasive trend in American schools in the last two decades has been the push for accountability. Beginning in the late 1960s and early 1970s with an emphasis on schools documenting their effectiveness, this accountability movement has developed into two more recent phenomena: minimum competency testing and the testing of teachers.

The impetus for the accountability movement came out of public dissatisfaction with the schools. Some have described this dissatisfaction as part of a larger conservative thrust in America which included the taxpayers' revolt and the Proposition 13 movement. Public dissatisfaction with the schools centered around lax standards and a lingering doubt as to whether the schools were really teaching students well or enough. The basic premise of the accountability movement was that professional educators should be held responsible for how much children learn (Alkin, 1972).

As originally conceived, accountability was to occur at three levels. At the highest level, school boards were held responsible for the goals and objectives in that school district. At the administrative level, superintendents and principals were held responsible for meeting the goals established by the school board. And, finally, teachers were held responsible for the learning outcomes of students in their classrooms. The proposed method of measuring these learning outcomes was through pre- and post-achievement tests.

Teaching Alignment: Matching Curriculum Instruction and Tests

A significant development coming out of the accountability movement has been the move toward teaching alignment. Included within this movement is curriculum alignment, an attempt to match curriculum with instruction and testing (Levine, 1982), and instructional alignment, efforts to link teaching procedures with testing. You'll recall that in Chapter 1 we defined good teaching in terms of the congruence of goals, instruction, and evaluation components; teaching alignment is the formal attempt to institutionalize these efforts at the state or district level.

The move toward alignment is a direct by-product of the accountability movement; if educators are to be held accountable for important learning outcomes, these outcomes needed to be clearly defined and measurable on tests. Efforts in the first direction—to clearly specify important learning outcomes in key academic areas—have resulted in state and district curriculum guides in virtually every state in the union. In addition to curriculum guides, a number of states and districts have moved one step further, developing and administering tests matched to these guides. The impetus for this development can be seen in some recent research.

One major way of measuring student progress is through the use of standardized achievement tests; these are a yearly ritual in most elementary classrooms. Research on the match between these tests and the curriculum—at least as defined by content in textbooks—revealed major problems (Berliner, 1987). In one study of fourth-grade math texts, researchers found that, in the best case, there was only a 70% overlap between the text and the test; 30% of the content on the test was not discussed in the text. In the worst case there was only a 47% overlap between text and test; over half of the content in the text was not measured by the test. Students and teachers using these texts were operating against a stacked deck.

Alignment problems also occur because of instructional variability. In one study, researchers found differences in time allocation for daily math instruction ranging for 25 to 60 minutes a day; students in some classrooms had well over twice as much math instruction as those in others. Similar differences were noted in reading (Berliner, 1987). Differences in terms of topics covered were also documented.

The interpretation of these results, as well as the general concept of alignment in teaching, is controversial. Advocates of alignment point to efficiency and fairness; students ought to be given opportunities to learn the material they'll be tested on and to do better when tested. Research on instructional alignment attests to the efficiency argument; studies that matched instruction to the test produced dramatic test gains (Cohen, 1987).

Opponents of the alignment movement focus on several potential problems (Bracey, 1987). Fragmentation and narrowing occur when teachers teach only to the test, ignoring other important outcomes. Trivialization occurs when only easily measurable outcomes are included on tests and selected for instruction. Finally, other workers in the area have criticized the deprofessionalization or neutering of teachers (Bullough, Goldstein, & Holt, 1984; Frymeier, 1987). These critics have argued that instructional alignment robs teachers of the opportunity to create and implement their own teaching program.

Where does this leave the classroom teacher? At a minimum a teacher ought to be clear about district expectations, both in terms of curriculum guides and tests. These should be examined early during the planning process so that these elements can be incorporated into professional planning, if necessary. In addition, these guides should also be compared with texts to identify areas of congruence and areas where existing materials need to be supplemented.

Minimum Competency Testing

As educators tried to implement these ideas they encountered major problems in linking learning outcomes to a particular teacher. They found that the performance of a given class on an achievement test at the end of the year was not only dependent on the teacher's actions during that year. Instead a number of variables such as a student's previous academic background, motivation, as well as the resources available to the teacher were major determinants of student performance.

Because of these problems, the responsibility for learning performance shifted from the teacher to the student. If students were to progress from grade to grade and ultimately graduate with a high school diploma, they were expected to achieve a minimum level on competence tests that were administered at different grade levels. This is the basic idea behind minimum competency testing. Minimum competency testing takes many forms. In some states such as Florida the testing is centralized, with all students in all districts receiving the same test at the same level. In other states, such as Utah, districts are responsible for designing and implementing their own tests. In New Jersey, a minimum competency test at the ninth-grade level is used to identify students for remediation, while in Tennessee students who do not pass the final competency test for graduation are awarded certificates of attendance (Pipho, 1982).

Advocates of minimum competency tests stress the beneficial effect of these tests on curriculums and students. Advocates claim that the tests can help clarify the major goals of a school system by specifying what these goals are on the tests. This sends a clear message to students about what they should be learning, and performance on these tests allows the public to see what the schools are doing and their level of effectiveness (Popham, 1981).

Opponents of these tests contend that the cut-off scores are arbitrary and that the instruments used are too crude to be a basis for making crucial decisions about individual careers. In addition, they point out that these tests have disproportionate adverse impact on minorities and that these tests encourage teachers to teach toward the test, ignoring broader, more important and sometimes hard-to-test competencies and skills (Madaus, 1981).

Despite these arguments against minimum competency tests, it appears that they are here to stay in some form for the near future. By 1984, 35 states had taken some type of action to mandate setting minimum competency standards for elementary and secondary students. (Equity/Excellence, 1986). In a variation on this idea a number of states (e.g., Texas, South Carolina) and dozens of school boards have instituted no-pass, no-play approaches to extracurricular activities (Pipho 1986). This highly controversial policy holds that students must maintain a *C* average to participate in activities such as athletics. Proponents see the rule as a way of encouraging academic performance; critics contend that participation in these extracurricular activities is essential in motivating academically marginal students, and the rule is punishing the very students who need alternative ways to excel. The state of Idaho has taken this idea one step further, requiring a *C* average in core subjects to graduate; the class of 1988 was the first affected.

As mentioned earlier, Florida instituted a statewide minimum competency testing program in 1978. Critics of this program focused on the test's content, contending that items on the test had not been presented in the curriculum and thus were invalid. The U.S. Fifth Circuit Court of Appeals agreed (*Debra P.* v. *Turlington,* 1981). They ruled that tests affecting the obtaining of a high school diploma must be fair in terms of asking questions on topics that have actually been taught (Popham & Lindheim, 1981).

Implications for test constructors are clear; they must ensure that the content of tests matches syllabi and curriculum. The implications for classroom teachers are not as clear. Are classroom teachers legally obligated to teach the content of the tests? At a global level we would say no. However, contractual agreements with the employing district may require teachers to teach the content described in district curriculum guides. Teachers should read their contracts carefully to clarify their contractual obligations in the classroom.

EXERCISE 12.1

Discussion Questions

1. How does minimum competency testing affect teachers' autonomy in the classroom? Is this a good or bad effect?

2. In the text we said that minimum competency tests are beneficial to students because they tell students what they should be learning. Can you think of any other positive or negative effects from a student's perspective?

3. What are the advantages and disadvantages of a statewide minimum competency system versus a districtwide system?

Teacher Testing

Another outgrowth of the accountability movement has been an increased public interest in the quality of teachers entering the profession. This interest has resulted in a number of legislatures passing laws requiring teachers to pass a test before becoming certified.

Teacher competency tests have occurred in two forms—national and local. The National Teachers Exam (NTE), a nationally standardized test designed by Educational Testing Service, is currently used by 21 states, with these states clustering in the South and Southeast (Equity/Excellence, 1986). There are two basic kinds of NTE exams: the core and content areas tests. The content area tests assess a teacher candidate's knowledge of specific subject matter areas such as math or biology. The core exam consists of a test of professional knowledge, a test of general knowledge, and a test of communication skills, with subtests on listening, reading, and writing. Scores for all of these are reported as raw scores and as percentiles, in which the test taker's performance is compared with a national sample.

Some states and even school districts have elected to develop their own competency tests. Currently, 17 states use locally constructed teacher certification tests, and two additional states are considering their use (Madaus & Pullin, 1987). One developed in Florida is typical of these. The Florida test, used since 1980, has subtests on math, reading, writing, and professional education knowledge.

Key considerations in teacher testing are knowledge of content and methodologies.

Recent developments in this area include performance testing for beginning teachers in actual classroom settings, provisional certification for beginning teachers, and testing for experienced teachers applying for recertification (Madaus & Pullin, 1987; Woolever, 1985). In several states beginning teachers are required to demonstrate their competence in actual classroom settings; in some states (e.g., Georgia) this is done in a formal evaluation setting, whereas in others (e.g., Utah) evaluation is part of the normal first-year supervision process. In both instances progression from temporary, provisional status to regular certification is contingent upon successful teaching performance.

Other states (three in 1987) have required pencil-and-paper tests for recertifying experienced teachers. Typically paper-and-pencil measures, these tests have been highly controversial, both in terms of their necessity and cost (Shepard & Kreitzer, 1987). Critics in Texas, where one such test was used, contend that both pass rates (over 99%) and total cost (over $35 million) are strong arguments against their continued use.

The impact of these tests on beginning teachers is obvious. In the past the majority of states belonged to a reciprocal certification agreement in which certification in one state would automatically qualify a candidate for certification in another. This no longer holds. Persons seeking certification in a state should contact the certification division of the state office of education to find out what tests are required. Doing this ahead of time is essential, as the NTE and many other state tests are only offered at certain times of the year and at certain locations.

EXERCISE 12.2

Discussion Questions

1. How well can paper-and-pencil tests measure teaching competency?

2. If you were developing a teacher certification test, what would be its major components?

3. What are the advantages and disadvantages of testing teachers in actual classrooms?

DIVERSITY IN AMERICAN SCHOOLS

A major trend in American schools has been increasing recognition of the diversity of the school population. Dimensions of this diversity come to us from different perspectives.

The area of special education focuses on exceptional students needing special help to realize their full potential in today's schools (Hardman, Drew, & Egan, 1987). Classroom teachers routinely work with both gifted students and students with mild learning and behavior disorders. Experts estimate that up to 13% of the student population falls into this latter category and requires some type of extra help to succeed in the regular classroom. This assistance occurs most often in mainstreamed classrooms, where these students are integrated into the normal flow of school life. The next section in this chapter deals with this topic.

Another dimension of diversity in American schools relates to the unique cultural backgrounds students bring to the classroom. Multicultural education, which deals with ways of using this diversity to enhance learning in the classroom, is the topic following the mainstreaming section.

Learning styles, and research on left and right hemispheres of the brain, approaches diversity from a learning strengths/preferences perspective. Educators have long acknowledged that no two students learn the same way, and recent research on learning styles has suggested ways to deal with this dimension of diversity. Let's turn now to mainstreaming and the integration of special populations into the regular classroom.

MAINSTREAMING

The 1970s brought a number of changes to U.S. schools, one of the most significant being enactment of the Education for All Handicapped Children Act of 1975. This law, often called P.L. 94–142, had a number of important provisions, the most important of which was the requirement that handicapped children be provided with free and appropriate education. The overall impact of the law was creating the practice of mainstreaming, or including handicapped children in the regular classroom. Before we discuss the concept of mainstreaming, let's examine the other provisions of P.L. 94–142 more carefully.

As just mentioned, the most far reaching provision of the law was that all students, including handicapped students, are entitled to a free and appropriate education (Hardman, Egan, & Landau, 1981). This law put an end to a practice prevalent in many states of requiring parents to provide financially for extra educational services for their handicapped children. These services included transportation to and from school, psychological testing and diagnosis, occupational and recreational testing, and counseling.

A second major provision of this law was a requirement for nonbiased testing. In the past, some of the instruments and procedures used to identify and place students into special education classes turned out to be culturally biased, relying too much on white middle-class language and concepts. This law has focused attention on the need for evaluation procedures that are multidimensional and sensitive to cultural differences.

Probably the most far reaching component of P.L. 94–142 was the requirement that handicapped students be provided with the *least restrictive* educational environment. This term means that educators must make every effort to give handicapped students a learning environment that provides them with the best opportunity to succeed. This might be a residential classroom, a self-contained special education class, a resource room, or the regular classroom. The important element here is that each child be considered individually in terms of his or her needs and capabilities.

In doing this an essential element is the Individualized Education Program (IEP). An IEP is a comprehensive description of an individualized curriculum designed for each student. It must include (1) a statement of goals, (2) a description of the educational services to be provided in relation to these goals, (3) a specification of when these services will begin and end, and (4) a delineation of the evaluation procedures to be used in placement and in the assessment of the program's effectiveness. The construction of each student's IEP is a team process involving a number of participants, including parents, the classroom teacher, a special education teacher, and the student. A major thrust of the IEP is to help clarify what special services will be provided to the handicapped children and by whom.

A final provision of P.L. 94–142 is the assurance of due process procedures for handicapped children and their parents. Procedural safeguards are required to protect students and their families from decisions and procedures that could negatively affect their present education and their futures. These due process safeguards require that parents be notified in advance of important educational decisions, that they have input into the decision, and that they have an opportunity to be heard if they have grievances. An important part of the due process provision is the requirement that all services for handicapped children be reviewed annually. This review evaluates the effectiveness of the present educational procedures and examines whether the student should be placed in a less restrictive environment.

In a study of 25 programs implementing the major provisions of P.L. 94–142, Bogdan (1983) found considerable variability in the way mainstreaming was implemented. In some schools the researchers found students with autism and severe disabling conditions side by side with nonimpaired peers, while in others, mainstreaming amounted to a class of mentally retarded junior high students eating lunch in the cafeteria with other students. The researchers also found differences within classrooms. In some classrooms, handicapped students sat beside peers but remained segregated in other respects, while in other classrooms, these students were not only seated in the class but participated in it. The researchers concluded that what goes on behind the scenes is more important than the IEP itself. Schools that were most successful in mainstreaming were those in which the schools themselves changed in response to these new students as opposed to those schools that just integrated handicapped students into the regular procedures.

What impact does all this have on the regular classroom teacher? In all likelihood you will be involved in the mainstreaming of exceptional students in your classroom. What this means is that handicapped children who can benefit from regular classroom instruction will spend part or all of their day mainstreamed into the regular classroom. In addition, students already in the regular classroom who are not successfully functioning because of some learning handicap may also be identified as needing special help. Here the classroom teacher's help is essential. These handicaps may range from speech and language disorders to hearing or visual impairments to mild learning and behavioral differences. Because of these differences the curriculum and teaching methods may have to be altered in significant ways.

A major help to the teacher in adapting her curriculum to the needs of these students is the mainstreaming team (Hardman, Drew, & Egan, 1987). Prior to the mainstreaming of handicapped students into the regular classroom, a multidisciplinary team consisting of administrators, parents, special educators, counselors, schools psychologists, and the teacher meet to discuss the needs of the individual child. This team's function is to assess the student's strengths and weaknesses and to design an IEP compatible with these characteristics and able to be administered by the classroom teacher.

The role of the classroom teacher in these meetings begins with explaining conditions in his or her classroom and exploring how these conditions might help or hinder the student's success in the classroom. In addition, if the teacher has already dealt with the student in the classroom, the teacher can be a valuable source of information in the diagnosis of the student's problem. In addition, as the IEP is constructed, the teacher can help to ensure that the demands of the IEP are consistent with classroom practice and realistic in terms of the classroom's resources.

Finally, the teacher has an essential role as implementor of this IEP and evaluator of its effectiveness. As mentioned previously, these plans are reviewed annually to ensure that they are accomplishing the goals established.

Research on the effects of mainstreaming confirm the claims of its advocates. In a review of a number of studies of mainstreamed students, Madden and Slavin (1983) concluded that "for most students with mild academic handicaps, the best placement is in a regular class using individualized instruction or in a regular class supplemented by well-designed resource support" (p. 544). The benefits of mainstreaming were seen in both academic achievement and in beneficial effects on mainstreamed students' self-esteem, behaviors, and attitudes. The researchers cautioned, though, that these positive effects were dependent upon students receiving additional support as outlined in IEPs.

EXERCISE 12.3

Discussion Questions

1. Does P.L. 94–142 mandate that all students be mainstreamed? Which students might not be included?

2. There has been some resistance on the part of some teachers to the idea of mainstreaming. What might these reservations be, and how could they be addressed?

3. In the text the noncognitive benefits to mainstreamed students were mentioned. What might these be, and how are they enhanced in the mainstreamed classroom?

MULTICULTURAL EDUCATION

The United States has always been a nation of immigrants, but the recognition of the impact of this cultural diversity on schools and schooling is a fairly recent development. During the late 1800s and early 1900s, the concept of the "melting pot" predominated; the cultures that immigrants brought to America were to be assimilated into a homogeneous American society. This didn't occur, and educators recognized that this diversity both posed problems and offered the potential for enriching the school curriculum. This recognition has resulted in the concept of multicultural education.

Multicultural education is a multidisciplinary program that has the following as its goals:

1. Recognition of the strength and value of cultural diversity
2. Development of human rights and respect for cultural diversity
3. Legitimation of alternate life choices for people
4. Social justice and equal opportunity for all
5. Equitable distribution of power among members of all ethnic groups (Sleeter & Grant, 1987)

As can be seen from the list, these goals extend beyond any one classroom or subject matter, encompassing the total school.

This approach to multicultural education developed out of earlier, less comprehensive strategies, one of which, teaching the culturally different, focused on helping minority students develop competence in the public culture of the dominant group. Major criticisms of this approach focus on its narrow emphasis on cultural diversity and inadequate exploration of other dimensions of diversity such as values and life-style. It also tends to leave the values and practices of the dominant group unexamined.

A second approach—focusing on human relations—also proved unworkable. This approach focused on ways of helping students of different backgrounds communicate, get along with each other, and feel good about themselves. A major problem with this approach is that it encapsulates multicultural education into a class or unit, failing to permeate or influence the whole school environment.

In contrast to these narrower approaches, cross-disciplinary multicultural education attempts to infuse the goals of multicultural education into all aspects of the curriculum (Banks, 1984, Sleeter & Grant, 1987). The concept of *culture* could be explored from various discipline perspectives, for example, with reading and literature focusing on fiction and literary works, art and music examining aesthetic products, and home economics looking at the foods of different cultures. The coordination of these different themes could occur at the class level in elementary schools and at the school level in junior high and high schools.

Teachers in American classrooms can expect to teach in culturally diverse classrooms. Probably the most important response to this diversity is the creation of a classroom environment in which all students are welcomed and in which there are positive expectations that all can learn. The research is clear on the subtle ways that teacher expectations can directly and indirectly influence learning (Good & Brophy, 1987). Clear positive expectations for all voiced at the beginning of the school year and implemented with equitable distributions of opportunities to learn are powerful factors influencing learning for culturally different students. Questioning strategies discussed in Chapter 6 aimed at active involvement of *all* students are powerful tools here. Cooperative learning, another powerful tool to build upon this diversity, is described in the next section.

EXERCISE 12.4

Discussion Questions

1. Is American society likely to become more or less culturally diverse? What effects might this have on schools and teaching?

2. Is the need for multicultural education greater at some levels than others? Are there some subject matter areas that lend themselves better to multicultural themes?

3. What are some ways that teachers can communicate positive expectations for all students?

Cooperative learning encourages students to work together.

COOPERATIVE LEARNING

Cooperative learning is a generic term for teaching strategies designed to foster group cooperation and interaction among students. These strategies are designed to eliminate the competition found in most classrooms, which tends to produce "winners and losers" and a classroom pecking order and which discourages students from helping each other (Slavin, 1988). Cooperative learning strategies are specifically designed to encourage students to work together and help each other towards common goals, and because of this, they have been found to be successful in fostering positive intergroup attitudes in multicultural classrooms.

Cooperative learning takes many forms. One of the simplest, peer tutoring, uses students as supplementary instructors in basic-skills areas. The teacher's role is to present material as she normally would; structured exercises and worksheets are then used by student pairs to reinforce the new material. In Student Teams Achievement Divisions (STAD), high- and low-ability students are paired up on evenly matched teams of four or five; team scores are based upon the extent to which *individuals* improve their scores on skills tests (Slavin, 1988). The important feature in STAD is that students are rewarded for *team* performance, thus encouraging group cooperation.

Cooperative learning can also be used to promote higher-level learning. Group investigations place students together on teams of three to six to investigate or solve some common problem. Examples here might include a science or social studies experiment, a home economics project, or the construction of a diorama or collage in art. Students are responsible for developing group goals, assigning individual responsibilities, and bringing the project to completion. Cooperation is fostered through common group goals and grades are assigned to the total project.

In a variation on this idea, the so-called jigsaw technique places students in small groups to investigate a common topic. These are typically broad enough in scope (e.g., the country of Mexico in geography, reptiles in science, or diseases in health) that individual members of the team can be assigned subjects within the topic. Individuals are then responsible for researching and learning about their area of specialization and teaching about this to other members. All students are expected to learn all the information on the topic, and comprehensive quizzes can be used to supplement group reports to insure that this happens.

These different forms of cooperative learning are summarized in Figure 12.1.

Strategies	Content Goals	Structure
Peer Tutoring	Facts, skills, goals	Drill-&-practice supplement to regular instruction
Student Teams Achievement Diversions	Facts, skills	Heterogeneous team reinforced for team performance
Group Investigation	Group problem solving/inquiry	Heterogeneous, with teams assigned to group projects
Jigsaw	Group investigation of broad topic	Individual team members assigned to facets of large topic

Figure 12.1. Cooperative Learning Strategies

LEARNING STYLES AND HEMISPHERIC
BRAIN RESEARCH

A third dimension of diversity relates to the ways students like to learn. Anyone who has worked with students soon recognizes that the ways in which students prefer to learn and the ways they learn best vary significantly. Some students learn effectively from textbooks, whereas others find this medium unappealing, if not uneducational. Workers in the area of learning styles have attempted to categorize these preferences and provide suggestions about ways to accommodate these differences.

One of the most popular approaches to learning styles was developed by Ken and Rita Dunn (1978). These educators found that the students they worked with differed in terms of their response to four key dimensions of learning: environment (e.g., sound, light, and temperature), support, (e.g., tightly versus loosely structured course requirements), peer interaction, and modality (including oral versus written). As they applied these dimensions to students, they found clear individual differences in terms of learning preferences and recommended the creation of multifaceted programs that provide students with choice. The mastery learning framework, with its alternative learning activities, as described in Chapter 8, is one effective way of accomplishing this.

Research on the left and right hemispheres of the brain also provides us with some insights into individual differences. The left hemisphere specializes in logical, sequential, analytical, and temporal processing of information; the right hemisphere focuses more on nonverbal, concrete, spatial, emotional, and aesthetic processing (Torrance, 1982). Both parts of the brain are used in virtually all learning situations, but research in this area has identified learning-style preferences and matching educational approaches (Boyle, 1986). For example, a person with a preference for abstract sequential thinking learns best when the instruction is verbal and organized, like a well-sequenced lecture, whereas someone with a concrete random style likes to play around with data and might do best with one of the discovery or inquiry strategies described in Chapter 7.

But what is a teacher to do with a diverse class with a broad spectrum of learning styles/preferences? One of the most promising solutions is McCarthy's (1983) 4MAT system, which systematically provides both concrete and abstract experiences in a unit. For example, a unit on following written directions alternates active and more traditional learning activities. Students begin the unit by writing their own directions and trying these out with other students. Then they analyze these directions, discuss general characteristics of good directions, and develop strategies for following directions. The teacher's role in this process alternates between information dissemination and group facilitation. This integration of thinking and doing provides students with opportunities to use their preferred mode of thinking while strengthening the other.

COMPUTER LITERACY

Computers have definitely become a facet not only of American life but also life in school. Some experts have estimated that 75% of all jobs involve computers in some way (Jones, Jones, Bowyer, & Ray, 1983). In education, the impact of computers is just as great. In a 1982 survey, it was found that American schools have access to 325,000 computers (Toch, 1984). Three years later this figure tripled to over 1 million computers *(Computer Survey Newsletter,* 1986). The average number of computers in a high school was 21; in a junior high, 14; and in an elementary school, 6. Average weekly time-use figures showed similar trends, with high school students using computers 85 minutes per week (doubled from the previous survey) and elementary students using computers 35 minutes per week (up from 20 minutes). Most of this time was devoted to *computer literacy.* Let's take a moment to define this concept.

As you can imagine in a new and developing area there are many different conceptions of computer literacy. Jones et al. (1983) define computer literacy as "an appreciation of the general principles which underlie computer hardware, software, and the application of computer technology to various science, business, education, government and entertainment objectives" (p. 4).

The hardware mentioned in this definition refers to the machine itself—the metal, silicon, and plastic components that do the work. Typically, hardware consists of four major parts (Radin & Lee, 1984). An input device is typically some type of keyboard device, much like a typewriter, which allows a person to type in data and interact with the computer. Inside the computer, we have the central processing unit and memory. The central processing unit performs operations such as addition and subtraction with the data you type in, while the memory component stores information or data that have been entered. The fourth component, the output device, is typically a cathode-ray tube which works like a TV screen and allows the user to see the information put into the computer as well as the products or solutions to the computer's operations.

The number of central processing units and their sophistication determine the number and kind of operations that a computer can do. Basically, there are three main sizes here: mainframe computers are the largest, minicomputers are next in terms of the size of their central processing unit, and microcomputers are the smallest. Most of the computers found in homes and schools are microcomputers.

The software mentioned in the definition are the programs that tell the computer what to do. These programs include, for example, the capability to do word processing, to store and average test scores, and to compute personal income taxes. Software typically comes in tapes, disks, or cartridges that plug into the computer.

In addition to an understanding of hardware and software, other experts feel that computer literacy should include some insight into the history of computers and the impact of computers on society. A final component of computer literacy has been termed computer control and includes the ability to actually use computers in a variety of settings.

Stallings and Blissmer (1984) suggested a three-step approach to teaching computer literacy. The first step is to have students read about computers, both in general terms and specifically about the particular computer with which they will be working. This should be followed by actual experiences with computers which could include games, drill-and-practice, or word processing. An easy way to introduce students to computers is through the use of a tutorial, a piece of software that teaches the fundamentals of working with a computer through hands-on experiences. Finally, these authors advocate that students have some exposure to trying to write a program in languages such as BASIC or Logo.

The implications for teachers are clear. Teachers must not only become computer literate themselves but must also understand how to integrate computers into their classrooms. Anderson (1983) recommended the following list of competencies for teachers:

1. The ability to read and write simple computer programs
2. The ability to use computer programs and documentation that is educational in nature
3. The ability to use computer terminology, particularly as it relates to hardware
4. The ability to recognize educational problems that can and cannot be solved using the computer
5. The ability to locate information on computing as it relates to education
6. The ability to discuss the historical development of computer technology as it relates to education
7. The ability to discuss the moral and human-impact issues as they relate to the societal use of computers, as well as the educational use of computers

The movement toward computer literacy has already left an impact on teacher preparation programs. A recent survey of teacher education programs showed that 63% of the institutions contacted have already included a computer education component in their program; in most instances this was a three- or four-hour course (Kull & Archambault, 1984). The most common topics in these new courses were integrating computers into the classroom, software evaluation, and some type of computer language such as BASIC or Logo. The most commonly used computers in these programs were the Apple II+ and IIe and the TRS-80.

Probably the fastest-growing instructional use of computers is in the area of computer-managed instruction (CMI) (Bluhm, 1987). Computer-managed instruction typically consists of a program that assists teachers in the myriad of record-keeping tasks encountered in classrooms. These programs allow teachers to enter student scores on quizzes and tests, then automatically compute the averages and weigh them according to the teacher's goals, and keep an ongoing record of quizzes and assignments. Such programs are invaluable in figuring grades at the end of the term and in keeping students up-to-date on their current performance.

A second application of CMI is in the creation and management of test banks. Once placed into the system, items can be stored and analyzed after each test, then refined and retained for later use. Teachers using computer test files management programs report that their tests are better and the time required to construct them is reduced.

Beginning teachers entering the schools in the near future should expect to find computers in them. The study mentioned earlier (Toch, 1984) found that 68% of the schools surveyed used at least one microcomputer for instruction. This percentage varied from state to state, with Minnesota having the highest percentage of schools with computers (92.8%) and Hawaii having the lowest (26.6%).

EXERCISE 12.5

Discussion Questions

1. In addition to helping students become computer literate, how else could computers be used in the classroom?

2. The trend has been to place more computers in secondary than elementary schools. Do you agree with this emphasis? Why or why not?

3. Should computer literacy be defined the same way for students with different ability levels? Why or why not?

REFERENCES

Alkin, M. (1972). Accountability defined. *Evaluation Comment, 3*(3), 1–5.
A nation at risk. (1983). New York: Carnegie Corporation.

A nation prepared: Teachers for the 21st century. (1986). New York: Carnegie Corporation.

Anderson, C. (1983). Computer literacy: Changes for teacher education. *Journal of Teacher Education, 34*(5), 6–9.

Banks, J. (1984). *Teaching strategies for ethnic studies* (3rd ed.). Newton, MA: Allyn & Bacon.

Berliner, D. (1987). Simple views of effecting teaching and a simple theory of classroom instruction. In D. Berliner & B. Rosenshine (Eds.), *Talks to teachers* (pp. 93–110). New York: Random House.

Bluhm, H. (1987). *Administrative uses of computers in the schools.* Englewood Cliffs, NJ: Prentice-Hall

Bogdan, R. (1983). Does mainstreaming work? *Phi Delta Kappan, 64,* 427.

Boyle, M. (1986). Hemispheric laterality as a basis of learning: What we know and don't know. In G. Phyle & T. Andre (Eds.), *Cognitive classroom learning* (pp. 21–45). New York: Academic Press.

Bracy, G. (1987). Measurement driven instruction: Catchy phrase, dangerous practice. *Phi Delta Kappan, 68*(9), 683–686.

Bullough, B., Goldstein, S., & Holt, L. (1984). *Human interests in the curriculum.* New York: Teachers College Press.

Cohen, S. (1987, November) Instructional alignment: Searching for a magic bullet. *Educational Researcher,* 16–20.

Computer Survey Newsletter. (1986). Center for Social Organization, Baltimore, MD: Johns Hopkins.

Debra P. *v.* Turlington, 664 F. and 397 (5th circuit, 1981).

Dunn, K. & Dunn, R. (1978). Teaching students through their individual learning styles. Reston, VA: Reston Publishing Company.

Equity/Excellence. (1986). *AACTE Briefs, 7*(2), 10–12.

Frymeier, J. (1987, September) Bureaucracy and the neutering of teachers. *Phi Delta Kappan,* 9–14.

Good, T., & Brophy, J. (1987). *Looking in classrooms* (4th ed.). New York: Harper & Row.

Hardman, M., Drew, C., & Egan, W. (1987). *Human exceptionality* (2nd ed.). Boston: Allyn & Bacon.

Hardman, M., Egan, W., & Landau, E. (1981). *What will we do in the morning?* Dubuque, IA: W. C. Brown

Jones, W., Jones, B., Bowyer, K., & Ray, M. (1983). *Computer literacy.* Reston, VA: Reston Publishing Company.

Kull, J., & Archambault, F. (1984). A survey of teacher preparation in computer education. *Journal of Teacher Education, 35,* 16–19.

Levine, D. (1982). Successful approaches for improving academic achievement in inner-city schools. *Phi Delta Kappan, 63,* 523–526.

Madaus, G. (1981). NIE clarification hearing: The negative teams case. *Phi Delta Kappan, 63*(2), 89–91.

Madden, N., & Slavin, R. (1983). Mainstreaming students with mild handicaps: Academic and social outcomes. *Review of Educational Research, 53*(4), 519–569.

McCarthy, B. & Leflar, S. (1983). 4MAT in action. Oak Brook, IL: Excel.

Pipho, C. (1982) Stateline. *Phi Delta Kappan, 64,* 157–158.

Pipho, C. (1986). States support academic rigor. *Phi Delta Kappan, 68*(3), 189–190.

Popham, J. (1981). The case for minimum competency testing. *Phi Delta Kappan, 63*(2), 89–91.

Popham, J., & Lindheim, E. (1981). Implications of a landmark ruling on Florida's minimum competency test. *Phi Delta Kappan, 63,* 18–20.

Popham, J. (1987). The merits of measurement-driven instruction. *Phi Delta Kappan, 68*(9), 679.

Radin, S., & Lee, F. (1984). *Computers in the classroom.* Chicago: SRA

Shepard, L. & Kreitzer, A. (1987). The Texas teacher test. *Educational Researcher, 16*(6), 22–31.

Slavin, R. (1988). *Educational psychology* (2nd ed.). Englewood Cliffs, NJ: Prentice-Hall.

Sleeter, C., & Grant, C. (1987). An analysis of multicultural education in the United States.. *Harvard Educational Review, 57*(4), 421–444.

Smith, D. (1980). *The classroom teacher and the special child.* Guilford, CT: Special Learning Corporation.

Stallings, W., & Blissmer, R. (1984). *Computer annual.* New York: John Wiley & Sons.

States moving to assess competency. (1982, Winter). *NTE News,* p. 4.

Toch, T. (1984, April 18). Numbers of computers in schools doubles. *Education Week, 3*(30) 1, 14.

Torrance, E. (1982). Hemisphercity and creative functioning. *Journal of Research and Development in Education, 15*(3), 29–37.

Woolever, R. (1985, March/April). State mandated performance evaluation of beginning teachers: Implications for teacher educators. *Journal of Teacher Education,* 22–25.

Index

About the Authors

DAVID A. JACOBSEN is a full professor of education at the University of North Florida and a member of the graduate faculty of the University of Florida.

Dr. Jacobsen received his Ed.D. from Arizona State University and has held faculty positions at Auburn University and the University of Georgia. He has served as classroom teacher, curriculum specialist, grants director, and college administrator.

In addition to his senior authorship of *Methods for Teaching: A Skills Approach,* Dr. Jacobsen has authored three textbooks in the areas of curriculum and instruction.

PAUL EGGEN received his bachelor's degree from Northern Montana College and his master's degree and Ph.D. from Oregon State University. Dr. Eggen holds the rank of professor of education in the Department of Elementary and Secondary Education at the University of North Florida. In addition to being a coauthor of *Methods for Teaching: A Skills Approach,* Dr. Eggen is the senior author of *Strategies for Teachers.* He has also authored and coauthored numerous journal articles and given professional presentations.

DON KAUCHAK received his bachelor's degree from Indiana University in the field of zoology. He taught science, language arts, and social studies in an elementary school for two years while working on his master's degree, which he received in secondary education from Indiana University. He then returned full time to graduate studies and received an Ed.D. in curriculum and instruction from Washington State University in 1973. Since 1973 he has taught at the University of North Florida in Jacksonville, and the University of Utah in Salt Lake City where he is presently head of graduate programs in the Department of Education Studies.

Dr. Kauchak has coauthored several education texts, including *Strategies for Teachers* and *Exploring Science in the Elementary School,* and is presently doing research on the subject of reading in the content area.